The Devil You Know

The Devil You Know

The Surprising Link between Conservative Christianity and Crime

Elicka Peterson Sparks

Prometheus Books

59 John Glenn Drive
Amherst, New York 14228

Cover images © Shutterstock.com
Cover design by Grace M. Conti-Zilsberger

Inquiries should be addressed to
Prometheus Books
59 John Glenn Drive
Amherst, New York 14228
VOICE: 716–691–0133
FAX: 716–691–0137
WWW.PROMETHEUSBOOKS.COM

20 19 18 17 16   5 4 3 2 1

Library of Congress Cataloging-in-Publication Data Pending

Names: Peterson Sparks, Elicka, 1967-
Title: The devil you know : the surprising link between conservative Christianity and crime / by
    Elicka Peterson Sparks, Ph.D.
Description: Amherst, NY : Prometheus Books, 2016. | Includes bibliographical references and
    index.
Identifiers: LCCN 2015037575| ISBN 9781633881501 (hardcover) | ISBN 9781633881518 (e-book)
Subjects: LCSH: Christianity and politics—United States. | Christian conservatism—United States. |
    Religious right—United States. | Crime—Religious aspects—Christianity.
Classification: LCC BR516 .P43 2016 | DDC 277.3/083—dc23 LC record available at http://lccn.loc.
    gov/2015037575

Printed in the United States of America

33614059717453

For Maggie Sparks

CONTENTS

8   CONTENTS

ACKNOWLEDGMENTS

Many people helped, supported and encouraged me in the completion of the research for this book, and I would especially like to thank Maggie, Jessica, and Megan Sparks, Cathy Marcum, Kit Gruelle, Brian Ellison, Jennifer Kopolow, Rose Hepworth, Janet Kernis, Julia Kent, Renee Scherlen, Julianne Stone, Kenna Quinet, Sunny Townes Stewart, Laura McCune, Shelly Wilson, Bonnie Berry, Rick Rosenfeld, Janet Lauritsen, Alissa Ackerman-Acklin, and my colleagues in the Department of Government and Justice Studies at Appalachian State University. I have the best friends and colleagues in the world. Thanks also to my editor, Sheila Stewart, who made this a better book. To my parents—thanks for putting up with me. We all know that this particular apple fell *really* far from the tree, but I'll always be glad you're my Mom and Dad. Thank you all so much.

CHAPTER ONE

WHEN DID CHRISTIANS GET SO MEAN (AGAIN)?

A fundamentalist is an evangelical who is angry about something.

—George M. Marsden,
in *Understanding Fundamentalism and Evangelicalism*

The Bible does not guarantee human rights. At the time of the fall, man lost all rights except the right to die. . . . What this means is that all protection, all justice, all compassion, and all fairness are given to men on the basis of grace and an adherence to the Scriptures, not on some nebulous and subjective notion of rights.

—George Grant, from *The Changing of the Guard: The Vital Role Christians Must Play in America's Unfolding Political and Cultural Drama*

Do not think that I have come to bring peace upon the earth. I have come to bring not peace but the sword.

—Matthew 10:34 (New American Bible)

W riting this book has been unsettling for several reasons. First, I consider myself fairly well-informed, yet I remain stunned by what I have discovered in the last four years about the extent to which the religious right has managed to impact political and social systems in the United States. Like most Americans, I noticed the movement in this direction: Michelle Bachmann's assertions that homosexuals are trying to legalize child sexual abuse, the number of Republican politicians proudly proclaiming their belief in creation rather than evolution, fights over books and scientific curriculum in schools, an Oklahoma political hopeful unapologetically expressing his desire to see LGBT people stoned to death, and skirmishes over Ten Commandment statues on government property. Stories such as these are ubiquitous and make it fairly clear that the United States remains a bastion of Christian fundamentalism, despite secular progress.

But impacting the realms of politics and policy is a far cry from infiltrating these systems with the aim of creating a theocracy or fundamentalist Christianity having an unintentional criminogenic impact, and, prior to this project, I felt utterly secure that anyone suggesting the latter idea likely needed fitting for an aluminum foil hat. I do not wear recyclable headgear, but I confess that there have been innumerable times in the course of researching this theory about the impact of the religious right on violent crime that it has felt more than a touch surreal that this striking movement has received so little attention in the mainstream media.

The second unsettling thing about addressing this topic is that the religious right, a powerful and vocal special-interest group in America, is unlikely to be thrilled with the theory I am positing about the impact of conservative Christian ideology on crime, and some of them do wear tinfoil hats. While there will probably be few members of the religious right who will read this book, those who do are unlikely to be happy about it and will likely do so in the service of either trying to discredit it or looking for evidence to further advertise the idea that fundamentalist Christians are persecuted in this country. The Christian right seems to have an "ignore it or deplore it" dichotomy in their response to information they find threatening to their belief system, and attorney Wendy Kaminer had it right in saying that, in the United States, "making fun of religion is as risky as burning an American flag in an American Legion Hall."[1] While I am not actively making fun of fundamentalist Christians, the facts are not always flattering, so it is difficult to imagine a positive reaction toward this work from their camp.

However, both the historical and current truth is that this movement spends more time in the service of persecuting others than in being persecuted, and it is amazingly adept at harnessing feelings of persecution to its advantage.[2] Part of this mechanism is fueled by three teachings of the Beatitudes from Jesus's Sermon on the Mount, which blesses those who are persecuted for the sake of righteousness, as well as those who are insulted, persecuted, or falsely accused of evil for following Jesus.[3]

People who suffer such earthly attacks are promised great rewards in heaven.[4] This is one of the primary reasons why this movement is extremely resilient to adversity: Defeat only strengthens their resolve, as it lends credit to the notion that they are underdogs in a spiritual war against a wicked world. In this respect, I might escape persecution for writing this book. After all, I am providing grist for the idea that Christians are put upon, and the mill is gravely lacking in real grist, because mainstream religions in the United States are sheltered from even deserved scrutiny through the accommodation of the American media, politicians, and citizenry—all of whom are rightly reluctant to be accused of picking on Christians. I am sympathetic, truly, as wearing kid gloves with respect to religion has become deeply engrained in our culture as synonymous with being respectful.

We will talk about this more later, but, for now, know that (a) I think this preferential treatment goes too far and is even a bit dangerous, and (b), given this, I urge politicians, journalists, criminologists, and the American public to start earnestly examining this brand of religion at their earliest convenience. It is uncomfortable to consider addressing negative consequences associated with a religion, due to our ethos of religious liberty, but it is necessary, and not a threat to liberty. The religious right has absolutely no problem grumbling about having to use politically correct (i.e., respectful) terminology in interactions with other groups—or even viciously attacking other groups—but appear to have no compunction in insisting that we bestow preferential treatment on them. This has to stop.

When you think about it, it is somewhat surprising that religion has not been researched to death in the context of crime, but it has not, and, while it is clichéd to say that more people have died in the name of religion than for any other cause, it is likely true with respect to crime as well as terrorism. As criminologists tend to be fairly interested in homicide, the relative dearth of scholarly attention is perplexing. As you will see later in this book, there is too little academic work on the intersection of religion and crime, particularly where the research attends to the conflation of religion and conservative ideology. There is *no* criminological research on the specific focus of this book: Christian nationalism in the context of violent crime.

So you know what you are getting yourself into here, the *Reader's Digest* version of the theory posited in this book is that fundamentalist Christian ideology is criminogenic—in other words, it actually causes crime. The United States has more fundamentalist Christians than any other comparable nation. The United States also has a very high rate of violent crime—and particularly high rates of lethal violence—compared to other similarly situated nations. In this book, I am positing a criminological theory suggesting that this is not a coincidence. Focusing on the United States necessitates focusing on Christianity, but it should be noted that this focus would shift in considering several other countries in which the theory could apply, such as Israel and many other countries in the Middle East.[5] Similar books might be written about the criminogenic impact of fundamentalist Islam or Judaism in other parts of the world.

In offering this theory, I will show how a distinctively American brand of conservative Christian ideology called Christian nationalism has both a direct and indirect impact on the crime problem in the United States. In a direct manner, this belief system—and the culture it inspires—lends itself to many types of criminal activity, including the promotion of violent crimes against a variety of victims, terrorism against those of different faiths,[6] and even crimes against the environment.[7] There are some types of crimes, and especially delinquency, that are mitigated through at least some kinds of religious involvement, though they tend to be far less serious crimes, such as drug and alcohol use in adolescents. The results are modest and mixed, but I believe other researchers have missed the greater influence of Christian nationalism due to measurement issues that will be discussed in chapter four.

On the second, indirect, front, conservative Christian ideology provides tremendous cultural and political support for criminal justice responses that are, in themselves, criminogenic. The so-called wars on drugs and crime, and a plethora of other "get-tough" policies, have resulted in shocking rates of incarceration and capital punishment in the United

States, at a staggering expense both in human and economic terms.[8] There is nothing compassionate about the Christian right's response to crime, and that response has resulted in incredibly high recidivism rates that perpetuate and amplify our crime rate.

Despite the fact that it receives very little attention, Christian nationalism (also called dominionism or Christian reconstructionism) is incredibly pervasive in America and is unwittingly supported by many people completely unaware of its goals, harms, and, indeed, much of its ideological underpinnings. Adherents to this ideology can be identified by a number of their beliefs, which should ring a bell as natural extensions of common right-wing political messages. Though rank and file members of the Christian nationalist movement are largely unaware of the extent of its goals and its history, this postmillennial[9] theology was the brain child of Rousas John Rushdoony in the early 1900s. Chief among these beliefs are the following convictions:

- The idea that the Bible is the literal word of God, and thus incontrovertible and authoritative in its assertions.
- That the Bible should serve as the sole foundation for every facet of American life—including governance and law.
- That the United States was formed as a Christian nation and must be restored to its original status as what essentially amounts to a theocratic society (something of a neopuritan model).
- That separation of church and state was not intended by the framers of the Constitution.
- That theology conveys a superiority to conservative Christians, who have dominion—the right to rule—over America vis-à-vis Genesis 1:28.[10]
- That the United States was once a great country, but that the liberal agenda of secular humanism has steered it in an ungodly direction that must be corrected.
- Issues such as marriage equality and legalized abortion have become central in mobilizing this movement, though appeals to the three Fs of American conservative Christianity—family, flag, and faith—are also routinely engaged with considerable success.

This movement harkens back to the Great Awakening of the mid-1700s, with the current resurgence gaining its initial momentum around the issue of desegregation, though a convincing case might be made that the movement received on-the-job training pushing Prohibition. In fact, the John Birch Society, an early Christian nationalist organization, led a drive to impeach Chief Justice Earl Warren, railing against the judicial tyranny of the liberal courts.[11] The modern equivalents to the Birchers include James Dobson's Focus on the Family, the late Jerry Falwell's Moral Majority, D. James Kennedy's Center for Reclaiming America and (with James Dobson) Alliance Defense Fund, David Barton's WallBuilders, Rick Scarborough's Vision America, and Lou Sheldon's Traditional Values Coalition, among many other euphemistically creative organizations.[12] The doctrine disseminated by groups such as these are the object of this study of crime.

After years of research, I believe that this form of religiosity is a powerful—and largely ignored—variable in the study of violence. Further, the increasingly strong influence of Christian nationalism has set the United States on a dangerous course with respect to both crime and human rights, and this influence has not been subject to the attention and debate necessary to stem the tide of social problems it is creating. Thomas Jefferson pointed out that "error of opinion may be tolerated where reason is left free to combat it."[13] Checks and balances are key features in our system of government with good reason: Problems arise when people do not speak out to challenge errors of opinion, and, as I mentioned previously, both the mainstream media and politicians of all stripes are clearly shying away from meaningful discourse about the conservative Christian influence in America to avoid charges of anti-Christian liberalism.

This silence is largely unilateral, and when we shy away from reasoning with one another, tolerance itself becomes a threat to maintaining the balance necessary to protect ourselves from tyranny. As a criminologist, it is difficult to observe the state of crime and what passes for justice in this country without wanting to do something about it.

Though my critics will inevitably have much to say about this, I am not a rabid hater of Christians. I am not even a casual hater of Christians, actually—I have a number of wonderful people in my life who exemplify the remarkable fruits possible through a loving, thoughtful, and reasoned approach to faith. And while some Christians may be a little too prone to see discrimination and persecution against them, while busily and often simultaneously dishing it out, I think it is ridiculous to say that discrimination against them does not exist. While their influence is great, the religious right represents only a small portion of citizens who identify themselves as Christians in this country. In fact, depending upon how you define conservative Christianity, it is estimated that this group accounts for only 8 to 35 percent of the general population,[14] though this feels incongruous given their tremendous impact in the public realm.[15]

There are extreme edges to most social groups—radical feminists, rabid Republicans, knee-jerk liberals, Rush Limbaugh—but, historically, most have held limited sway over policy and culture as a whole. This is no longer the case. Partly, the ideology of Christian nationalism has managed to infiltrate American culture and processes to the extent that it has because a more moderate and liberal Christianity is already firmly engrained in our country's history and identity. Thus, Christianity is familiar and garners support based upon common language and ideals that do not appear alarming at first blush. Similarly, patriotism is certainly nothing new in the United States, so appeals to the flag do not tend to cause much concern.[16] The great irony with respect to patriotism is that Christian nationalists do not really love America—in fact, they believe that we are something of a modern-day Sodom and Gomorrah. What they love is a wholesome vision of America as they believe it once was and will be again: A Christian nation straight out of *Mad Men*, but without all the sinning and angst.

Additionally, many Christians who embrace a quieter faith likely feel uncomfortable speaking out against this vocal fundamentalist minority given that minority's penchant to label those with different ideas as substandard Christians—or because some tenets of their ideals and doctrine are shared. But we have reached a moral threshold in America, and the danger of tolerating intolerance is something with which the left and center must come to grips.

As I write, Barack Obama is finishing up his second term as president of the United States, and, to most, the tide would seem to have changed dramatically, to the extent that this discussion might no longer seem relevant. But despite recent victories for mainline and progressive ideology in America, the influence of the religious right is always more likely to grow than wither under a progressive leadership. Examples where political setbacks have served to fuel the fervor of the religious right abound in recent years, as this faction draws strength from the perception that they are engaged in a holy war against a powerful enemy aimed at their destruction. Count them out at your peril.

President Obama's emphasis on change in his first campaign spoke directly to another strong motivating factor for the American Christian movement: an ideology that romanticizes the traditional values of the past while demonizing the progressive ideals of the present. In fact, it was during the Clinton years that this movement picked up much of its momentum and made the bulk of its progress in developing the organization necessary to gain the footholds that came to fruition with the Bush administration. You can bet that the current political landscape will serve to motivate adherents, and, just as they failed to learn anything from the debacle of the Bush years, it is likely that moderate and liberal Americans will fail to reflect upon how these interests grew so powerful in the first place. Such is the history of ignoring history—it is an equal-opportunity folly.

Readers should resist the urge to assume the purpose of this book is antireligious, as it is not my intent to promote negative feelings toward any religion or religious people. You will make up your own mind about what you read here, and I encourage you to check my research if you ever feel I have strayed from the facts or taken unfair contextual liberties to advance the theory I will present here. Instead of being antireligious, this is a book about the intersection of crime and a particular brand of ideology that conflates political power and patriotism with tenets of conservative Christianity. I am not examining this relationship to be antireligious but rather because this connection warrants close attention and has garnered little notice.

Many theologians are also concerned about this shift in fundamentalist ideology in the United States, but, again, have been unable to wake the masses to the dangers of this movement. One of the biggest problems with Christianity—one shared by almost all major religions—is that it speaks to the deepest fear and insecurity of human existence: death. Insomuch as religion is primarily a means to insulate oneself from trepidation over this inevitable event, it will inspire a fierce defensive response in its followers. If one is saved from death through their belief in a particular doctrine, then competing doctrines threaten their most fundamental sense of security. The desire to extinguish that threat naturally follows.

In the wake of this research, I have come to the conclusion that Christians are right to avoid exposing themselves to too much information about their religion—it does not lend itself to easily maintaining a faith in their God, which is a frightening prospect for people with huge psychological and social investments in being Christians. I was not terribly surprised to learn that a 2002 meta-analysis of forty-three studies on the relationship between IQ and religiosity resulted in the finding that people with higher IQs are less likely to be religious in all but four of the studies.[17] Religion shows a similar correlation with educational level. But despite the impact of intelligence and education, the strongest predictor of religiosity is parental religiosity.[18] The combo platter of childhood indoctrination, loyalty, and social pressure tends to keep people religious—or at least quietly nonreligious.

In researching this topic, I have also found myself continually challenging my own biases. The Bible is full of suppositions I find difficult to accept as the Word of a God not created by man. During this project, I have thought repeatedly of the story of Winston Churchill, reading the Bible for the first time as an adult, slapping his side and chortling, "God! Isn't God a shit!?"[19]

After nearly four years of research for this book, I can definitely relate. Of course, many Christians would likely point out that God works in mysterious ways beyond human understanding, but this feels a bit pat in light of biblical examples that are completely at odds with the notion of a loving and all-powerful God. Actually studying the Bible has left me unable to believe that the Bible is the Word of God in any literal sense, or that it was not shaped to serve many agendas at both its inception and in subsequent interpretations by human beings. If they did not keep such information carefully concealed in books, the Christian faith would be suffering an even greater defection rate.

I came into this project believing that the Bible contains a number of moral truths that are still relevant and that its overall message could and should be construed as loving and redemptive, despite much of the violence it contains—though I had less faith in people's ability to *rightly divine the word of truth*.[20] However, I have come to a point where I believe the bad far outweighs the good. Especially since the positive messages are easily arrived at without the aid of the Bible. Moreover, I have even fewer doubts as to whether combining governance with religion will result in anything good; certainly history has shown that this particular relationship tends to end badly. Those who long for such a state would do well to remember that in such cases religion tends to end up in service to political power rather than the reverse.

So there you have it. If you sense a bias in this book, I have done my best to ensure that it is due to the findings of my research, rather than my personal beliefs regarding Christian ideology, even as those personal beliefs are more the result of my research rather than the impetus for it. That said, I will not be surprised if negative intent is inferred by some readers, who may view my suggestion that this conservative Christian doctrine has criminogenic consequences as more than an indictment of the negative consequences of Christianity.

I am still holding out a vain hope to do more than preach to the choir here, though I understand that my chances for success to this end are extremely limited. I am sure that people on the other end of this spectrum feel the same at times. Honest examinations of the impact of religion in society have rarely found fertile ground in the minds of the deeply religious or the deeply irreligious. If you are a reader who falls into either of these camps, I beg you to consider that few things in this world exist without negative consequences: Even life-sustaining, overwhelmingly beneficial things such as the sun also cause harm in the form of skin cancer, droughts, and a role in global warming. I hold little hope of effecting a degree of influence on Christian nationalists, but a more modest and attainable goal is simply to motivate the choir to sing out their concern about these issues in order to make our country a safer and more just place to live. Americans who are not deeply religious or conservative must step up in both their involvement and influence with respect to these issues or suffer the consequences and costs of a continued failure to respond to the problems of crime and injustice with rational, effective programs and policies.

Christianity has a long and sometimes bloody history in reaction to scientific inquiry, and, indeed, toward academia as an institution.[21] But really, our goals should not be antithetical: Scholars seek the truth. If one's faith cannot withstand the light of factual information, it does not necessarily mean the facts are wrong, or that the person reporting those facts did so from a desire to persecute those for whom the facts are inconvenient. I cannot think of a more diplomatic way to put this—and I realize this is not nearly diplomatic enough—but the animosity between academia and religion is perhaps best understood as tension between people seeking the truth and those who believe they already know the truth and thus do not care to be confused by the facts. For me, the idea of a six-thousand-year-old earth, for example, can only be embraced at the expense of reason—a return to such a belief akin to insisting that the world is flat.[22]

This animosity has become bilateral over time. It is difficult to remain impassive when you feel threatened, but this is the key to maintaining the open mind that is necessary to learn. As an academic, I have been ashamed to see colleagues clearly discriminate against religious people—and particularly fundamentalist Christians—at a couple of points in my career. I have listened to people who would rather pull their own eyelashes out than make a racist comment make outlandishly condescending comments about fundamentalist Christians without even noticing the hypocrisy of it. I do not think anti-Christian bias is the last acceptable prejudice by any means—moving to the South will disabuse you of that idea quite quickly—and I do not mean Southerners' prejudices so much as the prejudice against them.[23] That will not be a popular statement, but it is true. I think it is a case of both sides expecting the worst from one another, and, too often, this results in having that expectation realized. Discrimination is ugly on any front, and the adversarial relationship between academia and religion is another way that the denizens of conservative Christianity thwart attempts to develop rational and effective criminal justice responses to crime.[24]

As humans, we have a biological need to believe in a variety of things in order to have a sense of meaning and peace in our lives; this is not necessarily a bad thing—and in understanding this, both sides may find common ground that results in constructive discourse rather than a pissing match unlikely to result in anything other than frustration and discord. In truth, the antipathy toward science on the part of fundamentalist Christians would likely dissipate instantly were scientists to find tangible proof for tenets of Christianity. At that point, Christians would likely broadcast such a finding to as wide an audience as possible, and I think this lays the crux of the issue bare.

We seem to be living in a time where pointing out problems in our country is viewed by conservatives as tantamount to not loving it, unless those "problems" are moral in nature. Nothing could be further from the truth. A key component to loving something is recognizing its potential to improve, and the first step in that process is necessarily an honest assessment of both its strengths and weaknesses. Christian nationalism is a call for an American theocracy cloaked in comforting allusions to a safer, simpler time. Ironically, those simpler times were not safe nor simple in most respects, so these are really allusions to illusions, but we will have a look at that soon.

Historically, such movements thrive in times of uncertainty. Currently, the United States is barely out of a war in which there could have been no real victory at a staggering cost in both lives and dollars. Our educational system is an expensive embarrassment. Far too many Americans still live without proper healthcare and either beyond their means or with no means. Our security at home is questionable at best, despite astonishing expenditures. We do not give proper care to our veterans and our poor. We contribute disproportionately to the problems of global warming and pollution. The United States' economy is an unmitigated disaster. We have too much crime, too little justice, and too many people sitting in prisons trying to pay their debt to society with the worthless currency of human suffering. And yet we are also a nation of great ideals, and I am indeed grateful for every opportunity and freedom I enjoy as a citizen.

So . . . when *did* Christians get so mean again? Is the fundamental message of Christianity violent—or loving? Is the doctrine one of fear and vengeance—or forgiveness and mercy? Christian nationalism unquestionably peddles fear as a means to swell the ranks of Christianity; the promise of eternal life in a utopian paradise versus burning in hell for an eternity is something of a no-brainer if you accept the premise. Being human is a scary proposition because it is a limited time offer, and who would not be tempted to try to avoid believing this, given an option with tremendous social acceptance and support?

The problem is that our beliefs related to death, though not immutable, make us resistant to other views; more often than not, this leads us to reject and discount a person holding alternative views, and sometimes this rejection produces violence. This is another means in which Christian nationalism is criminogenic. Further, modern conservative Christians seem to focus on the negative almost exclusively, defining themselves far more through whom they oppose than through what they stand for as a group. They are against abortion, contraceptives, comprehensive sex education, the media, competing religions, anything that smacks of political correctness, socialists, gays and lesbians (along with their right to marry, adopt or have children, and enjoy legal protection from discrimination), academics, anyone who is anti-war, immigrants, feminists, communists, human and animal rights activists, Democrats, secular humanists, criminals, intellectuals, activist judges, foreigners, environmentalists, poor people, people with differing or no religious beliefs, people having sex out of wedlock, and liberals of any stripe.

They are strong proponents of family values, a pursuit that sounds positive on its face—until you realize that the pursuit of "family values" simply amounts to insulating families from those perceived as threats to conservative Christianity—which takes you right back to the list of people conservative Christians are against, a list that represents a significant portion of the American population. If they simply disagreed with the views of others, it would not be at all problematic; this is one of the rights we hold dear as citizens. But this brand of Christianity goes further, and proponents are not looking for a spirited debate. At its heart, Christian nationalism includes the language of war, theocracy, and even fascism.[25]

Conservative Christians got mean when they embraced political power as an instrument of religious coercion. They do not play well with others, because a significant feature of their ideology holds that others must convert to their views or perish. And prior to perishing, those who refuse to embrace their beliefs are labeled as enemies to be vanquished. If someone holds an opposing worldview, they are not simply disagreeing with a set of religious beliefs—they are on the side of the devil.[26] How far beyond such thinking lies the justification for violence?

CHAPTER TWO

JESUS LOVES YOU,
BUT WE'RE HIS FAVORITES

The Christian church has left a legacy, a world view, that perme-
ates every aspect of Western society, both secular and religious.
— Helen Ellerbe, *The Dark Side of Christian History*

I tremble for my country when I reflect that God is just: that his
justice cannot sleep forever.
— Thomas Jefferson, *Notes on the State of Virginia,* 1781

Christianity started out in Palestine as a fellowship; it moved to
Greece and became a philosophy; it moved to Italy and became
an institution; it moved to Europe and became a culture; it came
to America and became an enterprise.

— Anonymous[1]

A central tenet of American individual liberty is religious
freedom, for which "Christian nation" enthusiasts can scarcely
avoid hypocrisy.
— Stuart Whatley, "Democratic Values, Islam and the
Judeo-Christian Tradition Fallacy," *Huffington Post*

Our culture is superior. Our culture is superior because our reli-
gion is Christianity, and that is the truth that makes men free.
— Pat Buchanan, speech to the Christian Coalition, 1993

Throughout this book, I will argue that a close relationship between
Christianity and nationalism accounts for our unimpressive standing
in the world with respect to violent crime, especially in light of how punitive we are where street criminals are concerned. Using the United States

to illustrate this theory is simply a way to more expediently and clearly make my case. In fact, if the theory is correct, comparing crime rates in countries with similarly close ties to any religion to those without such ties would be one of several means to test the theory.[2] As such, I am in no way proposing that fundamentalist Christianity has a monopoly as a causative factor in violent crime; they definitely have some nasty competition. Frankly, I am also focusing on the United States, and thus Christian nationalism, because the task would have been overwhelming for one person to address on an international level in addition to presenting these ideas and thoroughly researching this religious phenomenon in the United States.

Further, there exists a number of highly regarded works in criminology that attempt to explain the global standing of the United States with respect to its high rates of violent crime, based upon everything from our particularly enthusiastic brand of capitalism, to our deep indoctrination in the American Dream, to our affinity for guns and punishment, among other factors.[3] I have never heard of a theory that tries to account for our crime rate as a byproduct of our obesity, but I would not be surprised if there is one, given the amount of attention this question has received. Certainly all of these attempts to account for our violence touch upon important, relevant factors, but none have ever struck me as truly causative, in that there are always countries with which we might be fairly compared boasting similar features and dynamics—but without a concurrent higher level of violence. Given that the question still remains open to debate, I felt inclined to weigh in with this alternate explanation, because God has blessed America—with a lot of crime.

I hope to avoid a key feature in many past discussions about US crime rates in not being ethnocentric or implicitly arrogant in my explanation: There is more than a touch of condescension in the idea that the United States is such a great, wealthy, advanced, democratic nation that our high rate of violence is somehow more shocking than in the cases of other countries with the same problem. We are not immune to problems, we are far from wealthy, and nor do we treat our citizens better than the governments of many other countries. Why should we be immune from having a serious crime problem? Lately, about the only thing we are number one for is incarceration. We are not even number one for obesity anymore, so perhaps we should start approaching the rest of the world as something closer to equals.[4]

In this chapter, I will lay out two important underpinnings to this new theory that Christian nationalism is criminogenic, and I will try not to bore you to death in the process. Actually, I will shoot for not boring you at all, and I think I am up to the task, because trying to figure out why people do—and do not—believe in religion is interesting, as is the psychology behind belief, the impact of religion on believers, and the politics that pervade the movement. And crime is flat fascinating. I will address a number of issues that will have to be settled right up front—such as why I am calling the United States a Christian nation, and why I am focusing on Christian nationalism instead of picking on some other religion. There are, in fact, so many to choose from.

IS THE UNITED STATES A CHRISTIAN NATION?

The answer to this question is stickier than people on both ends of the religious spectrum seem willing to admit, but, for the purposes of this book, I am going to argue that the United States is *enough* of a Christian nation to warrant an honest examination of Christianity in the context of important national issues, such as crime. Though no one finds it particularly convenient, there exists ample evidence to use in a rational defense of either position—both that we are, or are not, a Christian nation—based upon law, custom, culture, the population of religious adherents, Lockean and Hobbesian philosophies underlying the Declaration of Independence and the Constitution, the Barbary coast treaties, disputes over the religious beliefs and civic intent of the founding fathers, and a multitude of other factors. My contention is based mostly on our cultural identity—and the influence and impact of that identity—rather than any assertion that America is explicitly Christian with respect to the creation of its government, though I will touch on that issue in an effort to avoid misunderstanding.

To further muddy the waters, this debate has become so polarized along political lines that it makes it difficult to discern the truth and unlikely that anyone would care to hear it at any rate. Like most politicized arguments mired in dogma, both camps can easily point to ignorant assertions and overstatements at the far edges of opposing arguments to buttress their own view as correct. The traditionally liberal standpoint is that the country was not really founded as a Christian nation, with conservatives arguing the reverse. Let's have a look at our history.

HISTORICAL ARGUMENTS

I am *not* arguing that the United States was founded as a Christian nation in the sense that our government was or is explicitly based upon Christian doctrine, or that it was designed to protect, promote, or exalt Christianity to the exclusion of other religious views. I will even add that most arguments to the contrary are steeped in a combo platter of misinformation and propaganda. In fact, most arguments to this end are so devoid of historical awareness or understanding as to boggle the mind.

For example, Christians often cite references to God in the Pledge of Allegiance and on our national currency as proof that ours is a Christian nation and cite controversies over the inclusion of these phrases as liberalism gone wild with a side of revisionist history. These accusations are almost comical in light of the truth: Christian nationalists only successfully amended the Pledge of Allegiance to include the words "under God" in 1954, and, similarly, were successful in first adding the phrase "In God We Trust" to US coins through an act of Congress in 1837. Paper currency did not bear the term "In God We Trust" until 1957, when it was added as an anticommunist flourish in the waning era of McCarthyism.[5]

People who tend to engage in this argument often seek to either minimize or maximize the impact of Christianity in the creation and history of the United States. Such issues have become so deeply politicized and polarized that several key points have been lost. First, at its root, this argument is not even about the role of Christianity in US history at all: *It is about what role people wish to see Christianity play in the United States and trying to justify that role.* The conservative view that Christianity should play a greater role now is based largely on the historical argument that Christianity enjoys an inherent position central to the creation of our country and a primary status as something of a national religion.

I would say that the bulk of the historical evidence suggests that this is incorrect. I would characterize the position of Christianity in America as the dominant religion culturally but not in any official capacity. It was not intended as a national religion in any sense by any of our country's framers, who were far too concerned about the religious tyranny they had just escaped to set the groundwork for making the same mistake again so quickly.

Even an amateur's look at the history of our founding fathers makes it clear that most were products of the European Enlightenment rather than biblical Christianity.[6] A couple even leaned precariously close to agnosticism or atheism at a time when talking about such beliefs would be social suicide, but most were clearly Deists.[7] I will include John Adams, Benjamin Franklin, Alexander Hamilton, John Jay, Thomas Jefferson, James Madison, and George Washington as founding fathers for the purpose of this discussion.[8]

John Adams made more than a few comments in his time that raised eyebrows—and should raise doubts that this was a man who thought that America was, or should be, a Christian nation. He also made a point that is germane to this discussion, in saying, "Facts are stubborn things; and whatever may be our wishes, our inclinations, or the dictates of our passion, they cannot alter the state of facts and evidence."[9] John Adams said many things about the separation of church and state, including his comments in the Treaty of Tripoli about the US government not being "in any sense founded on the Christian religion,"[10] but I think this one speaks very directly to the matter at hand, as well:

> The United States of America have exhibited, perhaps, the first example of governments erected on the simple principles of nature; and if men are now sufficiently enlightened to disabuse themselves of artifice, imposture, hypocrisy, and superstition, they will consider this event as an era in their history. Although the detail of the formation of the American governments, is at present little known or regarded either in Europe or

in America, it may hereafter become an object of curiosity. It will never be pretended that any persons employed in that service had interviews with the gods, or were in any degree under the influence of Heaven, more than those at work upon ships or houses, or laboring in merchandise or agriculture; it will forever be acknowledged that these governments were contrived merely by the use of reason and the senses.[11]

Benjamin Franklin's Deism was fairly clear, though he wisely chose not to trumpet it. These passages from a letter to a friend shortly before his death show the tension between his beliefs and the accepted doctrine of the time:

You desire to know something of my religion. It is the first time I have been questioned upon it. . . . I believe in one God, Creator of the Universe. That He governs it by His providence. That He ought to be worshipped. That the most acceptable service we render Him is doing good to His other children. That the soul of man is immortal, and will be treated with justice in another life respecting its conduct in this. These I take to be the fundamental principles of all sound religion, and I regard them as you do in whatever sect I meet with them. As to Jesus of Nazareth, my opinion of whom you particularly desire, I think the system of Morals and his Religion, as he left them to us, the best the World ever saw or is likely to see; but I apprehend it has received various corrupt changes, and I have, with most of the present Dissenters in England, some doubts as to his divinity. . . . I see no harm, however, in its being believed, if that belief has the good consequence, as probably it has, of making his doctrines more respected and better observed; especially as I do not perceive that the Supreme takes it amiss, by distinguishing the unbelievers in His government of the world with any particular marks of His displeasure. . . . I confide that you will not expose me to criticism and censure by publishing any part of this communication to you. I have ever let others enjoy their religious sentiments, without reflecting on them for those that appeared to me unsupportable and even absurd.[12]

This is Deism with a side of kindly Agnosticism. Pretty much everyone was religious at the time, so it is not hard to find references aplenty to religion in the writings of our founding fathers. It was really the only language available—and acceptable—with which to express thoughts on the natural world prior to Darwin hitting the scene. His request that his friend keep his beliefs under his hat speaks to the prominent role of religion at the time. It is also clear that reason was at the forefront in our forebearers' decision-making, to which Benjamin Franklin famously said, "The way to see by Faith is to shut the eye of Reason."[13]

Alexander Hamilton appears to have been a pretty devout Christian, though there is more evidence of this in his youth than later in life. Having read a bit on the topic, I am going to characterize attempts to say that he lost his faith as an adult as dubious.[14] While I think there is more evidence that the man was a Christian, and likely not only in the sense of Deism, it is also clear that his faith did not blind him to the potential danger in religion, as evidenced by this quote: "In politics, as in religion, it is equally absurd to aim at making proselytes by fire and sword. Heresies in either can rarely be cured by persecution."[15] It is hard to imagine someone capable of making a statement such as this supporting the ideology of Christian nationalism, despite his own religiosity.

John Jay was deeply religious, and of that there is no credible doubt. That his Christian beliefs were fundamental and biblically rooted is equally clear, as this quote suggests: "The Bible is the best of all books, for it is the word of God and teaches us the way to be happy in this world and in the next. Continue therefore to read it and to regulate your life by its precepts."[16] Moreover, John Jay could fairly be characterized as a Christian nationalist in many opinions he expressed, such as: "Providence has given to our people the choice of their rulers, and it is the duty—as well as the privilege and interest—of our Christian nation to select and prefer Christians as their rulers."[17] And: "Whether our religion permits Christians to vote for infidel rulers is a question which merits more consideration than it seems yet to have generally received either from the clergy or the laity."[18] Not surprisingly, John Jay's beliefs get a lot of play among Christian nationalists as the most conservative of the bunch, but it is important to remember that his beliefs were clearly in the minority among the founding fathers and, more importantly in this debate, are not at all reflected in the Constitution.

Thomas Jefferson is easy to characterize at the other end of the spectrum. If he were alive today, he would likely be sitting in a coffee shop reading Christopher Hitchens. He was a Deist and Unitarian, though he grew up in the Anglican church.[19] He did not believe in the Bible and had many negative things to say about it; he was even attacked by political opponents in his consideration for the presidency as an infidel and a "howling atheist."[20] His views on religion with respect to the state are equally unequivocal, as is evident in this passage from his first inaugural address:

> And let us reflect that having banished from our land that religious intolerance under which mankind so long bled and suffered, we have yet gained little if we countenance a political intolerance, as despotic, as wicked, and as capable of bitter and bloody persecutions.[21]

I do not think we need to delve too much further into the man who said, "Question with boldness even the existence of a god; because if there be one he must approve of the homage of reason more than that of blindfolded fear."[22]

Federalist James Madison was a big fan of the separation of church and state: "And I have no doubt that every new example will succeed, as every past one has done, in showing that religion and government will both exist in greater purity, the less they are mixed together."[23] If that was not clear enough, he got right down to it addressing the Virginia General Assembly in 1785:

> What influence, in fact, have ecclesiastical establishments had on society? In some instances they have been seen to erect a spiritual tyranny on the ruins of the civil authority; in many instances they have been seen upholding the thrones of political tyranny; in no instance have they been the guardians of the liberties of the people. Rulers who wish to subvert the public liberty may have found an established clergy convenient allies.[24]

The father of the Constitution definitely believed in a secular nation, with a government that would not be infringed upon by religion, and both his public and private writings provide no doubt of this.[25] He was fairly private about his own faith, but most seem to consider him a Deistic Unitarian.

I ran across an interesting story while checking some facts on James Madison, and I cannot resist including it because it will illustrate several points I need to make in one shot. The first point is that the beliefs of our founding fathers are highly politicized and that the Christian right lies in making cases for the things they believe in. The example of this I will discuss involves David Barton, who I could call the revisionist history expert of modern Christian nationalism (if I did not think he would be pleased). Barton actually created and disseminated several fictitious quotes that he attributed to James Madison, among other historical figures, in his popular book, *The Myth of Separation.*[26]

I do not really need to give Barton a title in the Christian nationalist movement, as he has been lauded by so many people on the right for his "scholarship." The reality is that it appears he specializes in discovering quotes that no historian has ever seen, and that he cannot produce, to prove that we were founded as an expressly Christian nation. His sideline is showing how the Constitution comes directly from biblical passages, most of which are not remotely related to any particular examples of Constitutional passages he cites. He is also the founder and president of Wall-Builders, an organization devoted to bringing America back to its standing as a Christian nation. Sadly, I have run across many such examples of these sorts of shenanigans in the last few years of research for this book.[27] Here is one of the "James Madison" quotes David Barton used in his book that turned out to be a fabrication:

> We have staked the whole future of American civilization, not upon the power of government, far from it. We have staked the future of all of our political institutions upon the capacity of each and all of us to govern ourselves . . . according to the Ten Commandments of God.[28]

That would be a nice quote to support the case that we are a Christian nation. Not proof, by any means, especially given the role of religious terminology in public life at the time, but a nice little piece of anecdotal evidence along the lines of the quotes I am using here—*If it were true,* and if it accurately characterized Madison's views. It is difficult to be certain about many of the facts in this story because most of the sources reporting it could easily be accused of having a bias—groups protecting the separation of church and state and atheist groups top the list[29]—so I have spent a great deal of time fact-checking in an effort to avoid repeating Barton's mistakes in relating this story. The scandal received very little mainstream media attention, though Keith Olbermann covered the story on MSNBC,[30] and it was mentioned briefly in a *New York Times* article (and, as such, was likely never read by a single person who believed in Barton's version of history in the first place).

The second point that this story illustrates is that Christian nationalists do not back down in the face of mere facts, and scandals such as this are viewed as a badge of credibility, especially when someone is rebuked by scholars. I cannot find anything to *conclusively* confirm numerous stories that Barton admitted flatly that the quotes were false, and the WallBuilders website maintains that claims that he did so are untrue. I will give him the benefit of the doubt on that, though, frankly, his admission would have gar-nered a touch more respect than the defensive gymnastics on his website.[31]

It is also difficult to get to the bottom of how this all came about, but there is an article on the WallBuilders website that lists what they call "unconfirmed quotations"[32] from Barton's book. I found allusions on various websites to the idea that he was required to do this in some legal sense, but, again, I was not able to confirm that with certainty, and, in fair-ness, it seems likely that I could easily verify the story if that were the case. However it came to pass, the list is a study in not admitting quotes were invented, while grudgingly admitting that they did not appear in the sources he said they did in his book, or, for the majority of the quotes, in any source on James Madison that anyone has ever seen.

There are silly suggestions that some of the quotes might still show up in an old trunk somewhere, as though their eventual, unlikely discovery in the future would somehow exonerate Barton. With respect to the quote I included here, the defense they offer includes a typical assertion: "Madison could have easily offered the thought."[33] Given the fact that Madison was practically a zealot on the separation issue, this is a tough sell, but it is such a ridiculous defense in the face of fabricated quotes from historical figures that this point is superfluous. It is a fairly shifty list, and most of the defenses are about as compelling as asserting "well, he *might* have said it—you cannot prove conclusively that he did not say it . . . only that we cannot offer any proof that he ever did."

Finally, this quote from the WallBuilders list bears sharing. In response to another Barton quote attributed to James Madison—"Religion . . . [is] the basis and foundation of government"—that even the WallBuilders site concedes is "inaccurate," the website offers the following explanation:

> Taken from Madison's *Memorial and Remonstrance*, this quote has proven to be inaccurate. The actual phrase refers to the "Declaration of those rights 'which pertain to the good people of Virginia, as the basis and foundation of Government.'" Thus the subject of the statement is the Virginia Declaration of Rights, not religion. One may only speculate as to how the error was made.[34]

One can, indeed, speculate. All of this would be less disturbing if Barton had not garnered so much attention in the conservative media and political world for his book—and were he not still getting it. But that is not the case.

His controversial book was written in 1989, and these issues were noted shortly after that, but his dance card has remained pretty full since then. In 2004, he worked as a political consultant for the Republican National Committee, mobilizing Evangelical Christian voters on behalf of George W. Bush. In fact, he was the vice-chairman of the Texas Republican Party from 1997 to 2006.[35] Among others, Newt Gingrich, Mike Huckabee, Bill Frist, and Michele Bachman have all met with and praised Barton and his "scholarship." He was even named as one of *Time* magazine's twenty-five "most influential evangelicals in America" in 2005. He is a darling of the right-wing, Christian nationalist media, where his radio and television appearances include interviews with Glenn Beck, D. James Kennedy, Pat Robertson, and James Dobson, among others. This man has a significant amount of social and political influence, and he is busily out there spreading his message.

The WallBuilders website decries the "scurrilous effort to discredit" Barton, but even some religious groups are clearly taking issue with him, much to their credit. In a lecture series sponsored by the Baptist Joint Committee for Religious Liberty, Purdue University historian Frank Lambert had this to say about the revisionist history of such "ultracon-servative, highly partisan, sectarian" Christian nationalists, as reported by Jeff Huett:

> The claims made by the evangelical "historians" include that America was founded as a Christian nation by Christian men on Christian prin-ciples; secular ideas and concerns are disregarded as having any role. Second, modern-day liberals and secularists, especially academic histo-rians, are the ones who have distorted the place of religion in American society. Third, partisan sectarian "historians" claim that the separation of church and state is a myth created by liberals and secularists because it is not in the Constitution. Lambert said these authors of bad history include Tim LaHaye, David Barton, William Federer and John Eidsmoe. "Rather than being historians, these are partisans. And when they write, they write as partisans, not historians who are trying to understand and explain history in context," he said.[36]

Lies and misrepresentations have muddied the waters of American history to the extent that you have to be very careful where you get your information. That is a shame, and it really says something about the scope of the cultural battle being fought in the United States on religious grounds. If you are guessing that David Barton has been discredited and relegated to joke status over this debacle, you would be mistaken: In 2012, he released another book, *The Jefferson Lies*,[37] which was a *New York Times* bestseller, despite being voted the "least credible history book in print" and eventually being pulled from further publication.[38]

Finally, we turn our attention to George Washington, who was fairly closed-mouthed about his own religious beliefs, but who clearly believed both in respecting all religions and in the separation of church and state. In 1795, he had this to say on the topic:

In politics as in religion, my tenets are few and simple. The leading one of which, and indeed that which embraces most others, is to be honest and just ourselves and to exact it from others, meddling as little as possible in their affairs where our own are not involved. If this maxim was generally adopted, wars would cease and our swords would soon be converted into reap hooks and our harvests be more peaceful, abundant, and happy.[39]

Washington is a founding father routinely cited to support both sides of the Christian nation argument, and he provided fodder for misinterpretation by dominionist historians in his frequent allusions to God. The proof, however, is in the pudding, as they say, and the Constitution is the pudding.

Having had experience with a state church in England, the founding fathers were obviously averse to reviving such a venture. As the founding document of the United States, the Constitution only mentions religion in terms of limiting it—which it does in article 6, section 3: "no religious test shall ever be required as a qualification to any office or public trust under the United States." If the founding fathers had intended the United States to be a Christian nation, does it not it seem likely that they would have at least mentioned it in this meticulous document defining our principles as a nation?

The Bill of Rights addressed religion in the first amendment, but, again, this document does nothing to advance the claims of Christian nationalists in that it clearly draws a line between the government and religious practices: "Congress shall make no law respecting an establishment of religion, or prohibiting the free exercise thereof . . ."[40] The fact that Congress is prohibited from making laws establishing religions makes no sense in light of claims that the United States was created as a Christian nation but makes perfect sense in the context of avoiding England's model.

Similarly, the Supreme Court's 1892 ruling in the *Church of the Holy Trinity v. the United States* (143, U.S. 457) did not legally define the United States as a Christian nation, as many Christian nationalists contend. In fairness, the decision also held far more implications for the place of Christianity in our country than many secular sources care to acknowledge in characterizing it as a simple immigration and labor case. In fact, the full text of the case reveals that the justices spent a great deal of time contemplating their decision in light of American culture and found ample evidence that American culture clearly reflected a Christian orientation:

> If we pass beyond these matters to a view of American life, as expressed by its laws, its business, its customs, and its society, we find every where a clear recognition of the same truth. Among other matters, note the following: the form of oath universally prevailing, concluding with an appeal to the Almighty; the custom of opening sessions of all deliberative bodies and most conventions with prayer; the prefatory words of all wills, "In the name of God, amen;" the laws respecting the observance of the Sabbath, with the general cessation of all secular business, and the closing of courts, legislatures, and other similar public assemblies on that day; the churches and church organizations which abound in every city, town, and hamlet; the multitude of charitable organizations existing everywhere under Christian auspices; the gigantic missionary associations, with general support, and aiming to establish Christian missions in every quarter of the globe. These, and many other matters which might be noticed, add a volume of unofficial declarations to the mass of organic utterances that this is a Christian nation.

CULTURAL ARGUMENTS

This Supreme Court opinion speaks very directly to the manner in which the United States can be considered a Christian nation: many of its long-standing cultural tenets and customs. In a recent call to jury duty, I was reminded of this phenomenon when I entered the jury room to find a Bible on every chair in preparation for the oath we would shortly be required to take. Americans who are not Christians are often sorely aware of the extent to which our culture is steeped in such tradition—and reminded of it often—particularly in parts of the country in which Christianity has more of a stronghold. This is something that tends to be invisible to those raised as Christians of any stripe, who would have to imagine a copy of the Koran on each chair to even grasp the discomfort inherent in the presumption.

The supposition is not that everyone is a Christian, certainly, nor that the American government is explicitly Christian in any sense; the assumption is that Christianity is the norm.[41]

The favor, protection, and privilege enjoyed by Christianity in the United States speak to a special relationship that few are willing to contest (at least openly). While America features a plurality of religion and secularism, the predominant religion is definitely Christianity, and the influence of Christianity is profound and pervasive. It permeates American life to such an extent that we often fail to notice it. Further, most Americans believe its Christian culture is superior to that of other countries, topping the list for agreement with the statement that "Our people are not perfect, but our culture is superior to others" in an international Pew survey. About half (49 percent) of Americans felt culturally superior to other countries, with Germany coming in second at 47 percent. While the French take a lot of heat from Americans for a perception that the French feel smug and superior, research shows that we are the ones with the snooty attitude—only 27 percent of French citizens thought they were culturally superior to other countries.[42]

Another measure of America's Christianized culture is found in the importance Americans afford the role of religion in their lives relative to Western Europeans. In this respect, Americans really stand out, with a full 50 percent reporting that religion is "very important." Spain is the closest contender at 22 percent for agreement with this assertion, followed by Germany (21 percent), Britain (17 percent), and France (13 percent). In this same survey, we find that Americans also place far greater importance on believing in God as necessary to being "moral and having good values": 53 percent of Americans reported this belief, compared to 33 percent of Germans, 20 percent in Britain, 19 percent of Spaniards, and 15 percent in France. This is a tremendous attitudinal difference.

Though fundamentalists rant against the secularization of holidays such as Christmas and Easter, the mere fact that these holidays are so prominent in United States culture compared to the attention paid to holidays belonging to other religions makes "secularized" versions a testament to the prevailing position of Christianity in the United States. Jesus is the reason for the season, by definition. No amount of capitalistic effort to cash in on the popularity of these holidays, no matter how tacky, undermines the fact that we are not overwhelmed by gaudy Hanukkah or Ramadan displays in American stores. Similarly, Christmas is a federal holiday, and I have yet to work at a state university that does not suspend classes for an Easter break—or that does provide a break for Passover. As Alexis de Tocqueville noted in 1831, "There is no country in the world where the Christian religion retains a greater influence over the souls of men than in America."[43]

Complaints from Christians about attempts to cash in on Christ have to be taken with a grain of salt, at any rate. The array of "Christ-honoring" products available for purchase in the United States—by far the largest market for such goods—is dizzying. We are not throwing the money-changers out of the temple anymore. In fact, most modern megachurches feature stores selling a wide variety of Christian bling, books, and movies in the vestibule.[44] Catering to Christians is big business in America.

The influence of the Christian right in politics can hardly be over-stated. Since Reagan discovered, in 1968, their then-latent power to cause Nixon some early discomfort, their impact on conservative politics has been transformational to the Republican Party, which barely resembles its early twentieth-century platform. Faith-based voters hold considerable sway over the GOP, even reshaping their mission to usurp earlier defining concerns, such as reducing governmental spending and involvement. George Bush's election in 2000 and 2004 served as official notice of the power, funding, and organization conservative Christians now possess, and their reach exceeds much further than even most well-informed political junkies know.[45] The results are clear, however, even if there are few people fully aware of how the agenda was realized: The face of political discourse has morphed almost overnight into a strategy of polarization, in which two warring camps duke it out for power and control over the government. Pulitzer Prize–winning journalist and academic Thomas B. Edsall describes what he calls "leveraging anger" in this environment:

In this political arena, the Republican Party has successfully enlisted support for its program by tapping and exploiting the anger and cultural anxiety of middle- and lower-income white Americans. The GOP has courted those white voters whose interests are overwhelmingly focused on tempering, if not altogether rolling back, the civil rights movement, on forcibly stemming the tide of migrants from developing countries, on seeking to decelerate or reverse libertarian cultural trends, and on re-establishing what they see as a "decent and honorable" society. To this end, the GOP and its allies in the conservative movement have focused on hot-button appeals concerning moral values such as "the homosexual lifestyle," the rights of the unborn, or "illegal" immigration.[46]

A great many books have been written about the political influence of conservative Christians, as well as their general impact on culture in the United States, and I am discussing the topics too briefly here out of necessity. Suffice it to say that it is through culture that I contend that the United States is a Christian nation.

Our founding fathers were clearly more concerned with creating a government that would protect Americans from religious tyranny than in establishing a homogeneous Christian state, and anyone arguing differently does so at the expense of incontrovertible evidence. The irony that the opposite of this contention serves as an underpinning for most brands of Christian nationalism, a form of religious tyranny, is not lost upon me—and should not be lost upon Americans intent upon upholding the secular foundation of our country.

STATISTICAL ARGUMENTS

Another means to support my contention that the United States is Christian to the extent that it bears examination in light of religiosity and crime rests on comparisons to levels of secularism in many comparable nations. Christianity is the world's largest religious denomination, with a membership of just more than a third of the global population, or roughly 2.18 billion people.[47]

In the United States, 79.5 percent of Americans identify themselves as belonging to a Christian denomination, with 26.3 percent belonging to "evangelical" Protestant churches, and the South boasting the greatest concentration of evangelical Protestants by an extremely wide margin.[48] Regional distributions of Christians worldwide have been impacted greatly by population growth in recent years, with sub-Saharan Africa accounting for a significant portion of recent growth in adherents to Christian denominations. The findings suggest that Christianity is not concentrated in a few places but rather is truly global in character; I am not contending that we are the only Christian outpost—I am simply contending that we are a particular stronghold, especially among developed countries, and the data more than support this contention.

In 2014, a Gallup Values and Beliefs survey revealed that 42 percent of Americans still believe that God created human beings in their present form about ten thousand years ago. Roughly half of Americans believe humans evolved, with the majority of these holding that God guided the evolutionary process (31 percent).[49] While the numbers who believe that God was not involved is rising (19 percent), this still paints a fairly clear picture of American religious beliefs. The discontinuity between the general scientific consensus and the beliefs of Americans is striking, as are both the presence and the patterns in these beliefs in a developed nation. There is movement, albeit slow, in these numbers: The strict secularist belief that God had no part in the creation of humans has doubled since 1999, while the creationist view has held fairly steady over time. Younger Americans are less likely to believe in a creationist perspective, and there is a sizable gap between college-educated individuals (27 percent believe in creation) and those with no more than a high school education (57 percent).

Survey findings in support of my contention that the United States has a Christian character are noteworthy in a couple of important respects: First, the United States contains the largest population of Christians in the world. And second, the United States also has the largest population of evangelical Christians in the world, which is not surprising in light of the fact that the movement began here.[50]

10 Countries with the Largest Number of Christians

Countries	ESTIMATED 2010 CHRISTIAN POPULATION	PERCENTAGE OF POPULATION THAT IS CHRISTIAN	PERCENTAGE OF WORLD CHRISTIAN POPULATION
United States	246,780,000	79.5%	11.3%
Brazil	175,770,000	90.2	8.0
Mexico	107,780,000	95.0	4.9
Russia	105,220,000	73.6	4.8
Philippines	86,790,000	93.1	4.0
Nigeria	80,510,000	50.8	3.7
China	67,070,000	5.0	3.1
DR Congo	63,150,000	95.7	2.9
Germany	58,240,000	70.8	2.7
Ethiopia	52,580,000	63.4	2.4
Subtotal for the 10 Countries	1,043,880,000	40.4	47.8
Total for Rest of World	1,140,180,000	6.3	52.2
World Total	**2,184,060,000**	**31.7**	**100.0**

Population estimates are rounded to the ten thousands. Percentages are calculated from unrounded numbers. Figures may not add exactly due to rounding. See Appendix C for details on the range of estimates available for China.

Pew Research Center's Forum on Religion & Public Life • *Global Christianity*, December 2011

Table 1: Used with permission from Pew Research Center, http://www.pewforum.org/2011/12/19/global-christianity-exec/.

Overall, the United States tops the list in terms of Christianity, with respect to the percentage of the world's Christian population, providing a compelling basis for examining crime in the United States in light of Christian religiosity, and for comparisons with other countries on this basis, as well. Christian principles play a far greater role in the public lives of Americans than they do in most similarly situated countries. The phrase "In God We Trust" on currency reflects this Christian undercurrent in American culture, and there is a concurrent and pervasive belief that God somehow favors the United States over other countries. The term "superpower" takes on a new meaning in this context, and it is not at all surprising that we are often criticized for our arrogant and paternalistic response to other nations when we hold this attitude of superiority.

It is a more difficult task to flesh out the numbers of Christian nationalists, as less research has been conducted to the end of identifying this particular belief system within the wider population of those identifying as Christians, or even Evangelical Christians. The biggest difficulty in this task lies in the fact that Christian nationalists are distinguished by their adherence to a particular belief system rather than their membership in a particular denomination. In fact, Christian nationalism is present across a wide variety of denominations, from Protestant-based faiths to Mormonism and Catholicism.[51] Despite the difficulty in directly fleshing out Christian nationalism, agreement on other measures that reflect Dominionist beliefs, such as God favoring the United States in particular, show that they are a sizable minority in America.

One could certainly argue with this major underlying assumption for my theory, and I willingly concede that such a debate could involve good points on both sides, but it is clear that, both culturally and statistically, the United States stands out in its Christian character. The theory that I will be presenting here is more cultural than structural, though culture always influences structure to some degree, and the numbers of Christians in the United States doubtless make for a greater influence than in places where Christianity holds less sway.

THE CONTINUING INFLUENCE OF CHRISTIANITY IN THE UNITED STATES: THE EXAMPLE OF NONBELIEVERS

Christian nationalists like to refer to discrimination against Christians as the "last acceptable prejudice" in the United States, but that clearly is not the case, and is almost comical in light of the discrimination they actively promote against other groups.[52] The idea that Christians are persecuted serves an important purpose in promoting group cohesion, and this is likely why the idea persists even in American society, where Christians enjoy far more than tolerance. Candida Moss, professor of New Testament and Early Christianity at Notre Dame, and author of *The Myth of Persecution*, points out:

> When disagreement and dissent are conflated with persecution, dialogue, collaboration and even compassion become impossible. You cannot

reason with your persecutors, you have to fight them. If persecution becomes a badge of honor and a sign of moral superiority then what reason is there to try and persuade others of one's arguments? Framed by the myth that we are persecuted, dialogue is not only impossible; it is undesirable.[53]

Within this framework, nonbelievers are persecuted while simultaneously being cast as persecutors of Christians.

The case of American attitudes about nonbelievers makes claims to persecution even more ridiculous, as Christians clearly hold the title for inflicting persecution on others in the United States, and the most virulent proponents of this treatment are Christian nationalists.[54] Attitudes about nonreligious people have long been employed as an index of social and political tolerance in various countries, and survey research about these attitudes in the United States casts doubt on our claim to openness and enlightenment. While various denominations of Christianity and other religions eye one another with skepticism, it appears that not believing in *any* God excites a heightened level of animosity and distrust that far exceeds that reserved for groups who believe in the "wrong" conception of God, despite the increasing numbers of Americans willing to openly admit a complete lack of religious faith.

A recent University of Minnesota study sheds unflattering light on the thriving prejudice against atheists, examining the results of a national survey of 2081 citizens. Among other findings, sociologists Penny Edgell, Joseph Gerteis, and Douglas Hartmann found that:

Americans draw symbolic boundaries that clearly and sharply exclude atheists in both private and public life. From a list of groups that also includes Muslims, recent immigrants, and homosexuals, Americans name atheists as those least likely to share their vision of American society. They are also more likely to disapprove of their children marrying atheists.[55]

It is very telling that atheists pose such a threat in light of the idea that the United States is generally so tolerant of religious differences, and these researchers concluded that the lines between various denominations and belief systems have become blurred to the extent that religious people view themselves as "us" versus a nonreligious "them." One bond here is likely the belief system of Christian nationalism, which explicitly counts nonbelievers as outsiders in a Christian country.

Further, atheists appear largely immune from the general trend toward increasing acceptance by Christians of out-groups, such as homosexuals, recent immigrants, and Muslims, leading the researchers to "rethink some core assumptions about Americans' increasing acceptance of religious diversity."[56] This certainly calls into question arguments that we are not a religious country, as Edgell and her colleagues aptly characterize in noting that "Americans construct the atheist as the symbolic representation of one who rejects the basis for moral solidarity and cultural membership in American society altogether."[57]

Another strong indicator that the nonreligious are the true lightening rod for acceptable prejudice is found in survey research conducted by Gallup to determine Americans' willingness to vote for presidential candidates based on a variety of characteristics. The characteristics included in the survey consisted of candidates who were black (96 percent), female (95 percent), Catholic (94 percent), Hispanic (92 percent), Jewish (91 percent), Mormon (80 percent), gay or lesbian (68 percent), and Muslim (58 percent). Atheists (54 percent) ranked at the bottom of the list of candidates that Americans would be willing to vote for, though the results of this 2012 survey put them over the halfway mark for the first time since these attitudes have been measured.[58]

All of these findings suggest that the United States has considerable room for improvement in terms of prejudice against the faith-free among us. These findings are even more disturbing in that the percentages of people admitting that they would not consider voting for a candidate based on these attributes came despite the hypothetical presidential candidates being presented as both "well-qualified" and "nominated by their own party."

Additionally, as with all survey research on topics such as this, it is also highly likely that many respondents were less than forthcoming about their prejudices, so these findings should be viewed as conservative estimates.[59] Not surprisingly, the Gallup findings differed along political lines, and the fact that the Republican Party had a Mormon candidate running for the presidency at the time of this survey likely influenced results for that group compared to previous surveys. Even results among Democrats shifted on the Mormon question, suggesting that respondents of both parties were probably thinking about their specific willingness to vote for Mitt Romney rather than any highly qualified Mormon candidate. Not surprisingly, Republicans were significantly more likely than Democrats to say that they would not vote for a highly qualified candidate who was gay, Muslim, or an atheist.

In an age where Christian nationalists have managed to put a candidate's faith at the forefront in presidential races, this emphasis on religiosity bears close examination. Interestingly, a look at the faith of past presidents results in the conclusion that faith does not predict Christ-like behavior once a president takes office. In fact, presidents widely regarded as less religious may act more in accordance with Christian principles— especially New Testament principles—than those regarded as devoutly Christian.[60] A few examples bear discussion in exploring this point.

While this is hardly a point of pride in conservative Christian circles, the contemporary president with the most impressive Christian credentials was arguably Richard Nixon, who called himself "a lifelong Quaker and a church-going Christian."[61] He played piano in church, taught Sunday school, and attended revivals. His mother thought he would become a missionary, while friends thought he was destined to be a preacher.[62] The history of his presidency speaks for itself, resulting in Watergate, a web of deception and crime that brought shame to both the office and the man. The foul-mouthed, mean-spirited Nixon revealed on tape in the wake of his presidency does not square easily with his image as a church-going Christian.[63] George W. Bush, a president who also parlayed his zealous Christian faith into a base of support without which he would not have won two terms,[64] supported the use of torture, revealed a conservatism that was less than compassionate in handling Katrina, and involved America in a war in Iraq resulting in the loss of 4,421 American lives, 31,934 Americans wounded, and 85,694 Iraqi civilian deaths from 2004 to 2008.[65] Lyndon

Johnson, who grew up in and was affiliated with the Baptist and Disciples of Christ churches, almost certainly stole his first election to public office, lied about United States involvement in the Vietnam war, and cursed so frequently that reporters had difficulty quoting him directly.[66]

If we go back further, Andrew Jackson likely takes the "all-time most devout president" title, as a daily Bible reader who built a chapel in his home and attended two churches almost without fail while in Washington. Despite his deeply held Presbyterian beliefs, Jackson once killed a man in a duel and was known for his violent temper, was a rich slaveholder, and killed enough Native Americans for numerous historians to characterize his policy as genocidal.[67]

Jimmy Carter is the best example of a devout Christian who lived up to the tenets of the New Testament in his presidency, but his faith was more moderate and oriented toward social justice.[68] Barack Obama has faced more scrutiny surrounding his faith than any other modern president (Thomas Jefferson and George Washington received similar treatment from the conservative Christian element in their times), though there is no doubt whatsoever that he is not a Muslim, and is, indeed, a liberal Christian.[69] His healthcare reform, support for gay and lesbian marriage rights, and desire to end the war in Iraq are thought to stem from his liberal Christian beliefs—though, of course, this contention is controversial.

The bottom line is that the role of faith in presidential elections highlights the importance of Christianity in the United States and will undoubtedly continue to do so, despite the fact that it appears to matter little once a candidate is in office. Mitt Romney's presidential bid should have proved interesting in this respect, as Mormonism has a rocky relationship with Christian nationalists of Protestant-based religions, despite sharing much of the same cultural belief system. Romney would likely have faced far more negative scrutiny if his opponent was less an anathema to the Christian right, and it is possible that his failure to ignite the conservative base stemmed to some extent from his Mormon bona fides.

That this obsession with the faith of politicians is so pervasive in light of the fact that history clearly demonstrates that it is a lousy predictor of morality in office is not surprising given the Christian culture of the United

States, and it is unlikely to change the goal of Christian nationalists to keep faith at the forefront in elections. Arguments based on history, and data showing that traditional Christian beliefs are a questionable litmus test for future ethical behavior, are unlikely to find fertile ground in the minds of Christian nationalist adherents.

The threat of atheism and agnosticism is quite easy to understand, even beyond its unconscious utility in defining insiders in American society through defining who is excluded. Atheists are threatening to Christianity in even suggesting that there is an alternative to embracing their beliefs, and Christianity has a long history of vilifying and silencing them due to this threat, along with others with different religious views.[70] I will not belabor this point, as even most Christians are hard-pressed to discount the litany of examples, including the Crusades, the Inquisition, Reformation, witch hunts, and the Christian Identity movement.[71] Sadly, this list barely scratches the surface, and, sadder still, among Christian nationalists these warnings are clearly forgotten or viewed as not applicable to their aims.[72]

As a result of the near-taboo on disbelief, it is believed that many people with atheistic and agnostic beliefs keep such beliefs to themselves, or simply describe themselves as nonreligious, while avoiding the question of God. Given the downside of incurring distain, many people likely dodge the question personally as well as publically.[73] It is possible to "pass" in society without being identified with this group, but survey research clearly shows that atheists and agnostics may be tiring of the shadows.

There are enough atheists in the United States to count them among other, more influential and visible minorities, such as Jews, who account for 1.7 percent versus the 1.6 percent of atheists in the American population. When you consider that another 2.4 percent report that they are agnostic, and a further 12.1 percent report their religion as "nothing in particular," you begin to form a picture of a much larger minority of nonreligious people in the United States.[74] While this has been a very silent minority in the past, as mentioned previously, this group may now be finding its voice. Many recent books and films signal this group's weariness with hiding what they view to be rational and ethical beliefs in the face of a vocal majority. This group's greater participation in public life will likely take time, but closely resembles the gay and lesbian population's road toward greater visibility and power in both politics and society. Christopher Hitchens and Richard Dawkins have served as inspiration, and a number of celebrities have been tentatively coming out of the closet as nonbelievers. This shift will likely impact rates of violence in the United States in a positive way, but the road will surely be rocky. At this point, there is every indication that the closet may be pretty full of atheists: In 2009, the Pew Research Center's Forum on Religion and Public Life reported that while 5 percent of respondents in the US Religious Landscape Survey said they do not believe in God or a universal spirit, only a quarter (24 percent) of these nonbelievers call themselves atheists,[75] which is not surprising with prevailing attitudes toward this formal label so strongly negative.

Probably the greatest threat to Christianity posed by atheists is that they tend to be much more educated about Christianity, and other religious traditions, than the adherents of Christianity themselves. The Pew Center's Forum on Religious and Public Life conducted a survey of religious knowledge that revealed that atheists and agnostics out-performed adherents of all religions, followed closely by Jews and Mormons, controlling for factors such as educational levels.[76] In response to these findings, current president of the nonprofit organization American Atheists, Dave Silverman, expressed no surprise:

> The simple truth is this; the more someone knows about religion, the more likely they will reject it as mythology. Consider the books of Leviticus, Job, or Revelations. These are not books of love, but rather of barbaric rules, ruthless torture, and threats from a petty and bloodthirsty god. Islam is no different, placing a pedophile on a pedestal of perfection. . . . Many religious people do not read their holy books for fear of finding things they don't like, which will force them to consider whether those easy answers are valid, and whether death is in fact permanent. In other words, religious people already have doubts, and avoid reading their Bibles to avoid addressing those doubts. . . . So please, dear readers, read your Bible. Before you pay your preacher another penny, or get on your knees to beg your god for something you know very well he's not going to give you, read your holy book, cover to cover, alone. I dare you.[77]

What I found most surprising about this quote was where I found it: On the Fox News opinion page. (The comment feature was disabled, but who can blame them?) Silverman's observation is common among atheists and agnostics, who frequently cite religious studies as the impetus for their lack of belief.

Scientific advancement and greater knowledge about religions have certainly played a role in the decline of religiosity in better-educated parts of the world. It is difficult to argue with the idea that people who are less knowledgeable generally are also less knowledgeable about religion, but the Pew Forum survey dispels any lingering doubts to that end. In a segment of the religious knowledge study that received far less media attention, surveyors asked respondents a set of nine questions on topics other than religion—two political, three scientific, and four about historical and literary topics. These were not the type of questions one would need to study for: Questions included asking respondents who the vice-president of the United States is (59 percent knew it was Joe Biden), whether or not lasers work by focusing sound waves (40 percent thought that was the case), and who wrote Moby Dick (this one was multiple choice, and 42 percent correctly chose Herman Melville; though it is scary, I cannot resist noting that 4 percent chose Stephen King). Once again, atheists and agnostics were at the head of the class, with Jews close behind, showing the strong correlation between scoring high or low on the religious and general questionnaires.[78] It becomes inescapable to conclude that if you want to increase membership in religions it is best to keep people dumb. Atheists and agnostics are a real threat to that goal, and God, being omnipotent and all-knowing, must have known that when he forbade eating fruit from the tree of knowledge.[79]

The antipathy between science and religion is at play in the case of nonbelievers, and the same bellicose reactions come into play for the same reasons: Religions do not benefit from people knowing more about them or about the world they live in. For people who have built their lives around their faith, atheists and agnostics are the snake in the garden. Luckily for religious leaders, they have done a good job of presenting an unquestioning faith as the most godly variety and knowledge as an evil antithesis to faith.

Overall, if the United States were not a Christian nation, nonbelievers would hardly experience such negative public attitudes. Nonbelievers would also feel more comfortable expressing their views on the compelling issue of faith without fear of consequence, and we would not live in a world in which so many situations feature an assumption of Christian belief.

CHAPTER THREE

WHY PICK ON
CHRISTIAN NATIONALISTS?

You can safely assume that you've created God in your own image when it turns out God hates all the same people you do.
—**Anne Lamott**, *Bird by Bird*

The ultimate goal of Christian nationalist leaders isn't fairness. It's dominion. The movement is built on a theology that asserts the Christian right to rule. That doesn't mean that nonbelievers will be forced to convert. They'll just have to learn their place.
—**Michelle Goldberg**, *Kingdom Coming*

An avidity to punish is always dangerous to liberty. It leads men to stretch, to misinterpret, and to misapply even the best of laws. He that would make his own liberty secure must guard even his enemy from oppression; for if he violates his duty, he establishes a precedent that will reach to himself.
—**Thomas Paine**,
Dissertation on First Principles of Government

The idea that Christianity is the underpinning for violence is not new, and most with an appreciation of history clearly see the negative consequences of zealous religiosity in wars, crusades, genocides, and many other cases of bloody persecution throughout human history. But surprisingly little scholarly attention has focused on Christianity as having a causal connection with violent criminality, and what attention the subject has received has tended to focus almost exclusively on the question of whether religious involvement serves as insulation from committing criminal acts, mostly in the context of religion as a form of social control.[1]

The vast majority of this research has also focused on a couple of very specific types of nonviolent criminality, such as drug and alcohol use, where religion often imparts a positive impact.[2] In itself, this orientation seems rooted in the view of Christianity as synonymous with strong, intact families, discipline and structure, and an emphasis on moral instruction that would likely inhibit forays into delinquency and crime. But is this really the case? Or is this an idealized view of self-avowed conservative Christian families that is based more in cultural lore than modern realities? There is evidence that Christian values in America, and the actions they inspire, are something less than advertised in terms of inhibiting bad behavior.

As such, my theory does not approach Christianity on its own terms or accept the premise that faith results in more moral behavior. There is a case for assuming this skepticism in debunking many myths widely perpetuated by Christian nationalists regarding everything from their strong, intact families to the idea that modern Christians reflect the Protestant work ethic in more than disgust for the "undeserving" poor, to the idea that Christians are morally superior and better Americans than non-Christians.[3] In short, I propose a theory that deals with the reality of Christianity in America, rather than the rhetoric. While the reality of Christianity encompasses many positive features, it also includes a number of features that are criminogenic (crime-producing) in nature.

Of all the denominations and flavors that fall under the auspices of "Christianity" in most survey data on religiosity, Christian nationalism most reflects the aspects of religion that I believe to be criminogenic. Before we look at those factors, however, it will be helpful to more carefully define what I mean by Christian nationalism, also known as dominionism, and discuss the terminology for the various theologies and belief systems that it encompasses to varying degrees.

A CULTURAL MOVEMENT

One difficulty that arises in defining what is encompassed by the term "Christian nationalism" lies in the fact that much of the group's character is not strictly religious but rather incorporates a strong cultural identity, including many secular aspects that are loosely related to a perception of religiosity. These aspects can be conceived of as a belief system common to most adherents of Christian nationalism—whether they know they are Christian nationalists or not. Importantly, it is likely most Christian nationalists would not even be familiar with this term for their belief system and might not even see their beliefs as part of a unified system flowing from—or through—their fundamentalist Christianity. There are a variety of religious groups that adhere to a significant number of Christian nationalist views and few—if any—who would actually call themselves such. But a rose by any other name still has thorns. Evangelical, charismatic, fundamentalist, traditionalist—there are many terms applied to religions that tend to include a significant number of Christian nationalists.

But Christian nationalism is not a religious denomination, a political party, or an explicit ideology—it is more of a movement incorporating all of these facets. Jeff Sharlet, author of *The Family: The Secret Fundamentalism at the Heart of American Power*, described some central tenets of the Christian nationalist belief system as such:

> The Christian nation of which the movement dreams, a government of those chosen by God but democratically elected by a people who freely accept His will as their own, is a far country. The nation they seek does not, at the moment, exist; perhaps it could in the future. More important to fundamentalism is the belief that it did exist in the American past, not in the history we learn in public school and from PBS and in newsmagazine cover stories on the Founders but in another story, one more biblical, one more mythic and more true. Secularism hides this story, killed the Christian nation, and tried to dispose of the body. Fundamentalism wants to resurrect it, and doing so requires revision: fundamentalists, looking backward, see a different history, remade in the image of the seductive but strict logic of a prime mover that sets things in motion. The cause behind every effect, says fundamentalist science, is God. Even the inexorable facts of math are subject to His decree, as explained in home-schooling texts such as *Mathematics: Is God Silent?* Two plus two is four because God says so. If He chose, it could just as easily be five.[4]

The key features in this description are a revisionist history of the United States, a longing for that imagined vision, and a desire to "return" the country to this hallowed past as a truly Christian nation. Add appeals to flag, faith, and family, along with the list of people who are perceived as threats, and you have a fuller list of the cultural tenets of Christian nationalism. Christian nationalists also tend to be white, by and large, and lower to middle class, though many of the leaders of the movement are of higher socioeconomic status (partly through capitalizing on their leadership roles).

Christian nationalism is pro-life, pro capital punishment, vaguely anti-contraceptive, and anti-gay. They are proponents of religious instruction, including creationism, and prayer in public schools. They seek the greater inclusion of Christianity in law and government as a guiding principle. They are against extramarital sex, and they spawned abstinence-only education and virginity-pledge movements as means to that end.[5] While fighting to expand the role of Christianity in public schools, they also support voucher programs for private schools, many of which have religious curriculums. Overall, the belief system of Christian nationalism has a tremendous impact on the culture, institutions, and political life of the United States.

ATTRIBUTES OF THE BELIEF SYSTEM

The following Christian nationalist convictions will be discussed in the context of violent criminality. In much the same manner as diagnoses in the DSM, an adherent need not agree with every tenet to warrant inclusion in the movement:

- The idea that the Bible is the literal word of God, and thus incontrovertible and authoritative in its assertions.
- That the Bible should serve as the sole foundation for every facet of American life—including governance and law.
- That the United States was formed as a Christian nation and must be

restored to its original status as what essentially amounts to a theocratic society (sort of a neopuritan model).

- That separation of church and state was not intended by the framers
  of the Constitution.
- That theology conveys a superiority to conservative Christians, who have
  dominion—the right to rule—over America vis-à-vis Genesis 1:28.
- That the United States was once a great country, but the liberal
  agenda of secular humanism has steered it in an ungodly direction
  that must be corrected.
- Gay marriage and legalized abortion have become the central issues
  used to mobilize this movement, though appeals to the three Fs of
  American conservative Christianity—family, flag, and faith—are
  also routinely engaged, and with considerable success.
- That Christians are required to spread the word of God through
  evangelism—or at least to have their beliefs known. At minimum,
  they should be easily identifiable through their belief system.[6]
- That good Christians must stand up against people and things deemed
  ungodly and have the right to identify that which they believe to be
  ungodly through the auspices of religious freedom.
- That Christians—and particularly those who hold fundamentalist
  beliefs—are persecuted and ridiculed in the United States.

These distinct Christian nationalist convictions make up the belief
system that differentiates this group from other religious groups in the
United States, many of which are more moderate or liberal. They also tip
the balance toward the various negative effects of religious life, particularly
in the case of violence, where such a belief system will have a measurable
impact if this theory is correct.

Again, it is important to note that Christian nationalists will likely
vary a bit in terms of their level of agreement with all of these tenets, and
undoubtedly there will be some who would disagree with a few of them. I
am hesitant to impose some arbitrary estimation of the level of agreement
necessary to trigger a label of "Christian nationalist," but certainly such
a distinction can be made.[7] I suspect that agreement with even a few of

these tenets would more than suffice, but future research on this phenom-enon will certainly need to incorporate a measure of these convictions in order to capture the independent variable of interest, rather than relying on proxy measures, such as church attendance, denomination, or whether people consider themselves "born again."

CRIMINOGENIC FEATURES OF THESE ATTRIBUTES

But how can these beliefs cause crime? For many, the idea that a Christian belief system promotes criminality is completely counterintuitive. Religious beliefs are steeped in the avoidance of sin, after all—how can they possibly result in "sins" so widely viewed as harmful that they are crimi-nalized in a democratic society? Christianity is, well, wholesome, and Christians exert a lot of energy extolling virtues that seem antithetical to my thesis. Further, conservative Christians have little tolerance for crimi-nals and tend to view harsh punishments for crime as both necessary and right. This also contributes to the perception that Christianity could not possibly lend itself to violent criminality.

Like many issues surrounding conservative Christianity, its impact on crime tends to be assessed along polarized lines that present two opposing views that are equally incorrect. Christian nationalists will undoubtedly see nothing but a positive effect, while rabidly anti-religious people will tend to focus only on the negative impact of religion. As with just about everything else in life, the truth is easier to locate at the center of the argu-ment. If we move beyond fodder for propaganda, we see that such beliefs have a more complicated effect.

Christian convictions have a number of specific crime-inhibiting effects—again, namely in the cases of drug and alcohol use and some less serious forms of delinquency—but for the moment, I will briefly focus on the argument that many of the beliefs common to Christian nationalism are criminogenic. I will reserve a fuller discussion of this phenomenon in terms of biblical justifications and the theological contradictions inherent to the issue for chapters four and five, but this treatment should be enough to get the reader oriented to the basics of why Christian nationalism is the focus of this theory. In broad strokes:

- A biblical justification and rationalization for violence are inherent in Christian nationalism. The Bible is rife with violence, and particularly violent retribution, as you will see in later chapters. When viewed as the literal word of God, this conveys God's blessing on the use of violence in the face of opposition to anything perceived as being God's will, along with many garden variety affronts. Christian nationalists tend to embrace a conception of God as judgmental and tough on social issues, eschewing the meeker social justice orientation of Jesus.[8]

The Bible contains a doctrine—and a God—that are fairly characterized as violent, even in the New Testament, which is milder in this respect than the Old Testament (though less so than many people seem to think). It is often overlooked that while there are certainly loving and redemptive passages in the Bible, those sentiments are reserved almost exclusively for adherents of the Christian faith, and, even there, a significant number of passages are punitive toward adherents who are judged unworthy for one reason or another. God is not above smiting folks who piss him off, and Christian nationalists tend to embrace many of the more rigid moral judgments and consequences in the Bible to a greater extent than Christians of more moderate and liberal faiths. At times, belief in these harsh "moral" doctrines seems almost a point of pride: Real Christians do not shirk the tough stuff, and they believe those who do have a substandard faith.

Biblical tenets that are particularly significant in their criminogenic impact will be discussed in more detail in chapter five, but suffice it to say that there is enough material to need a chapter five, and that I had to be selective even there in order to avoid confusing endurance with hospitality on your part. Overall, the Bible provides ample justification for violence.

- Christian nationalism promotes and reinforces right-wing beliefs in adherents, and those beliefs have become increasingly aggressive and aligned with the use of violence. Conservative political beliefs are part and parcel of Christian nationalism, and the beliefs that resonate most strongly with Christian nationalists include militarism, gun rights, aggressive foreign policy, weak domestic social supports, getting "tough" on crime, and moves to exclude and reduce the rights and power of groups garnering the displeasure of Christian nationalists, such as gays and lesbians, immigrants, criminals, liberals, nontraditional women, those of other faiths, and nonbelievers. It can be argued that right-wing politics have become something of a feedback loop for Christian nationalists, who both shape and are shaped by their political views. This growing political influence is on display in the usurping of the Tea Party's original intent, and the part this branch of right-wing conservative politics now plays in driving the GOP further to the right—and more in line with Christian nationalist aims.[9]

- Christian nationalism places certain groups of people in the category of deserving of victimization—or, at the very least, not deserving of much sympathy when they are victimized. Dominionism promotes intolerance and hatred. Groups viewed as threats to "traditional values"—which are the values of Christian nationalism—reap what they sow.[10] This extends beyond groups such as gays and lesbians to include victims of religious violence, such as abortion doctors, people viewed as unpatriotic, and the victimization of those engaged in behaviors deemed immoral or antiauthoritarian, among others. This feeling may not always reach the level of condoning such victimization, but it sets apart a category of people for whom victimization might be viewed as God's will.

Finally, Christian nationalism provides social support for prejudicial beliefs against other groups, legitimizing such views biblically, broadcasting them, and in diffusing their responsibility for holding the views.[11] Christian nationalists are, after all, simply engaging in their right to freedom of religion. But it is far easier to victimize people who have been dehumanized or, at minimum, deemed deserving of punishment, and in this manner Christian nationalist beliefs promote violence.

- Christian nationalism promotes vengeance-seeking, righteousness, and violence in the protection of the belief system, because it insulates followers from fear of death. There is a large body of research on a phenomenon called mortality salience (reminders of our own mortality) that strongly suggests that people react with hostility, and even violence, when beliefs that insulate them from their natural fear of death are threatened.[12] Fear of death is generally an unconscious fear, but there is significant evidence to support the rather obvious contention that it is powerful and primal. If someone adopts a belief that insulates them from this fear—and that is a primary function of religion—any threat to that belief tends to result in a strong, aggressive reaction.

If you think about that for a minute, it makes tremendous sense. The unknown of dying can be very frightening, especially when contrasted with the promise of eternal life in a godly utopia. This reaction is likely more intense if a person has adopted a belief in which heaven and hell are the only two options in death. If someone or something shakes the belief that God exists, the person doubting their beliefs experiences considerable discomfort, having been indoctrinated into a belief system in which they either believe in God and go to heaven or do not believe and go to hell. Purgatory has nothing on that sort of torment, and such beliefs are hard to comfortably shake. Pascal's wager likely seems like a smart bet in the midst of such anguish, and it is clear that many people take that wager. Given the discomfort of challenges to one's faith, it is not surprising that this fear leads people to insulate themselves from outside influences that might threaten that faith. This results in xenophobia and more homogeneous social circles, as well as the vilification of people with differing beliefs on the subject of the afterlife.

Religion as insulation from fear of death has a further component: Not only does the promise of eternal life serve to lessen fear but the experience of tying yourself to something greater—and more permanent—tends to lessen the fear of death, as well. Patriotism and religion both serve this purpose admirably, as the religious institution and the country will live on after your death. This is akin to having children, creating some monumental work, or in some way making a mark on mankind in an effort to show you were here after your demise and that you mattered.

For most, that goal is pretty elusive beyond the memories of our loved ones, but involvement in something that endures beyond us provides a powerful emotional proxy for this insulation. Overall, the sort of potent response invoked by reminders of the inevitability of death can be crimi-nogenic.[13] This is why patriotism swells when people feel their country is threatened, and it is why convivial conversations about religion are so rare among people of deep but different faiths.

- The survival of Christian nationalism, like most religions, requires adherents to reject the beliefs of others as wrong. People with opposing views are cast not as simply disagreeing, but as working on the side of Satan. This should not be surprising in light of the last discussion, and requires little further explanation. The difference in the antipathy toward a person holding an opposing viewpoint versus someone viewed as a force of evil is bound to be greater, and a handy justification for greater hostility, and even violence.[14] The rhetoric of labeling opposition as evil is pervasive, and this quote from televangelist James Robison is typical of such fare:

  > With God's help, believers can defeat the enemy's plan. We must join together to see hearts changed and fulfill the will of God. We can and must defeat the enemy's strategy. Remember, we are not warring against flesh and blood, but against spiritual powers and hidden sinister forces of darkness and deception. Satan is the father of all lies.[15]

  I could provide hundreds of examples of vilifying enemies to facilitate violent actions toward them, but I suspect the point is obvious. The bottom line is that, if you are fighting against evil, nearly any action is justified.

- Christian nationalism requires adherents to adopt their membership as a master status—a primary feature of both their group and personal identity.[16] This increases the intensity with which Christian nationalists defend their faith and belief system because it also serves as the foundation for their social universe. The social support and control exerted by membership in this type of movement is immense and has both positive and negative effects.

Christian nationalists are likely to situate the majority of their social lives in the movement. Their friends tend to be like-minded, and church activities play a significant role in their social life while promoting and reinforcing the belief system. Falling out of favor or leaving the group would leave an enormous void that would require a Herculean effort to fill. Further, this vivid social life is almost instant and portable, requiring only that the adherent become involved in a church, from which sociability is easy to attain and establish. Ironically, this is one of the reasons why it is difficult for criminals to reintegrate successfully into their communities in the wake of rehabilitative efforts; their social universe tends to be criminal, and the difficulty of walking away from everything you know is immense.

Involvement in these social circles and adherence to these beliefs also tends to limit entrée into other social circles—this belief system becomes a defining trait of the person, and human beings tend to be protective of their sense of who they are. We react defensively to threats against our sense of self and how we are perceived by others.[17] As such, it is far easier to stay within the confines of groups who agree with our views. One might rightly point out that this holds true for secularists, as well, but there is a key difference in that a secularists' political, social, and religious views do not necessarily constitute their master status, whereas being this sort of Christian does. This is not a quiet faith, but a faith characterized as a very public first priority in the adherent's life, whereas secularists might have a variety of interests at the forefront. Praying publicly, attending Bible study groups, socializing through church activities and with fellow church members, and a voicemail greeting admonishing people to "have a blessed day" are examples of the kind of extroverted religious expression that are common in Christian nationalists. These expressions tend to attract like-minded people, and repel those who are different—and most especially those who are deemed enemies of dominionist values. This has great utility in keeping people in the fold, as their beliefs are far less likely to be challenged in this insulated environment.

Patriotism plays a significant role in this social milieu, as well, forming a second aspect of the Christian nationalist culture. Research consistently finds that white evangelicals report feeling the most intense feelings of patriotism, with more than two-thirds (68 percent) sharing the opinion that they are "extremely proud" to be a US citizen.[18] White evangelicals are more likely than those of other faiths to believe that "God has granted the United States a special role in history" (a whopping 84 percent agree with this statement).[19] Compare this with people who are not religious, for which only 40 percent reported agreement with this divine bit of exceptionalism for the United States.

Religion is not necessarily the cause of this significant upsurge in jingoism, but it arises from a cultural crossroads in which religion plays a very large role. The researchers concluded that regional differences might account for the variation in patriotism, as well, with Dan Cox, the research director for the Public Religion Research Institute noting, "A lot of evangelicals live in the South, and flying a flag from your house or car, and singing the National anthem—not just standing for it—is infused in Southern life."[20]

I would argue that Christian nationalism has a greater foothold in areas where there are more self-professed evangelicals and "born-again" Christians, and that patriotism is simply a component of this belief system that one would expect to see in greater abundance, as well. As with the religious component of Christian nationalism, patriotism exerts an insulating influence on adherents, which also serves to deepen their commitment to the belief system. Xenophobia is limiting, and the fewer beliefs competing with a system of thought, the stronger that system becomes. There are marginal Christian nationalists, certainly, but not many.

- Christian nationalism encourages support for punitive criminal justice policies and legislation that are, in and of themselves, criminogenic. Christian nationalists respond readily to politicized calls to "get tough" on criminals, as they complement black-and-white thinking with respect to right and wrong.[21] "Getting tough" includes criminal justice policies that emphasize punishment as the primary response to crime. Contemporary examples of such policies include the death penalty,[22] mandatory sentencing (which includes three strikes and truth-in sentencing), zero-tolerance policies, stop-and-frisk, a general weakening of constitutional protections, and the elimination of rehabilitative programming that is not faith-based. In Christian nationalist circles, having nuanced views about crime is viewed as relativism, which is secular and antithetical to true Christianity. Due to this almost rote adherence to harsher punishment for criminals, they form a strong base for an ill-informed citizenry supporting for these policies.[23]

This would be less troublesome if not for the import of such beliefs. The landmark 1976 Supreme Court decision in *Gregg v. Georgia* (428 U.S. 153) not only reopened the doors for states to again use capital punishment, it also ruled that public opinion could be used as a legitimate basis for formulating public policy (428 U.S. 184).[24] At a time when the "New Christian Right" was gaining political strength, this led to penal policies borne of a "just deserts" philosophy and the abandonment of the rehabilitative model in corrections. While it can be argued convincingly that religion has always played a central role in philosophies of punishment, the impact of religious beliefs on punitive attitudes has largely been overlooked through an academic focus on conservative political leanings and the idea that the public believed nothing worked to rehabilitate prisoners, resulting in a paradigm shift toward retribution.[25] However, the latter assumption is based on the notion that the public was deeply influenced by faulty research proclaiming that rehabilitation was ineffective.[26] At best, that research likely served as justification for the belief system that really drove the change.

It makes perfect sense that conservatism and fundamentalist beliefs go hand in hand, and if offenders are evil it makes sense that religious conversion would be the only acceptable form of rehabilitation. Moreover,

Christian nationalists tend toward the Old Testament rather than the New when it comes to their biblical inspiration for criminal justice policy, so conversion takes a backseat to retribution in the scheme of things. For example, support for the death penalty is found in the Old Testament in the well-known "eye for an eye" passages, which are the earliest account we have for Lex Talionis, or the law of like for like.[27] Another underpinning for Christian nationalist support for harsh criminal justice policies is found in Proverbs, where God confers rich blessings upon those who convict the guilty and holds that a wise king sifts out the wicked and brings a threshing wheel over them.[28] Like all people reading the Bible, Christian nationalists tend to gravitate toward the scriptures that reinforce and justify their beliefs, and support for harsh criminal justice sanctions is simply easier to rationalize using the Old Testament.

Large majorities (77 percent) of white evangelical Christians support the death penalty, as do 84 percent of those identifying as conservative Republicans, and both groups will very likely reflect the views of Christian nationalists.[29] The list of nations keeping us company in our continued application of the death penalty should be enough to give us pause in and of itself, as it features such human rights garden spots as Russia, China, Iran, Pakistan, Saudi Arabia, Iraq, Syria, Somalia, Sudan, and North Korea.

Jean Hardisty sums up prevailing Christian nationalist views about responding to criminality in this way:

> The conservative view of humankind as sinful and in need of self-discipline, harsh punishment, and religious redemption to keep people on the correct path stems from a philosophical belief that society in its "natural" state is chaotic. . . . Rightists, despite their occasional adherence to values of love and charity, believe that humankind is divided into good (worthy) people and bad (unworthy) people. Bad or unworthy people are irresponsible and/or anti-social because of weakness, self-indulgence, and lack of the will to overcome their baser instincts. The definition of "good" and "bad" has many dimensions, including moral, cultural, economic, and political. The designation "unworthy" can be stark and unforgiving. Lack of discipline should earn a "bad reputation" and a watchful eye from law enforcement officials. . . . The theme of law and order, as it stems

from the conservative worldview, sets up a stark us/them dichotomy that makes it possible for "deserving" people to place "them" outside the boundaries of an orderly and godly society. From this perspective, once outside the boundaries of legitimate society, "the other" is no longer the responsibility of those who are good and worthy.[30]

Given this belief system, and the political sway held by Christian nationalists in conservative politics, it is not surprising that the United States has become the incarceration capital of the world: Here in the land of the free, we incarcerate more people per capita than any other nation; at a rate of 743 incarcerated persons per 100,000 in 2010, America recently surpassed even Russia for the number of people in jails and prisons— and we did so by a long shot, as even they only sport a rate of 577 per 100,000.[31] As Americans always suspected, we are number one. To put that into even greater perspective, the United States accounts for roughly 5 percent of the world's population but about a quarter of all the people in prison in the world.[32]

Our continued use of the death penalty also puts us at odds with a United Nations resolution calling for a global moratorium on capital punishment,[33] and we were on the list of the top five countries responsible for the bulk of all executions carried out in 2007.[34] Likewise, since 1990, Iran was the only country executing more people under the age of eighteen than the United States, a practice that is explicitly prohibited by international human rights laws.[35] No other democratic nation still employs the death penalty, but 2011 Gallup data show that 61 percent of US citizens still support its use in the case of murder, with a majority (52 percent) reporting that they believe it is applied fairly. While this level of support represents a thirty-nine-year low, it is stunning that we are so different in our punitive attitudes compared to citizens of other democratic countries.[36] The rates of support from fundamentalist Christians are clearly a factor, as is the cultural pervasiveness of fundamentalist Christian underpinnings for punishment.

I hope it is obvious by now that the notion that our crime problem is due to lenience in our criminal justice system holds no merit whatsoever. In fact, we have become so tough on crime that other countries often exclude us from international comparisons because we are such an outlier that we throw off results. If we lived in a safer country due to these practices they might be more defensible, but at present intelligent onlookers might rightly view our criminal justice policies as an example of Americans having more balls than brains. Getting tough is not the solution to our crime problem, or we would likely be among the safest countries in the world.

We are not among the safest countries in the world, though the good news is that crime has fallen drastically in recent years.[37] That said, rates of homicide in the United States consistently place us in an unflattering light respective to other wealthy, industrialized countries, to the extent that Canadians and Europeans have every right to look down their noses at us.[38] Our total crime rate is surprisingly high compared to other industrialized nations, especially considering the number of people we have locked up, but we only get noteworthy in these comparisons when you focus on violent crime.[39]

Aside from direct notions about the criminal justice system, a number of other beliefs impacted by Christian nationalism likely contribute to higher crime rates, such as abortion, abstinence-only education and teen pregnancy, welfare, and support for education and rehabilitation programs in prison. Overall, the belief system of Christian nationalists, and its impact on politics and criminal justice policies, tends to be another way in which Christian nationalism results in more crime.

- Where Christian doctrine contains conflicting messages, Christian nationalists will choose to adhere to the messages that best serve their spiritual and political agendas. In the case of Christian nationalism, this equates to a move away from inclusive, forgiving doctrines toward exclusive, punitive ones. The criminogenic impact of this phenomenon rests in the availability of suitable religious doctrines to justify social and political beliefs that are violent, punitive, and which provide the illusion of insulating followers from threats. This cafeteria-style approach to ideology is an underpinning for the belief system of Christian nationalism; if the movement were bound to adhere to all biblical tenets rather than only those proving convenient, it is likely that the movement would cease to exist, or at least exist only as a very small, fringe movement with little, if any, political and social capital.[40]

A host of revisionist history is tied to this category, as well, in that a number of beliefs held by Christian nationalists in the past that now have little mainstream support were biblically justified at the time. Slavery, banning interracial marriage, Sunday laws, and the forced sterilization of many American citizens are but a few examples of practices that have enjoyed considerable support from Christian nationalists historically, using the Bible.[41] A modern struggle to this end can be found in the so-called "intelligent design" versus natural selection educational debates, or in anti-gay-marriage initiatives.

The key point to remember is that arguing about biblical inerrancy, the literal word of God, or cherry-picking will get you nowhere. If a passage from the Bible is not something with which Christian nationalists care to associate themselves with, that passage is simply misinterpreted or a cultural artifact. If you disagree with a passage they choose to embrace, that passage is the clear will of God and still culturally relevant. In this manner, the Bible becomes tailor-made to maintain a movement with appeals to prejudice and fear, and to which violence is a very close cousin.

- Christian nationalism allows members to feel superior to others, which amounts to another motive for protecting the belief system. Identifying as a group with superior values has its rewards, and chief among them is the sense that you are a "good" person, or, better, a good, God-fearing American. Maintaining this facet of identity is much easier when you create a group for juxtaposition—"bad" people. In the context of this discussion, the usual culprits identified by Christian nationalists (gay people, secular humanists, liberals, and the like) are joined by criminals, who are the ultimate foil; law-breakers are a group ripe for comparison if you are looking to make yourself feel better about your status as "good" in society. Moreover, in the United States, they are particularly useful in this respect if you are a Christian nationalist, as they tend to be disproportionately of lower economic status, black, and Hispanic. Christian nationalists are likely to cluster around the lower to middle levels of the socioeconomic scale.[42] There is a considerable body of evidence that shows that a variety of prejudices—racism, xenophobia, homophobia, classism, sexism, and the like—are held more strongly by those closer to the status levels of the groups they vilify, mostly due to lower levels of educational attainment.[43] In other words, if I am closer to the lower end of the spectrum in terms of economic, social, and political power, I am more likely to support the notion that other groups of people should automatically be ranked beneath me.[44] This makes statistics about disparity in the criminal justice system seem less problematic than reinforcing, as these data are viewed as support for the belief that such people are inferior, or "bad," by comparison. Simply put, Christian nationalists believe that more minorities are arrested because more are breaking the law. Finally, nationalism tends to promote hate and violence, not to mention war. Charles de Gaulle put this elegantly in saying, "Patriotism is when love of your own people comes first; nationalism, when hate for people other than your own comes first." [45]

When a belief system serves to insulate people from fear of death, as do both patriotism and religion, there is a sense of superiority inherent in membership in that group. From their perspective, Christian nationalists know the truth, while the rest of us are both ignorant and hell bound. They are good Americans, and from their perspective, America is the greatest country in the world, so that certainly brings a sense of superiority, as well. If a system of belief promotes a positive sense of self, that system will be protected, and if one feels superior to others who are perceived as a threat to that feeling of superiority, aggressive behavior is likely to occur.

- Christian nationalism inhibits funding and support for programs and policies that would likely *deter* crime. In addition to supporting criminal justice responses to crime that are criminogenic, Christian nationalism results in a lack of support for preventative efforts that might also lower the rate of violent crime. The Bush administration's support for faith-based crime initiatives pushed this phenomenon to a new level, as many secular programs that had a significant impact on reducing delinquency and criminality had their funding cut or vastly reduced, while programs with religious components were given preference for funding. This took place even where evaluation research showed they were not as effective (or at all effective, or damaging). Funding cuts were even more likely in the case of programs sporting components running counter to Christian nationalist beliefs, such as delinquency programs or centers that offered sex education or contraception. This is not to say that faith-based initiatives do not work—many do.[46] I am simply contending that many good programs struggle for funding due to political pressure from the religious right, rather than evidence for their success or failure. Despite Christian nationalist claims that they are discriminated against in this context, the opposite appears to be the case. Funding for faith-based programs is actively and specifically solicited in advertising by government granting agencies in a manner that clearly suggests that such applicants will receive priority.[47]

- Christian nationalism encourages less respect for secular law. Judges are viewed as tools of secular humanism and liberal politics, bent on usurping the word of God, and, as we have already seen, the system is viewed as too soft on criminals. Ironically, the source of this discord does not stem from structural inequalities in the criminal and judicial systems that disadvantage minorities, as they do not believe in such inequity. Further, this is an instance of cafeteria-style Bible thumping. Most Christian nationalists believe that, in situations where the law conflicts with biblical teachings on a particular topic, biblical teachings hold precedence, as they have the weight of God behind them. Here are just a couple of scriptural examples that highlight the inconvenience of this notion:

> 1 Peter 2:13: "Submit yourselves for the Lord's sake to every human authority: whether to the emperor, as the supreme authority."

Romans 13:1: (Paul) "Let everyone be subject to the governing authorities, for there is no authority except that which God has established. The authorities that exist have been established by God."[48]

In cases such as antidiscrimination laws against gay and lesbians, the legality of abortion, the role of religion in public schools, and the like, Christian nationalists actively oppose the law, and, in some cases, resort to violence in doing so.[49] Even where legal means are used to fight against secular law, there is a clear ideology that the law has been usurped by the godless when there is faith-based disagreement. If God's Word is the ultimate authority, this can serve as a handy justification and rationalization for law-breaking.

- Christian nationalism impedes thoughtful public discourse about crime and the social problems associated with crime. Christian nationalists tend to take this a step further than many other movements, in ignoring inconvenient facts, discrediting researchers, public officials, and journalists who espouse information counter to their beliefs, and actively seeking to create "facts" that are more conducive to their ends. In these ways, Christian nationalists actively promote an atmosphere of distrust in public discourse, and are dogmatic in the face of credible proof for alternate ideas. They tend to get their information from sources that can fairly be characterized as propagandist, leaving little room for doubt—or facts in common—to spur true debate. When what passes for debate occurs, Christian nationalists tend toward a vitriolic style rather than fact-based discourse.[50]

Conservative politics in the United States have become a bastion of distortion, and Christian nationalists are among the groups eagerly sucking down this misinformation masquerading as news. Media sources who pander to this audience use a formula to hit talking points they want to hear, while avoiding or distorting unpopular information. As a result, the divide between what people think has grown so wide as to make thoughtful conversation about some of the most important issues facing the United States nearly impossible. Crime is one of those topics.

Figure 1: A Recipe for Righteousness

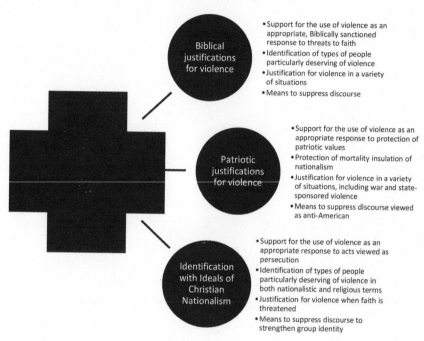

Overall, the Christian nationalist belief system exerts a strong influence over American culture, including the culture of those who do not embrace the belief system. This influence is growing, both despite and because of progress in opposition to their belief systems on a number of fronts.[51] Remember, Christian nationalism thrives on opposition, as it imparts the sense of persecution that motivates their base. This peculiar mix of patriotism and Christianity is the focus of this theory for all of these reasons, but it is important to remember that either aspect of dominionism would increase violence independent of the other.

CHAPTER FOUR

A THEORY OF
VIOLENT RELIGIOSITY

There were a lot of gods. Gods always come in handy, they justify almost anything.   —Margaret Atwood, *The Blind Assassin*

Most of the harm in the world is done by good people, and not by accident, lapse, or omission. It is the result of their deliberate actions, long persevered in, which they hold to be motivated by high ideals toward virtuous ends.
    —Isabel Paterson, *The Humanitarian With the Guillotine*

From the beginning men used God to justify the unjustifiable. He moves in mysterious ways: men say.
                —Salman Rushdie, *The Satanic Verses*

Extremism is so easy. You've got your position, and that's it. It doesn't take much thought. And when you go far enough to the right you meet the same idiots coming around from the left.
                —Clint Eastwood[1]

The only thing more dangerous than an idea is a belief. And by dangerous I don't mean thought-provoking. I mean: might get people killed.   —Sarah Vowell, *The Wordy Shipmates*

The take-home message is that we should blame religion itself, not religious extremism—as though that were some kind of terrible perversion of real, decent religion. Voltaire got it right long ago: "Those who can make you believe absurdities can make you commit atrocities."   —Richard Dawkins, *The God Delusion*

Extremists think "communication" means agreeing with them.
                —Leo Rosten, *Religions of America*

The proposed theory incorporates many facets of the Christian nationalist belief system (and the culture it inspires) in an attempt to make sense of several looming questions in the field of criminology. Of these questions, why the United States has such a high rate of violent crime relative to other similarly situated countries looms largest and has received an abundance of attention in a variety of works—focusing on everything from gun ownership to the ethos of the American Dream as the catalyst for our levels of violence. Here, I will add another explanation to the mix: The particular blend of nationalistic Christianity that holds such sway in the United States.

It remains to be seen how this theory will fair in garnering empirical support, but, at this point, the question of why the United States is so violent is far from settled. I contend that this aspect of social life in our country will reveal itself to be an important piece of the puzzle that has been largely ignored. Additionally, if this theory holds weight, it will shed light on several other important patterns in criminality, such as why the South differs from other regions in the country in producing higher levels of violence, why Black citizens engage in crime at a level disproportionate to their numbers in the population, and why men commit so much crime relative to women.

Details of particular interest to criminologists interested in researching the theory, such as the scope of what this theory can and cannot explain and ways it can be tested empirically, will be addressed at the end of the chapter, but the bulk of the discussion in this chapter will center on why this system of belief produces crime.[2] To this end, the most salient criminogenic aspects of Christian nationalism will be the main focus, as not all aspects of the belief system contribute equally—or at all—to promoting violent crime.

Most people probably fall into one of two camps in terms of their predictions about the impact of religion on crime. One camp views it as completely intuitive that formal religion causes violence, while the other views religion as antithetical to violence. Of course, the truth about almost anything having to do with human beings is rarely so tidily categorized, and the impact of religion is no exception. Neither view accurately reflects the reality of religion's impact on violent behavior, but nor is that impact a zero-sum proposition. Also, it is important to keep in mind that this explanation for violent crime is not meant to explain individual acts of violence, despite the fact that it sometimes does. In criminology, as with most social science, we deal in probabilities and patterns to which there will always be many exceptions.

As part of my continued effort at scrupulous honesty regarding bias in this book, you should know that I do not view the Bible as the literal word of God, or anything close to it. I view the Bible as fiction, and, worse, as largely plagiarized fiction, since almost all of the main elements of the story can easily be traced back to the stories of other "gods" that handily predate Christianity, and these elements are not presented as anything but original in the text of the Bible.[3]

There are many examples of Christ-like mythical figures who share significant allegorical features with Jesus, such as Romulus, Dionysus, Zarathustra, Mithra, Krishna, Baal, Horus, and Attis of Phrygia. These and other pagan gods share too much in common with the Jesus figure, and with many Bible stories, to preclude serious doubt about the veracity of any of these figures being real people with the biographical features attributed them—features such as virgin births, birth dates on December 25, the significance of the number twelve, their executions, and resurrections after three days, for example.[4] If you look further, it becomes even clearer that the Bible, like all these earlier stories, are allegories relating to astronomy and astrology, explaining and predicting natural occurrences and patterns, such as the winter solstice—the point at which the sun appears at its lowest point in the sky for roughly three days, before the days begin to grow longer.[5]

There are a variety of reasons why I do not believe in the Bible as anything more than an interesting reflection on an ancient human need for greater understanding of the world in the absence of knowledge about the workings of nature, in addition to a more enduring human need for structure, meaning, and a means to usurp the fear of death. I would imagine that this should more than suffice in making you understand that I am approaching this topic absent of Christian faith and beliefs. Christians with a strong faith do not tend to read materials such as this at any rate—or at least not in a spirit of open-minded assessment. If they did, they would likely not be Christians for long, and, for that reason, the Bible explicitly warns against an attitude of open inquiry.[6] In fact, eternal damnation is the price for blaspheming the Holy Spirit with such talk.[7] The idea that questioning whether the Holy Spirit is indeed inviolable is an irreverent act with the power to land one in hell is a powerful motivator to avoid open inquiry, but I have never been one to scare easily except where a snake is involved.

I clearly do not believe in God, but where my beliefs are strongest I tend to strive even harder to be fair and scrupulous in my presentation of facts, and I will do so here. I only mention my beliefs and biases so that you, as consumers of this information, can more easily weigh my assertions against my potential bias. With this in mind, we turn to how Christian nationalism causes crime.

THE BIG THREE: CRIMINOGENIC ASPECTS
OF CHRISTIAN NATIONALISM

Why does religion—especially religion imbued with the sense that it is somehow the dominion of a specific people—cause crime? What mechanisms are at play in causing violence and crime when the impact of such a belief system might be so positive? The three main features responsible for this phenomenon are (1) the explicit theology of violence present in fundamentalist religions, (2) the psychology attendant in insulating oneself from fear of death through religion, and (3) the promulgation of laws, policies, and programs to address crime that stem from this belief system. We will address each of these criminogenic factors in turn.

When I first came to this project, I did so with a belief common to many people: that the Christian religion is good and loving, at its root, and that the negative, vitriolic beliefs of many Christians represent a misinterpretation or departure from the true intent and meaning of Christianity. I held this view from early adulthood and embarked on this research with the sense that I would be exposing the error and social consequences of this sort of judgmental and harsh interpretation of Christian principles, rather than exposing anything about the underlying principles themselves. But being open-minded in evaluating all the materials that form the basis for this book resulted in a change of direction from this belief; having studied the Bible, and many other works of theology, I concluded that I was mistaken in believing that Christian theology is essentially loving and redemptive. In fact, the fundamentalist leaders of the Christian faith who appeared the most out of step with a loving interpretation of biblical teachings now strike me as being most in compliance to biblical representations of the Word of God. I now believe this to the extent that I find more moderate, liberal manifestations of Christianity more vulnerable to charges of selective interpretation than their more strident, conservative counterparts. This was a difficult adjustment for me.

Another bias I held coming into this project was an idea that the Bible is bifurcated in a manner that splits its message into the Old Testament, which is fundamentally a message of vengeance and judgment, and the New Testament, which represents a more progressive doctrine of forgiveness and social justice. In fact, while the New Testament does present many ideas at odds with American brands of evangelical Christianity, particularly in that it espouses a sort of biblical socialism, it is far less benign than I had previously gathered. An attendant belief was that Christianity was based more on the New Testament than the Old, setting it apart from Judaism. This, too, proved patently incorrect, of course—while all modern Christianity encompasses both Testaments as doctrine, Christian nationalists derive much of their social and political identity from the Old Testament.

While many Christians divorce themselves from discussions about the Old Testament when it comes to much of the violence and clearly incorrect information it contains, conservative Christians simultaneously rely on the Old Testament to justify positions and beliefs such as supporting the death penalty, the public placement of Ten Commandments statues, or being homophobic. You cannot have it both ways, so I will pull from both Testaments in making my points about the doctrines. I hope to address the Bible as fairly as possible here, and I will likely please no one in the process. Liberal Christians often accuse fundamentalist Christians of cherry-picking the Word of God to support the more negative features of their conservative belief system, but the reverse is also true. The idea that Christianity is all about unconditional love and forgiveness is no more complete than the notion that Christianity is all about judgment and damnation for those who are not "saved." Both perspectives miss the whole, regardless of the social benefits and consequences inherent in either view. With this in mind, we turn our attention to the Bible as the foundation for Christian nationalist beliefs.

A THEOLOGY AND CULTURE OF VIOLENCE

The Bible is a very violent book, full of very violent teachings. When people contend that its overall message is one of love, I can only guess that they (a) have not actually read it, (b) never grappled with more than fodder for Bible studies and Sunday school classes, or (c) watch Quentin Tarantino movies with their toddler. The survival of any religious system is no different than the survival of animals in the wild: It is a kill or be killed proposition. A belief system has to survive in order to spread, and historically that required violence to both protect adherents and to wipe out adherents of competing systems. With this history of violence, much of which is codified in the Bible, it would be surprising if religion did not beget violence.

Christian nationalism is steeped in the ethos of violence and conquest, but certain concepts, such as punishment, righteousness, and vengeance, have a disproportionate impact on criminal violence. The concept of punishment is also pervasive. For example, punishments meted out in the Bible include death, burning eternally in hell, stoning, being destroyed, raped, thrown into a lake of fire (fire and sulfur, in some passages), garden variety smiting,[8] ripping up pregnant women, being cut up with a sword, general wrath and fury, spreading dung on people's faces, eye-plucking, beheading, physical tribulation and distress, cutting off the hands and feet of the dead, dashing children to pieces, and eternal destruction, to name but a few.[9] I am not certain if there is another book containing as much violence, but the fact that this book serves as the basis for Christian nationalism makes my point easy to make. The Bible is rife with violent passages, along with the notion that some people deserve to be victimized in violent ways, and that it is godly to heap such retribution on them. "Vengeance is mine; I will repay, saith the Lord."[10]The Bible is something of a vigilante handbook, really, with the caveat that it is only permissible to do violence in certain, God-approved situations. But there are a lot of those situations, which include everything from being disobedient to your parents to wearing a cotton/polyester blend to simply rejecting the idea of the Christian God.[11] Christians are then left to interpret whether specific situations justify the use of violence, which is viewed as an acceptable response to an affront. Vigilantism encompasses far more than lynch mob-type justice; it is a subtle concept at play in a great deal of violent crime. The law serves to punish offenders, and *people* punish those whom they view as offending against them in a significant number of offenses.[12]

1 John 3:4 sums up another aspect of the theological argument for violent punishment: "Everyone who makes a practice of sinning also practices lawlessness; sin is lawlessness."[13] The idea conveyed in this verse encompasses several criminogenic aspects of Christian nationalist theology. First, equating lawbreaking with sinning makes it easy to justify harsh punishments and a lack of empathy for criminals, who are seen as deserving what they get. Because of this, Christian nationalists support policies that continually expand the reach of the criminal justice system to draw in more and more sinners.

Second, it advances the idea that sinners deserve punishment in a less formal setting. Most violent crime occurs between people who know one another to some extent and often involves a dispute. A sense of righteousness often accompanies disputes; someone believes strongly that they are right and that the other person is wrong. The violent act itself is thus viewed as retribution—a form of violent conflict resolution—and the template for this response can be found in the Bible. At their heart, most violent episodes are initiated by judgment.[14] One person judges another as being in the wrong, and punishes them for the affront using violence.[15] One of the reasons it is difficult to find repentant inmates in prisons is that many feel strongly that their actions were justified—that they, in fact, did the right thing in using violence against their victim, who deserved to be punished whatever the law has to say about it. Due to this belief, they view their own punishment as being the result of a legal technicality: Their act broke a law, but was not wrong, or was understandable, at least. From this standpoint, the other person holds the bulk of the blame for the offense. And this is not just post hoc rationalization at work: In a significant number of violent crimes, the victim does play a not insignificant role in their own injury or death.[16]

You might be bristling right now, and that is good. Victim-blaming, most commonly associated with the crime of rape, is certainly wrong-headed and often based on sexist cultural norms and expectations. Women bear the brunt of victim-blaming, despite being less likely to be victimized than men to the extent that there is a well-worn trope in which a male robbery victim is questioned about his choice in clothing, how much he had been drinking, and where he was hanging out, with an eye toward the questioner showing that he had "wanted" to be robbed.[17] I assure you, I am not victim-blaming.

I am, however, a criminologist, and in order to understand crime, we have to take the victim into account as one of three broad factors available to make sense of criminal events—the victim, the offender, and situational factors (such as the time of day, location, and whether other people were present or not).[18] I would be remiss if I limited my focus to the offender and the situation in which the crime occurred, while ignoring victims. And it turns out that there are robust findings in criminology and victimology showing that victims play a wide variety of roles in their own victimization, from what we conceive of as a completely innocent victim (fairly rare) to a victim due to ignorance (think of a tourist stumbling into the wrong neighborhood in an unfamiliar city) to a victim who is as guilty—in some cases even more guilty—than the offender in precipitating their own victimization. Here's a common example of a violent crime precipitated by the victim:

A very big, well-muscled man walks into a bar and has a drink. As he is making his way to the men's room, he bumps into a smaller, very inebriated man making his way through the crowd. The smaller man, thoroughly liquored up and feeling ten feet tall, starts yelling at the larger man over the perceived insult of being jostled. The larger man tries to shrug it off, but the other man is making quite a scene and eventually pushes the big guy to try to start a fight. The big man finally loses his patience, unwilling to take being physically and verbally abused in front of a crowd any longer. He punches the smaller man, who falls back and hits his head on the sharp edge of a table, seriously injuring himself. He dies of a cerebral hemorrhage on the way to the hospital. The big man is now a murderer, while the smaller man is the victim, but it is clear that the smaller man precipitated the violence.

You might be thinking that this is a clear-cut case of self-defense or that this is a freakish example that is not what you think of when you think of violent crime. While it might not be what comes to mind for the average non-criminologist, it is anything but uncommon. A fair share of "assaults" involve two people fighting—the winner is declared the offender, while the loser is designated the victim.

Further, the difference between an assault and a homicide can hinge on factors as mundane as falling a few inches to one side or another or how fast the ambulance gets an injured person to the hospital. The point is that a significant amount of violence is dispute-related and leaves the offender feeling justified in their actions, even if they are sorry for how things turned out. From the standpoint of the law, the event looks very different.

Much violence is moralistic in nature and feels righteous, even when it is terribly wrong. Christian nationalists know a little something about righteousness, and, aside from the literal messages in their scripture, their belief system makes them especially prone to feeling justified and on the side of right, which can play a big role in the escalation of interpersonal violence. If you come into an altercation feeling you are the member of an especially moral group and that you have the approval of God, how much more likely do you think you will be to engage in violence to defend your position or status? It is an interesting question for researchers to explore, and I predict that the more self-righteous a person is, the more likely they will be to engage in violent altercations. Obviously, there are other paths to expressing feelings of self-righteousness, but this measure alone should provide a means to test support for the theory.

A significant number of violent events are perpetrated by people in response to what they perceive as wrongdoing. Cheating, belonging to the wrong group, disrespect, and theft are just a few examples of offenses over which people commit violent acts, to the extent that several criminological theories address what is known as honor violence.[19] Violence is rare in the scheme of crime, but research reveals that motives such as this are very common in the violence that does occur. Despite what is portrayed in the media, crime is a fairly mundane, often almost silly, affair.[20] Serial killers and evil geniuses do not worry me and the vast majority of my criminologist colleagues very much at all because we know that they are too rare to worry about. If you are dead set on worrying about crime, worry about the people around you that you know to some extent—they are far more likely to victimize you than a stranger. The next most likely scenario to forward scary emails to your children about would be a dispute with a stranger. The common element here is conflict, and without conflict very little violence occurs. This conflict has received a great deal of scholarly attention in the framework of honor, but far less from the perspective of punishment.

Christian nationalism connects to such violence through the concepts of punishment, vengeance, and righteousness. Christianity is rife with it, as you will remember from the brief list of punishments mentioned in the Bible, and Christian nationalist culture is steeped in it. You might prefer to focus on the reward of going to heaven for accepting Jesus into your heart as your savior, but the bottom line is that there is a humdinger of a stick associated with that carrot. If you are not going to heaven, you do not simply cease to exist, get reincarnated, or take any other alternative path you might imagine in death: You simply go to hell.[21] You burn for eternity, suffering the torments of hell. It is a furnace or lake of fire, depending on the passage, you get no rest, and there is a lot of weeping and gnashing of teeth.[22] To those who say that a loving God would not be inclined to send people to such a horrible place, Christians are instructed to remind people that God is just; God does not send people to hell—they choose to go to hell through rejecting God.[23] This is both not charming and indicative of the fact that punishment is a central ethos in Christianity, and the list of those deserving of such punishment is long, and, like everything in the Bible, open to human interpretation. Take Revelation 21:8 as an example:

> But as for the cowardly, the faithless, the detestable, as for murderers, the sexually immoral, sorcerers, idolaters, and all liars, their portion will be in the lake that burns with fire and sulfur, which is the second death. (ESV)[24]

As is apparent, it does not even require interpretation to divine that there are far more people in the hell-bound category than outside of it, and all of them might seem to deserve what they get from God's perspective—and thus from the perspective of a Christian nationalist or even fundamentalist Christian. It makes the relative heat in partisan politics about social issues seem far more understandable. Virulent homophobia? Distain for people of other faiths and nonbelievers? People who oppose war? People you just do not like? Hate seems a perfectly natural response in this context, and we see this in hate crimes perpetrated by people professing to be Christians, despite right-wing propaganda that there is a "War on Christianity" being waged in the United States.[25] In fact, Jewish and Muslim people are far more likely to be the victims of hate crimes in America. (Jews account for 60 percent of all religiously motivated hate crimes, second only to black victims in all categories.)[26]

The Bible has even been the subject of hate crime legislation both in California (S.B. 777) and in Canada (*Saskatchewan v. Whatcott*), where the Supreme Court ruled that biblical passages promoting hatred against LGBT people were not protected under the right to free speech or freedom of religion because they were considered hate speech. In this decision, Justice Rothstein said that hate speech, characterizing

> the targeted group as a menace that could threaten the safety and well-being of others, makes reference to respected sources (in this case the Bible) to lend credibility to negative generalizations, and uses vilifying and derogatory representations to create a tone of hatred.[27]

Arguably the best-known verse in the Bible is John 3:16, wherein God provides the means for salvation to all in giving his only begotten Son to bring us eternal life. But this blissful focus on the carrot tends to overshadow the stick. And even the carrot is violent where it certainly would not have to be. I offer my Son to die for your redemption—an omnipotent, loving God could not think of a less horrible package for the gift of redemption for mankind? God could have chosen the carrot alone, but he did not, and this elementary example sheds light on why fundamentalist Christians embrace the stick with such enthusiasm.

If a huge part of your belief system focuses on punishment, it stands to reason that you might be inclined to dish some out, and anecdotally we see just that clearly in many hate crimes perpetrated by Christian national-ists.[28] But I am proposing that this effect might be present in a more diffuse manner, as well. There is a long biblical history in which God either pun-ishes people directly for sin or asks believers to do so for him. Among the best-known Bible stories, and a favorite for children, is the story of Noah's ark. This tale recounts the mass murder of the entire population of the earth, save Noah, his family, and two of each type of animal. We tend to focus on Noah to the exclusion of the entire rest of the population of the world, to the extent that we forget how terrible this story is. What kind of a person would God have to be to drown everyone else, including innocent children, animals without an ark ticket, and, well, everybody? Not so cute when you imagine thousands upon thousands of bobbing corpses.

Noah has a lot of gruesome company in the Bible, and it is not uncommon for the stories of punishments to transcend death in their awfulness. The message is not cut and dried, certainly, as the Bible also contains a plethora of passages about leaving punishment to God, along with numerous passages about violent death as the proper sentence for murder.[29] But an eye for an eye does not begin to constitute the last word on this topic. The average Christian is not terribly well-versed in the Bible, so it is unlikely that most have given much thought to the vagaries and inconsistencies inherent in biblical pro-nouncements about violence. Jesus warned against violence, as well, giving us the adage that whosoever lives by the sword shall die by it, but that message competes with a great number of explicit exhortations to commit violence.[30]

Finally, there is the matter of forgiveness, which seems like a concept completely at odds with committing violent acts at first blush, but which plays a part in this influence nonetheless. Christians are forgiven for their sins when they accept Jesus Christ as their Lord and Savior. Their sins are washed away, and they are exhorted to go and sin no more.[31] But what if you do sin again? What then? Obviously, I cannot speak to every interpretation, but a very common interpretation holds that, essentially, you do your best, but as a human being you are a sinner and will likely sin again (and again, if you are really fun). At which point, you will need to ask God's forgiveness and try again, but you are still saved from hell.

The bottom line is what is important here: No matter what you do, if you accept Jesus into your heart, you are saved from eternal damnation. There is no fine print when it comes to that promise. Sure, you will be judged when you get to heaven, and that could be unpleasant for those who sinned a lot, but you will still be suffering that discomfort in heaven, rather than burning in hell. If you commit a crime, you can always "get right with God" afterward, if you are not able to justify the offense to yourself using "eye for an eye" principles. Jesus is a lot like most grandmothers: he will forgive any sin, even those specified in the Ten Commandments. That is a good thing for the occupancy rate in heaven, given the prevalence of Christians breaking those Commandments.[32] This is important, because it speaks to the fact that Christian theology does not really have any deterrent power in terms of withholding its ultimate promise of cheating death. Further, it emphasizes sin in the notion that we are all sinners anyway, which is an easy rationalization for crime.

The Bible is viewed as the literal word of God by these believers, so the impact is profound, as Christian nationalist institutions and culture are steeped in this doctrine. We will discuss some specific cases where violence is more likely, such as that perpetrated against children and women, later in the book, but for now it should be clear that the theology of this brand of Christianity is not as loving and redemptive as you might have thought, and it might easily cause violence.[33]

THE PSYCHOLOGY OF THE FEAR OF DEATH

Christian nationalism also promulgates violence through its role as an insulator from the fear of death. This aspect of Christian nationalism is a key raison d'être in accounting for the violence inherent in this belief system. As I touched on in chapters one and three, the idea here is that people use certain things—and here we are focusing on religion and nationalism—to protect themselves from distressing thoughts about their own demise. This phenomenon, known as terror management, is largely unconscious but very powerful. Managing fear of death through Christian nationalism is achieved through two mechanisms:

1. Believing in the Christian doctrine of eternal life.

One of the greatest benefits of Christianity is insulation from the fear of death, and the founders of the religion knew what they were selling—and what a hot commodity it would be. Human beings are supposed to be unique among animals in our ability to comprehend that we eventually die, and this creates an existential crisis.[34] Most people adopt a defense against this knowledge, and believing that you are going to heaven is a particularly effective one. In this manner, one can avoid the crisis altogether, since one believes that they do not die at all, but rather go to live in a perfect place with God.

    1 Corinthians 2:9 presents heaven as something so wonderful that humans cannot even fathom it,[35] while Hebrews 13:14 reminds the faithful that there are no lasting cities on earth, and that they are to seek only the city that is to come after death.[36] The bottom line is that in God's house of many rooms there is a means to cheat death and have eternal life, which is not a bad prize for believing in God while you are living on earth.[37] This pay before you play doctrine is great, unless you have built your life around it and somebody starts punching holes in your conception of salvation; at which point, Christians tend to react aggressively. People can challenge this belief system in a number of ways, both intentionally and unintentionally.

Coming into close contact with competing doctrines can do it, especially where they boast differences with respect to achieving salvation. It is disconcerting for an adherent of any religion to come face-to-face with people who believe in a different path to eternal life as strongly as they believe in theirs. It presents a specter that calls beliefs into question if they allow themselves to consider the fact that there are many paths, and that theirs might not be the right one. Given the discomfort this would cause, most believers choose to reject and discredit the competing belief system—and its adherents—with vigor. Interdenominational feuding appears less petty when viewed through this lens, and makes far more sense; in the minds of those involved, it is their very survival that is at stake.

Similarly, nonbelievers can challenge this belief system. They might question adherents about their faith, either to challenge it or from an honest desire to understand it better. Sometimes just getting to know and like a nonbeliever can cause believers to question that they must go to hell according to the Bible. If the person is moral and admired by the Christian, it can be difficult to reconcile caring for this good person with the notion that the person is destined to burn in hell for eternity. If the believer allows this awareness to seep in—especially repeatedly—it starts to undermine the foundation of their faith. The same process can occur with Christian nationalists getting to know LGBT people personally—or others destined for hell vis-à-vis some personal characteristic or belief.

The best insulation against this erosion is to avoid the situation altogether. If you segregate yourself from people who challenge your faith, it is easier to maintain it. Nonbelievers are exempt from automatic scorn until they willfully reject God in the wake of evangelical efforts, at which point they become a threat to terror management through theology.

Conservatives are especially likely to see the world as a threatening place, at any rate, and their response to perceived threats is especially likely to be aggressive.[38] Cultural conservatism, fear of death, and a need for structure have been found to be significant predictors of dogmatic aggression.[39] This is evident in conservative support for war, an opposition to immigration reform, the contention that marriage equality is a threat to "traditional" marriage, a belief that openly gay soldiers would disrupt the military, the economic belief that regulating corporations will cause them to leave the United States or go out of business, the fear that LGBT people will molest children, the argument that helping the poor will result in abuse of the system and dependence, and the general, prolonged anxiety that the country is going to hell in a hand basket. When you view the world this way, the best defense might just be a good offense, and that is the strategy preferred by Christian nationalists.[40]

A great example of this is the response to the attacks on 9/11, which was predictably aggressive on the part of patriotic Americans.[41] Overall, a large body of research supports the idea that when people are reminded of their own mortality, they react aggressively toward people who are different—and particularly those of other, competing, faiths.[42]

2. Feeling a part of a larger, more permanent entity that will continue to exist after you die.

Aside from serving as what is believed to be a literal protection from death, belonging to a Christian nationalist group or church can provide a sense of belonging to an enduring entity that provides a sense of vicarious immortality.[43] As humans, attaching ourselves to something greater, which will continue on long after we die, lends a kind of continuation of ourselves as a part of the larger institution.[44] As humans, we feel less alone in that context, and subconsciously, that soothes the existential angst of being a limited time offer.[45]

The same sort of mechanism is at play when we write books, plays, or symphonies that will exist after we are gone. Any endeavor—from designing a building to fighting a war—serves to connect us to something that will outlast us on the mortal coil, and the more permanent that contribution, the better. Universities play upon this feeling to increase financial support for the institution, harnessing fear of mortality to attract named donors for buildings and other projects. Similarly, wealthy donors often honor a deceased relative through named buildings, memorials, and even plantings and benches. Less wealthy donors can be memorialized on bricks. Headstones serve this purpose, as well, and when people go this route they tend to purchase as permanent and substantial a monument as they can afford, as this is another way in which we can mark our existence. A traditional funeral, particularly involving embalmment, is an act of mortality defiance in and of itself. The idea that it continues to matter what our bodies look like, or that they not decay, speaks as directly as possible to the denial of death.[46]

The phenomenon of attaching ourselves to lasting institutions encompasses both the Christian church and the United States as a country. Researchers Sheldon Solomon, Tom Pyszczynski, and Jeff Greenberg first proposed the terror management theory in 1986 and have done much to advance our understanding of the mechanisms of death denial through their subsequent work.[47]

Solomon, Pyszczynski, and Greenberg predicted that a threat such as 9/11 would result in aggression that was not terribly rational, and they were right: We immediately went to war with the wrong people and for all the wrong reasons, we saw a spike in violence against people perceived to be Muslim, and many manufacturers sold out of American flags as people scrambled to reassert American spirit and dominance. Almost overnight, it became practically forbidden to voice dissent that, by any stretch, might be construed as anti-American. The Dixie Chicks, as the most obvious example, were pilloried for lead singer Natalie Maines's rather mild comment at a concert in England that she was ashamed that then-President George W. Bush was from Texas—and that was after it was clear that there were no weapons of mass destruction in Iraq.[48] Unfortunately for them, their fan base was right wing. If you are too young to remember, country music radio stations banned their music and held CD-burning parties. Some of the hatred directed toward them even included death threats. It does not make a lot of sense unless you look at it in the context of terror management. From that perspective it is still ugly and inexcusable but clearly the product of fear.

The Dixie Chicks were by far not the only victims of this phenomenon, with support for American aggression so strident that those in opposition were understandably afraid to speak up. Patriotism gripped the nation, and any suggestion that our country was anything but great ruined careers or garnered threats or actual violence.[49]

Research on this real-world event revealed a number of important findings that advanced understanding about terror management. One finding was that even subliminal exposure to the images and stimuli related to 9/11 brought thoughts of mortality closer to the surface in individuals. Then president George W. Bush had more than the Supreme Court fallback going for him in his second run for the White House—he had mortality salience on his side.[50]

When people are prompted to consider their own demise, they cling to people who seem to exude strength, charisma, and resolve. Charisma might not be a word that springs readily to mind when describing George W. Bush, but remember the alternative. Next to John Kerry, Bush looked positively lifelike. Unable to run on intellect, he ran on a sort of folksy charm, instead, and managed to come across as decisive and warm to some, which has great appeal to voters in a state of fear. Pulitzer Prize–winning anthropologist Ernest Becker had it right when he wrote:

> It is fear that makes people so willing to follow brash, strong-looking demagogues with tight jaws and loud voices: those who focus their measured words and their sharpened eyes in the intensity of hate, and so seem the most capable of cleansing the world of the vague, the weak, the uncertain, the evil. Ah, to give oneself over to their direction—what calm, what relief.[51]

There might not be a better description for John Kerry as a candidate than vague, weak, and uncertain compared to George W. Bush, who famously said that he did not "do nuance."[52] While another president might have appeared indecisive in the wake of an attack due to uncertainty over targeting the offenders, Bush jumped right into vengeance mode and never looked back. That was comforting to people who were reeling from the threat to our country as a reminder of their own inevitable demise. And who is most susceptible to this fear-induced reaction than people for whom patriotism is a hedge against mortality? Religion and country are two very powerful means by which people soothe their fear of death. When people are prompted to think about their death, they react violently against those who threaten these comforting symbols of permanence.

When people have unconsciously engaged these defense mechanisms against fear of death, they will resort to violence and aggression to defend mechanisms of death denial against anything perceived as a threat to it. Attaching ourselves to a cultural entity perceived as eternal shields us from feeling the bite of our eventual physical deaths, so it is not terribly surprising that this is the case. The reaction people have to such threats is automatic and powerful, and serves as another means by which Christian nationalism increases violent crime.

PROVIDING SUPPORT FOR CRIMINOGENIC STRATEGIES IN THE CRIMINAL JUSTICE SYSTEM

Given that none of us can throw the first stone, it is amazing how judgmental Christians can be when it comes to criminals. My colleagues and I often marvel at the "kill 'em all, let God sort 'em out" mentality of some of our students, and, through discussion when such attitudes are revealed, we discover that a significant portion of the students holding these views come from families that can easily be characterized as Christian nationalists. Just today, a student of mine who had previously (spontaneously) identified himself as a fundamentalist Christian commented both that mentally ill people who commit crime should be in prison with other criminals and with no special treatment, and that he did not believe in the legalization of marijuana because he believes it to be "against God's plan." Not knowing that God had a plan regarding weed, I was a bit taken aback by that, but the rather harsh view on the mentally ill was not surprising after more than fifteen years of teaching and the research I have conducted for this book.[53] This lack of empathy and compassion is a hallmark of Christian nationalists, much to the horror of more liberal and moderate Christians, who would prefer not to have such attitudes associated with their religion. You can hardly blame them.

This lack of charity is easiest to explain using an attitudinal scale called right-wing authoritarianism (RWA), which was developed by Canadian researcher Robert Altemeyer to explain group prejudice.[54] RWA essentially refers to the convergence of three attitudinal clusters that I contend are especially likely to be present in Christian nationalists:

1. Conventionalism: Adhering to a great degree to social conventions perceived to be endorsed by both society and established authorities.
2. Authoritarian Submission: Submitting to a great degree to authorities perceived as established and legitimate.
3. Authoritarian Aggression: A generalized aggression directed at a variety of people who are perceived as sanctioned and endorsed by society and established authorities.[55]

Not surprisingly, the presence of these attitudes leads to a high degree of hostility toward outgroups, and, I believe, violence. I am employing Altemeyer's list of RWA characteristics here to characterize the behaviors and beliefs of Christian nationalists because the shoe fits so comfortably and because it might be of use in future tests of the theory. Applying the scale to Christian nationalists, they are more likely to:

- Support weakening Constitutional guarantees related to liberty, such as in the Bill of Rights (with the notable exception of the Second Amendment).
- Admit they get pleasure out of punishing criminals.
- Severely punish street criminals in role-playing situations.
- Go easy on crime committed by authorities and people attacking minorities.
- Exhibit hostility toward gay, lesbian, bisexual, and transgendered people.
- Be supportive of "gay bashing."
- Show prejudice against many racial, national, ethnic, and linguistic minorities.
- Engage in hostility toward feminists.
- Voluntarily assist the government in persecuting almost anyone.
- Exhibit fear toward a world perceived as dangerous.
- Be mean-spirited toward people who have made mistakes and suffered.

- Strongly believe in the concept of loyalty and group cohesion.
- Enforce traditional sex roles.
- Employ Christianity to mitigate guilt for their actions.[56]
- Use Christianity to maintain a feeling of self-righteousness.
- Reside at the "fundamentalist" end of the religious spectrum.
- Serve as the most prejudiced members of the Christian religion.
- More easily accept unfair and illegal abuses of power by governmental authorities.
- Trust leaders who are untrustworthy (for example, Richard Nixon or a long list of Jimmy Swaggart-esque Christian leaders).
- Make incorrect inferences from factual evidence.
- Hold conflicting beliefs that cause them to "speak out of both sides of their mouths."
- Uncritically accept that many issues are the most serious problem facing society.
- Support their beliefs with insufficient evidence.
- Trust people who say what they want to hear on the grounds of personality rather than fact.[57]
- Employ double standards in their thinking and judgment.
- Be dogmatic in their thinking.
- Dominate others in a destructive and competitive manner in situations requiring cooperation.
- Behave like zealots.
- Bully when in a position of power over others.
- Cause and worsen intergroup conflict.
- Be hypocritical.
- Feel they have few personal failings.
- Be especially self-righteous.
- Fail to learn from their mistakes and failings.
- Support a conservative economic policy.
- Believe in social dominance.
- Oppose abortion.
- Support capital punishment.
- Be ethnocentric, highly nationalistic, and patriotic.

- Oppose gun control legislation.
- Undervalue equality and oppose measures to increase it.
- Give lip service to valuing freedom, while undermining the Bill of Rights selectively.
- Engage in compartmentalized thinking.

Most Christian nationalists can fairly be described as poster children for right-wing authoritarianism, and the addition of religion to the mix intensifies most of these characteristics to the extent that Christian nationalists should comprise a significant proportion of those deemed "high RWAs."[58] Altemeyer uses the term "right" in right wing in the literal sense of the word—proper, correct, lawful, and doing what authorities tell them to do.[59]

These traits of Christian nationalists account for their often inconceivable support for very punitive criminal justice policies in the face of Jesus's calls for the opposite. In fact, their ability to compartmentalize and inability to interpret information to draw the logical conclusion helps them to navigate their belief that the Bible is the infallible, literal Word of God—while they simultaneously reject much of the doctrine that does not fit with their cultural worldview and belief-system-driven preferences. Take, for example, Matthew 7:1–2: "Do not judge, or you too will be judged." This is pretty cut-and-dried, and it would certainly suggest more forgiveness and less punishment.

Yet, when Altemeyer asked a group of subjects what they thought about these passages, along with "When they kept on questioning him, he straightened up and said to them, 'Let any one of you who is without sin be the first to throw a stone at her,'" he still found that high Christian RWAs said that the Bible should be taken literally—and that we should judge and punish others. None of the subjects explained how these two views could be reconciled. Further, these same students scored high on many parts of the authoritarian aggression scale, indicating that they were, indeed, quick to judge and punish.[60] That plays out in real-world support for harsh punishment for criminals, despite the fact that many such punishments do not deter future criminality, and, in fact, are likely to increase crime rates as well as exacerbate other social problems.

Incidentally, there is no left-wing equivalent to RWAs. Though Alte-meyer tried, he did not find it. He developed a direct reflection of the RWA scale, but could not find anyone who scored over 50 percent on this LWA litmus. Contrast this with numerous people scoring 100 percent on the RWA scale. Liberal people represent a looser coalition on the left, with a variety of differing views within the group. This is actually a political advantage for the right wing, as their followers see the world very simi-larly—if not accurately—so it is far easier to appeal to their more unified base. Unfortunately, with the advent of Tea Party politics, the demands of this base have been amplified and their influence increased through the threat that even staunch right-wingers might be ousted by candidates even farther to the right. This righteous constituency, a boon when controlled, tolerates little in the way of compromise in politics, and thus has become a very effective obstructionist force in the United States.

This is why arguing logically about politics, nationalism, and reli-gion so often falls flat, failing to make a dent in dogmatic belief systems held by Christian nationalists. Similarly, it is why appeals to logic and facts to assess criminal justice system practices seem to fall on deaf ears. Because the concept of strength has permeated political discourse about crime—getting tough on crime, a war on drugs—it has become very dif-ficult for cooler heads to prevail in terms of creating rational policy in this area. Since the infamous Willy Horton attack ad in 1988 sank presidential hopeful Michael Dukakis, politicians have been trying to out-butch one another on the issue, with disastrous results.[61] Any failure in the system that could be connected to a candidate suddenly became fodder to be used by an opponent to paint a candidate as soft on crime, and the success of the tactic had politicians running scared (ironically, in a race to look tough). Since that period, we have expanded our prison system to an unprece-dented size—for any country—and make frequent use of the death penalty. We have stripped prisons of funding for anything remotely rehabilitative, and we seem to have forgotten that most criminals who go into prison come back out into our communities. The American underclass now tends to view the criminal justice system with extreme skepticism and fatalism.[62] So many people go to prison from their ranks that going to prison has lost most of its ability to stigmatize in those quarters, and the view of prison has become that of a massive warehousing complex that some people are unlucky enough to get caught in by token of their race or class.

Stop-and-frisk policies make walking in many areas a serious risk for the underclass. Ridiculous charges of loitering, failure to obey an officer, and the like actually land people under police control in this country—just rarely the kind of people who can afford to raise a stink about it.[63] Plea bargaining has become both necessary in a system processing alarming numbers of people, and another manner in which the system is rigged against the poor.[64] Mandatory minimum sentencing further exacerbates the overcrowding problems and helps ensure that more people leave the system less prepared to rejoin their communities as productive members.[65] Since Congress instituted mandatory minimum sentences in the 1980s, the federal prison population has grown from 24,000 prisoners to over 218,000 prisoners, to gain its title as the largest prison system in the country.[66]

Extreme racial and socioeconomic differences in enforcement and sentencing have instilled a deep distrust and antipathy toward the system in the lower classes.[67] Our system is huge—and in shambles—and even people in more privileged classes are starting to call foul over our prison industrial complex, which has also become a profit center in recent years.[68]

Not surprisingly, given their propensity for fear, judgment, and punitive attitudes toward criminals and people different from themselves, coupled with strict law-and-order sentiments, Christian nationalists are at the forefront of those pushing for the harsher sentencing that serves as the underpinning for the criminal justice system.[69] Having spent time in prison is the biggest predictor for recidivism.[70] Moreover, it has been firmly established that capital punishment does not have a general deterrent effect.[71]

Support for the death penalty—which runs extremely high among Christian nationalists, as I mentioned earlier—is an example of their comfort with lethal vengeance as a response to affronts. Capital punishment is so well-researched, and that research is so conclusive, that the American Society of Criminology issued a formal policy position on the issue in 1989:

Be it resolved that because social science research has demonstrated the death penalty to be racist in application and social science research has found no consistent evidence of crime deterrence through execution, The American Society of Criminology publically condemns this form of punishment, and urges its members to use their professional skills in legislatures and courts to seek a speedy abolition of this form of punishment.

The American Society of Criminology has only issued three policy statements through its entire existence, which should give you a pretty good idea of the level of empirical support for this stance.[72] Capital punishment is also far more expensive than a sentence of life in prison without the possibility of parole. According to Richard Dieter of the Death Penalty Information Center, research has "uniformly and conservatively shown that a death-penalty trial costs $1 million more than one in which prosecutors seek life without parole."[73] Most of these costs are incurred during and prior to capital trials, as well as in higher costs associated with housing death row inmates, rather than as the result of legal appeals (as many people believe). In addition to the greater financial cost, states that employ the death penalty consistently boast the highest homicide rates in the country, while only three states without the death penalty—Alaska, Michigan, and New York—even crack the top-twenty-five list.[74]

This discussion should have helped explain the reason why you are not hearing a deafening chorus of complaint from the right about the staggering amount of government spending on our criminal justice system—and on our correctional system in particular. You are not likely to ever hear objections about the expenditure, and certainly not about the amazing loss of liberty it represents from this group. Similarly, they will not be moved by obvious inequity in the system.

Their fearful worldview, coupled with an ability to compartmentalize that enables effortless hypocrisy and a desire to punish others, makes perfect sense in terms of support for harsh punishments, no matter what Jesus might have said about the matter. Conservatives are punitive, and certainly right-wing authoritarians are, but when you add Christianity and patriotism to the mix, that punitive attitude and support for punitive policies should be significantly higher.

One final note on Christian nationalist support for punitive and ineffective criminal justice policies involves nonprofit endeavors. Christian nationalists are perplexing in their inconsistencies when it comes to charity and compassion. They engage in too much charitable work as a whole to be fairly characterized as hard-hearted, but the charity tends to be very specific in terms of both who benefits and how the help is distributed. In other words, they support their Christian organizations, including their churches, and prefer to help people they deem worthy of their assistance. That generally boils down to Christians who have hit a rough patch (possibly church members) or people who are good candidates for converting to Christianity through the effort—and who are, preferably, also good people.[75]

With government spending drastically curtailed for anything remotely resembling rehabilitation in prisons, a lot of the slack is taken up by religious people coming into prisons to run groups and provide help, but these are generally not Christian nationalists. They tend to be Christians of a far more liberal stripe, and their work is admirable. Christian nationalists view inmates as other and tend to steer clear. When they do work with prisoners, it is through Christian nonprofits that often feature evangelizing as the core service they provide. To them, bringing people to God is the paramount reason for these efforts, and other services are secondary reasons for their existence.

This would not be a problem if Christian organizations were not taking a large portion of the funding available to help convicts reintegrate into society due to a preference for faith-based initiatives left over from the Bush era.[76] Moreover, no politician is willing to stand up and say that we should be giving less preference to faith-based initiatives, so this will likely continue to be the case for some time. In this manner, money gets diverted from programs offering more tangible benefits to people trying to make their way back into the world after prison, as funds are diverted away from prevention programs that are not evangelizing outfits in disguise.

PREDICTING VIOLENCE RELATED TO
CHRISTIAN NATIONALISM

We now come to the nuts and bolts section of the chapter, in which I make some specific hypotheses and suggestions to my colleagues with respect to empirical research on this theory. If you are not an academic, or being forced by some professor to read this, feel free to skip to the next chapter. I will not hold it against you. (Or continue reading—you are certainly more than welcome.)

An important underlying assumption of this theory is that the culture of the United States is deeply impacted by the ideology that we live in a Christian nation, where Christianity has a special influence in the public realm, reaching beyond believers. While a significant proportion of the population does not believe in Christianity, as we have already seen, the United States is characterized by great numbers of adherents to some variation of the Christian doctrine. Further, a fairly significant proportion of Americans believe that this country is somehow special in light of its standing as a Christian nation and that Christianity is a central tenet in the way the country interacts with the rest of the world. I discussed and outlined this Christian nationalist belief system in chapter two, along with the potential criminogenic impact of those beliefs in chapter three. Here, we will look at what impact we might expect that belief system to have on rates of crime, and why.

First and foremost, predictions based on this theory stem from the following overreaching hypothesis:

H1: The level of violent crime in any country will increase as the level of religious nationalism increases.

If correct, this hypothesis will account for a number of patterns that have long been a focus of criminological theorists. With respect to the United States, the patterns of interest will include the following predictions:

H2: Higher rates of violence in the South—where Christian nationalism has a stronger influence—versus other regions in the United States.

This difference should be more pronounced among Southern whites due to greater adherence to Christian nationalism, with less of a difference among Southern blacks relative to their counterparts in other regions. While black populations might run high for levels of religiosity, they should run lower on measures of nationalism, in large part because their treatment in the United States would likely dampen their enthusiasm a bit. Of course, this is not to say that you will not find very patriotic black people, and multitudes have served their country with distinction in the armed forces. I present the racial aspect of this prediction with an understanding of why there might be a difference, along with an understanding that the difference may be difficult to measure.[77]

Overall, I submit that the long-standing phenomenon of higher rates of violence in the South is a function of the geography of the Bible Belt, rather than considerations that have previously been posited, such as enduring bitterness over the loss of the Civil War, an exaggerated role of honor in Southern males, or vestiges of violence that remain from the institution of slavery.

H3: Higher rates of violence in the United States versus comparable countries where religious nationalism is less prominent culturally.

This is simply a more specific prediction based upon H1.

H4: Higher rates of violence among blacks versus whites in the United States.[78]

This is predicted due to the greater influence of evangelical Christianity in black versus white communities, rather than the influence of nationalism, which should be significantly less. The doctrine still has the potential to be criminogenic in the black community, even in the absence of nationalistic tendencies, and black churches tend to be conservative on social issues such as homosexuality, even while they tend toward social justice orientations on the issues of racism and poverty.

H5: Higher rates of violence among men versus women in the United States.

This is largely due to a difference in the emphasis placed on more and less violent doctrines that vary along gender lines, along with subjugated, passive roles for women in Christianity. That said, rates of violence should still be higher for women where the influence of Christian nationalism is greater versus those in more secular environments.

H6: A continuing decline in violence as secularization increases in the United States (or the opposite effect, if Christian nationalism gains a stronger foothold).

Christianity is taking a hit in the United States, following patterns seen elsewhere in developed countries. The number of nonbelievers is rising, to the chagrin of conservative Christians who have definitely noticed the trend. In fact, the 2009 American Religious Identification Survey (ARIS) revealed that the number of Americans claiming no religious identification has nearly doubled since 1990, while the number identifying themselves as agnostic or atheists has increased fourfold in that time.[79] This trend continues to deepen. In fact, while the rate of the increase in nonreligious citizens has slowed slightly since the 1990s, a period characterized as the "secular boom," there is every indication that the younger generation is increasingly eschewing the religion of previous generations, with males disproportionately doing so, the bulk of whom can be fairly characterized as "rational skeptics."[80] This phenomenon competes with many other explanations for declining crime rates in the United States.

In what is widely regarded as the leading explanation for higher levels of atheism in societies, political scientists Norris and Inglehart argue that they are correlated strongly with higher levels of societal health, such as low poverty rates, greater gender equality, strong public healthcare systems, adequate food distribution, and accessible shelter. Available survey data seem to support the idea that where life is less secure and safe there are higher levels of religious belief and vice versa.[81] While I am not attempting to explain why Christian nationalism has such a strong foothold in the United States, it is interesting to note that this country is a curious exception to this general pattern, and a number of explanations may account for this, from our unequal wealth distribution to a variety of political, cultural, and sociological factors.[82]

COMPARISONS TO A FEW COMPETING EXPLANATIONS

The United States' distinction for having absurd rates of violence is an open question in the field of criminology, and is not the function of anomalous variations over time: The *average* rate of homicide in the United States over the course of the twentieth century exceeded the *highest* rates of other Western, industrialized nations. Indeed, with few exceptions, our *lowest* rates exceeded their *highest* rates.[83] We are a very violent country in the scheme of things, especially where violence ends in death.[84] However, we are not as violent as some people think: People tend to under or overestimate violence in the United States. The real reason the United States is noteworthy is that, in the words of psychologist Steven Pinker, "Instead of clustering with kindred peoples like Britain, the Netherlands, and Germany, it hangs out with toughs like Albania and Uruguay, close to the median rate for the entire world."[85] So, we are not number one by a long shot—but we are worth gossiping about as the thugs in a very polite group. As such, we do not exactly set the good example expected from an advanced superpower.

The central task in explaining American violent crime rates hinges on correctly identifying a cause of this crime that is a distinctly American phenomenon, and this is precisely where many existing explanations are most open to criticism. That Americans are too well-armed is a good example of a problematic explanation, in that other countries, such as Canada or France, have very high levels of gun ownership but are not even in the same ballpark with the United States in terms of homicide rates.[86] Similarly, problems emerge when we look at violence among different racial and ethnic groups as an explanation for America's rates of violence.

Mainly, even excluding all deaths involving nonwhite perpetrators from the American homicide rates, we still have a rate of lethal violence that outpaces that of other comparable countries. That means that white Americans alone are more prone to lethal violence than people of all races in many other industrialized countries.

The idea that the ideology of the American Dream is a criminogenic force is intriguing, and likely has some explanatory power for economically motivated crime. This theory holds that the United States has a unique fixation on monetary success as a measure of personal achievement, coupled with a strong ideology that anyone can achieve success if they work hard enough.[87] The goal of getting rich is more widely disseminated than the means to get rich, which causes people with blocked access to avenues to succeed legally to innovate in criminal ways in order to advance. At a societal level, economic institutions become more powerful at the expense of institutions such as education, family, and religion, which serve as social controls against committing crime.

This condition results in a higher crime rate as people, unrestrained by other institutions, resort to criminal means to obtain wealth. The problem with this explanation is that it would predict higher rates of crime in the service of obtaining wealth, such as stealing, and the United States is not uniquely prone to higher rates of such crime. And while lethal violence certainly occurs in the service of obtaining wealth, this is rare compared to homicides that do not serve an economic purpose. In fact, the most common precipitating factor in American homicides is a simple argument that escalates.[88]

We are also not unique in that most countries have bloody histories as the underpinning for their emergence as distinct nations. Numerous examples similar to the American Revolution exist in countries with far lower rates of lethal violence. The history of world civilizations is fraught with countries emerging from oppression at the hands of other countries. Australia got its start as a penal colony, and still we kill more people. To say that our violent beginnings are unique is simply incorrect, and, as such, our history does little to explain our violent nature.

Obviously, this is a very quick and dirty overview of some of the explanations for America's violence relative to other similar countries, but I am not a fan of the obligatory chapter in theoretical books in which the work of other criminologists is denigrated in an effort to make the current offering look more appealing. Only research truly sorts out such matters in the end, and many explanations shed light on some facet of crime and thus are of value, while perhaps missing the key raison d'être that accounts for our greater use of violence. It is a tough question, and nobody making a genuine attempt to answer it has done so without contributing important ideas to the literature. As criminologists, you can easily discern where my theory differs from the existing work on the topic and whether you think it has merit.

SOME FINAL THOUGHTS AND SUGGESTIONS FOR RESEARCHERS

Church attendance has been used as a proxy for measuring religious beliefs in the past, and it has been found to be correlated with lower rates of some types of delinquency. From this finding, it has often been assumed that religion inhibits criminality, but this assumption rests on shaky ground, as church attendance is correlated with factors such as more engaged parenting, increased supervision of youth, and less free time—all of which reduce involvement in delinquency. Further, liberal and moderate variations of Christianity are not predicted to have the same effect as Christian nationalism, and church attendance does not begin to scratch the surface of the independent variable.

We also see much the same effect with participating in other organized activities that require parental involvement and assistance, and the extent to which religious ideologies are directly responsible for less delinquency is unknown. For these reasons, church attendance serves as a very poor proxy for Christian nationalism and really should not be employed. While I realize that this limits use of many existing data sets to address this theory, I do not believe that criminology will advance in its understanding of religion and crime unless we dig deeper to flesh out the belief system.

It would be easy to construct surveys that are sensitive enough to detect Christian nationalism, and the list of RWA characteristics would be helpful in developing such instruments, which could test support for criminogenic policies, attitudes about violence, the impact of built-in forgiveness, the relationship between theology and action, and many other possible angles. Another interesting research question would be to gather and compare statistics for people who went into prison with a Christian belief system, and what that belief system looks like, versus the number of people who become Christians while in prison or who are nonbelievers. The assumption is usually that people "find" Jesus while serving time, but what if that is not the case? Perhaps they just have more time to focus their attention on previously existing religious beliefs there and find it comforting under trying circumstances.

Another interesting question is whether Christian right-wing authoritarians commit more or less violent crime compared to their less religious left-wing counterparts, and whether the addition of religion to the authoritarian mix significantly changes these patterns. Where is this cultural ethos most likely to translate into violent crime? What types of crime are likely to occur as a result of Christian nationalism—and are Christian nationalists themselves likely to be the ones offending? While Christian nationalism is a movement, its pervasive influence spreads much further than the borders of its membership. We know that Christian nationalists are punitive, and a significant amount of violence is punitive in nature—is there a causal relationship where interpersonal violence is concerned? Beyond the realm of social interaction and culture, scientists are uncovering physiological differences between conservatives and liberals that might be precipitating a greater propensity to embrace Christian nationalism in some people. Is there a way to quell innate fears that might cause less harm? In chapter six, I offer some preliminary suggestions to address the criminogenic influence of Christian nationalism, but perhaps research on the theory will uncover further avenues to reduce violent criminality.

A preponderance of political scientists and psychologists are in agreement that the political disagreements between conservatives and liberals occur in part due to differences in personality, psychology, physiology, and genetics that make change far more difficult—if not impossible—to enact through the usual vehicles of persuasion and logic.[89] As it turns out, conservatives have a "negativity bias" in which they are more physiologically tuned into negative stimuli;[90] they react far more quickly to aversive and threatening stimuli, which is likely why fear-based political messages are so effective on the right. A need for certainty and intolerance for ambiguity are also key traits on the right.[91] John Jost, a respected social psychologist, and his colleagues summarized the state of the literature in this area in these terms:

> There is now evidence from a variety of laboratories around the world using a variety of methodological techniques leading to the virtually inescapable conclusion that the cognitive-motivational styles of leftists and rightists are quite different. This research consistently finds that conservatism is positively associated with heightened epistemic concerns for order, structure, closure, certainty, consistency, simplicity, and familiarity, as well as existential concerns such as perceptions of danger, sensitivity to threat, and death anxiety.[92]

Many of these characteristics have great potential to spur violence, especially when combined with a theology that is, in itself, violent. I have drawn from many disciplines in developing this theory, and I hope that my colleagues will take an interdisciplinary approach to testing it, as well.

Criminologists rarely conduct experiments to test theory—but why not? Statistical analyses and qualitative methodology will be extremely useful in determining support for this theory, but experimentation would likely prove helpful, as well. Will Christian nationalists prove more likely to act aggressively toward out-groups than other subjects? Are they more susceptible to mortality salience and death denial? Do threats to their doctrine make them more likely to resort to and support the use of violence? These are important questions to answer in determining the criminogenic impact of this belief system that permeates much of our country.

Finally, it seems important to comment on the lack of research in this area within the field of criminology. We study to death almost every social variable—education, marriage, gender, gun ownership, and the like—but research on religion and politics in the context of crime is relatively rare to nonexistent.[93] Almost all of the research that does exist uses church attendance as the measure of religiosity, with most focusing on a few types of delinquency (such as drug and alcohol use), and this research is sometimes funded by conservative Christian organizations.[94] It is time to stop tiptoeing around religion as a variable worth examination in the context of crime. Conservative Christianity is held up as a belief system that promotes moral behavior; it seems implausible that it has not warranted far more attention to determine whether it impacts criminality.

CHAPTER FIVE

THE BIBLE, CAFETERIA STYLE

*The Bible has noble poetry in it . . . and some good morals and a
wealth of obscenity, and upwards of a thousand lies.*
—Mark Twain, *Letters from the Earth*

*I think that we would be totally in the right to do it [stone gays to
death]. . . . Ignoring as a nation things that are worthy of death
is very remiss.*
—Oklahoma State House candidate, Scott Esk
(on Facebook in 2014)

*The God of the Old Testament is arguably the most unpleasant
character in all fiction: jealous and proud of it; a petty, unjust,
unforgiving control-freak; a vindictive, bloodthirsty ethnic
cleanser; a misogynistic, homophobic, racist, infanticidal, genocidal, filicidal, pestilential, megalomaniacal, sadomasochistic,
capriciously malevolent bully.*
—Richard Dawkins, *The God Delusion*

*With or without religion, you would have good people doing
good things and evil people doing evil things. But for good
people to do evil things, that takes religion.*
—Steven Weinberg, "A Designer Universe"

*Properly read, the Bible is the most potent force for atheism ever
conceived.*
—Isaac Asimov, letter dated February 22, 1966

THE WAR ON SIN

In this chapter, the Bible will be examined as a potential impetus for violent crime in more detail, drawing directly from the scripture, since Christian nationalists claim it as the underpinning for their beliefs and as the literal Word of God. I will not dwell on interpretation here—I am not a theologian and do not claim to be—instead, I will present verses relevant to violence against several categories of people who are especially likely to suffer due to this theology. My interpretation is as likely to be wrong as the next person's, outside of experts on the historical context in which it was written. I have read a lot of theological writings in researching this book and have often been surprised by interpretations of various passages; I think that is an important point, though: If experts draw completely different conclusions than the average reader, who is not likely to be delving into theological texts to aid in their interpretation, the Bible means what you think it means.

A good example of an average interpretation differing greatly from an expert one can be found in Matthew 10:34, in which Jesus says that he came "not to bring peace but a sword." In arguing that Islam is more violent than Christianity, Arabic expert Raymond Ibrahim asserted the following:

> Still, there are those who attempt to portray Jesus as having a similarly militant ethos as Muhammad by quoting the verse where the former—who "spoke to the multitudes in parables and without a parable spoke not"—said, "I come not to bring peace but a sword." But based on the context of this statement, it is clear that Jesus was not commanding violence against non-Christians but rather predicting that strife will exist between Christians and their environment—a prediction that was only too true as early Christians, far from taking up the sword, passively perished by the sword in martyrdom as too often they still do in the Muslim world.
>
> Others point to the violence predicted in the Book of Revelation while, again, failing to discern that the entire account is descriptive—not to mention clearly symbolic—and thus hardly prescriptive for Christians.

At any rate, how can one conscionably compare this handful of New Testament verses that metaphorically mention the word "sword" to the literally hundreds of Qur'anic injunctions and statements by Muhammad that clearly command Muslims to take up a very real sword against non-Muslims? Does this mean that no self-professed Christian can be anti-Semitic? Of course not. But it does mean that Christian anti-Semites are living oxymorons—for the simple reason that textually and theologically, Christianity, far from teaching hatred or animosity, unambiguously stresses love and forgiveness. Whether or not all Christians follow such mandates is hardly the point; just as whether or not all Muslims uphold the obligation of jihad is hardly the point. The only question is, what do the religions command?"[1]

I chose this nuanced discussion about the issue of violence in the Christian faith relative to that of Islam because it assumes a lot about adherents' understanding the use of metaphors in the Bible, while also making a point about interpretation.

First, let's look at the issue of understanding. Ever notice how many tattoos people have of swords? A good number of them are not there to mark the wearer as a *Game of Thrones* fan. They are also popular among the kind of Christian nationalists who get tattoos because of Matthew 10:34, and they are not celebrating their own martyrdom.[2] Christian nationalists are militant and militaristic, and they embrace this verse as something of a call to arms for Christians to defend their faith against outside threats. Their rough interpretation of this passage appears to be that Jesus wanted them to be tough and stand up for Christianity; that this does not mesh particularly well with any other utterance or action Jesus took tends to go unnoticed.

Jesus is a little problematic for Christian nationalists, and Matthew 10:34 is one of the mechanisms they use to blunt his impact where it is not welcome. He was something of a nonjudgmental, socialistic peacenik, which is inconvenient to a movement characterized by judgment, unfettered capitalism, and war. So Christian nationalists gave Jesus a makeover, combining the unflinching, violent judgment and punishments of the Old Testament with a Jesus who provides eternal life through his death and resurrection for our sins. I often wonder how Jesus would feel in a modern, evangelical megachurch, as he would have precious little ideology in common with his followers there.

Second, we turn to the issue of interpretation. In truth, there is no way to know whether the experts are correct in their interpretation of Jesus's statement in Matthew. If you are a Christian nationalist, that is one of the beauties of the Bible: It can be used to say anything you want. You can emphasize some passages, while claiming others are historical artifacts or metaphors, depending on your priorities. It is fascinating how much Sunday school time is devoted to the New Testament when Christian nationalists are so at odds with its message and pull so heavily from the Old as the basis for their socially conservative beliefs. My sense is that staring at the trees too closely must help obscure the forest lying beyond the text of redemption through Christ's sacrifice.

Ibrahim's contention that the message of Christianity is unambiguous in stressing love and forgiveness, that Revelation is clearly symbolic and descriptive rather than proscriptive, and that the sword is a metaphorical device strikes me as cavalier when applied to a lay audience.[3] The fictional Left Behind series, by evangelical authors Tim LaHaye and Jerry Jenkins, alone makes this point for me, and I do not want to belabor it, as I am certain it is clear. What Raymond Ibrahim glossed over is a plethora of violent passages, and passages that can be interpreted as violent. Similarly, his dismissal of the Old Testament in this argument glosses over the fact that Christian nationalists make ready and frequent use of it to support their more aggressive and judgmental urges, which greatly damages his argument that Islam is fundamentally more violent than Christianity. In contrast, religious studies professor and prolific author on the topic of Christianity, Philip Jenkins, had this to say about the comparison:

> In terms of ordering violence and bloodshed, any simplistic claim about the superiority of the Bible to the Koran would be wildly wrong. In fact, the Bible overflows with "texts of terror," to borrow a phrase coined by the American theologian Phyllis Trible. The Bible contains far more verses praising or urging bloodshed than does the Koran, and biblical violence is often far more extreme, and marked by more indiscrimi-

nate savagery. . . . If the founding text shapes the whole religion, then Judaism and Christianity deserve the utmost condemnation as religions of savagery.[4]

Obviously, it should be noted that I am picking and choosing from the Bible in much the same manner as Christian nationalists in presenting passages that illustrate my point—that the Bible is a violent theology—but I hope that the point is not lost in that fact. If I were pulling one passage, such as Matthew 10:34, to make this point, I would be rightly subject to a heap of criticism that I am making a mountain of a molehill. I ask simply that you withhold judgment until the end of the chapter. Entire facets of the Christian nationalist belief system, such as their enmity for gay people, are based on a very few verses, so the volume of biblical support for an idea is of little importance at any rate. What is important is the use to which those passages are put, though I think the prevalence of the violence will speak for itself.

LETHAL VIOLENCE IN THE BIBLE

I was sorely tempted to offer a short discussion of the actual violence in the Bible in this section, coupled with a very long appendix where I would include a collection of violent passages, but I decided to let the verses speak for themselves.[5] It is far more instructive to read the actual violence in the scripture, especially if you allow yourself to really think about the acts described and proscribed. Decide for yourself if the Bible is violent, and whether you think that God is compassionate and slow to anger.[6]

This list is by no means exhaustive, but it is a fair representation of the ubiquitous and explicit nature of lethal violence inherent in Christian theology. In order to make the task manageable, this list includes only violence ending in death; it does not include promises of other-worldly, lethal violence after death, or nonlethal violence, unless it occurs in the context of a lethal event or proscription. In a way, this is a list of instances in which capital punishment and murder appear in the Bible. Finally, I have listed the books in alphabetical order, rather than in their biblical order to make the section easier to use as a reference:

Acts 3:23
And it shall come to pass, that every soul, which will not hear the prophet, shall be destroyed. (KJV)

Acts 12:23
And immediately the angel of the LORD smote him, because he gave not God the Glory: and he was eaten of worms, and gave up the ghost. (KJV)

✳✳✳

1 Chronicles 21:1, 14
Satan rose up against Israel and incited David to take a census of Israel. . . . So the LORD sent a plague on Israel, and seventy thousand men of Israel fell dead.

✳✳✳

2 Chronicles 15:13
All who would not seek the LORD, the God of Israel, were to be put to death, whether small or great, man or woman.

✳✳✳

Deuteronomy 2:32–34
Then Sihon came out against us, he and all his people, to fight at Jahaz. And the LORD our God delivered him before us; and we smote him, and his sons, and all his people. And we took all his cities at that time, and utterly destroyed the men, and the women, and the little ones, of every city, we left none to remain. (KJV)

Deuteronomy 13:5

That prophet or dreamer must be put to death for inciting rebellion against the LORD your God, who brought you out of Egypt and redeemed you from the land of slavery. That prophet or dreamer tried to turn you from the way the LORD your God commanded you to follow. You must purge the evil from among you.

Deuteronomy 13:6–9

If your very own brother, or your son or daughter, or the wife you love, or your closest friend secretly entices you, saying, "Let us go and worship other gods" (gods that neither you nor your fathers have known, gods of the peoples around you, whether near or far, from one end of the land to the other), do not yield to him or listen to them. Show them no pity. Do not spare them or shield them. You must certainly put them to death.

Deuteronomy 13:12–15

If you hear it said about one of the towns the LORD your God is giving you to live in that troublemakers have arisen among you and have led the people of their town astray, saying, "Let us go and worship other gods" (gods you have not known), then you must inquire, probe and investigate it thoroughly. And if it is true and it has been proved that this detestable thing has been done among you, you must certainly put to the sword all who live in that town. You must destroy it completely, both its people and its livestock.

Deuteronomy 13:6–11

If thy brother, the son of thy mother, or thy son, or thy daughter, or the wife of thy bosom, or thy friend, which is of thine own soul, entice thee secretly, saying, Let us go and serve other gods, which thou hast not known, thou, nor thy fathers; Thou shalt not consent unto him, nor hearken unto him; neither shall thine eye pity him, neither shalt thou spare, neither shalt thou conceal him: But thou shalt surely kill him; thine hand shall be first upon him to put him to death, and afterwards the hand of all the people. Thou shalt stone him with stones, that he die; because he hath sought to thrust thee away from the Lord thy God. (KJV)

Deuteronomy 17:2–5

If a man or woman living among you in one of the towns the LORD gives you is found doing evil in the eyes of the LORD your God in violation of his covenant, and contrary to my command has worshiped other gods, bowing down to them or to the sun or the moon or the stars in the sky, and this has been brought to your attention, then you must investigate it thoroughly. If it is true and it has been proved that this detestable thing has been done in Israel, take the man or woman who has done this evil deed to your city gate and stone that person to death.

Deuteronomy 18:20

But any prophet who claims to give a message from another god or who falsely claims to speak for Me must die. (NLT)

Deuteronomy 21:18–21

If someone has a stubborn and rebellious son who does not obey his father and mother and will not listen to them when they discipline him, his father and mother shall take hold of him and bring him to the elders at the gate of the town. They shall say to the elders, "This son of ours is stubborn and rebellious. He will not obey us. He is a glutton and a drunkard." Then all the men of his town shall stone him to death.

Deuteronomy 22:20–21

If, however, the charge is true and no proof of the young woman's virginity can be found, she shall be brought to the door of her father's house and there the men of her town shall stone her to death. She has done an outrageous thing in Israel by being promiscuous while still in her father's house. You must purge the evil from among you.

Deuteronomy 22:22

If a man is found sleeping with another man's wife, both the man who slept with her and the woman must die. You must purge the evil from Israel.

Deuteronomy 22:23–24

If a damsel that is a virgin be betrothed unto an husband, and a man find her in the city, and lie with her; Then ye shall bring them both out unto the gate of the city, and ye shall stone them with stones that they die; the damsel, because she cried not, being in the city; and the man, because he hath humbled his neighbor's wife: so thou shalt put away evil from among you. (KJV)

Deuteronomy 24:7

If someone is caught kidnapping a fellow Israelite and treating or selling them as a slave, the kidnapper must die. You must purge the evil from among you.

✳✳✳

Exodus 12:29–30

At midnight the LORD struck down all the firstborn in Egypt, from the firstborn of Pharaoh, who sat on the throne, to the firstborn of the prisoner, who was in the dungeon, and the firstborn of all the livestock as well. Pharaoh and all his officials and all the Egyptians got up during the night, and there was loud wailing in Egypt, for there was not a house without someone dead.

Exodus 21:12–14

Anyone who strikes a person with a fatal blow is to be put to death. However, if it is not done intentionally, but God lets it happen, they are to flee to a place I will designate. But if anyone schemes and kills someone deliberately, that person is to be taken from my altar and put to death.

Exodus 21:15

Anyone who attacks their father or mother is to be put to death.

Exodus 21:16

Anyone who kidnaps someone is to be put to death, whether the victim has been sold or is still in the kidnapper's possession.

Exodus 21:17
Anyone who curses their father or mother is to be put to death.

Exodus 22:18
Do not allow a sorceress to live.

Exodus 22:19
Anyone who has sexual relations with an animal is to be put to death.

Exodus 22:20
Whoever sacrifices to any god other than the LORD must be destroyed.

Exodus 22:22–24
Do not take advantage of the widow or the fatherless. If you do and they cry out to me, I will certainly hear their cry. My anger will be aroused, and I will kill you with the sword; your wives will become widows and your children fatherless.

Exodus 31:14–15
Observe the Sabbath, because it is holy to you. Anyone who desecrates it is to be put to death; those who do any work on that day must be cut off from their people. For six days work is to be done, but the seventh day is a day of sabbath rest, holy to the LORD. Whoever does any work on the Sabbath day is to be put to death.

Exodus 32:27–29
Then [Moses] said to [the Levites], "This is what the LORD, the God of Israel, says: 'Each man strap a sword to his side. Go back and forth through the camp from one end to the other, each killing his brother and friend and neighbor.'" The Levites did as Moses commanded, and that day about three thousand of the people died. Then Moses said, "You have been set apart to the LORD today, for you were against your own sons and brothers, and he has blessed you this day."

Exodus 35:2

"For six days, work is to be done, but the seventh day shall be your holy day, a day of sabbath rest to the LORD. Whoever does any work on it is to be put to death."

✱✱✱

Ezekiel 9:5–7

As I listened, he said to the others, "Follow him through the city and kill, without showing pity or compassion. Slaughter the old men, the young men and women, the mothers and children, but do not touch anyone who has the mark. Begin at my sanctuary." So they began with the old men who were in front of the temple.

Then he said to them, "Defile the temple and fill the courts with the slain. Go!" So they went out and began killing throughout the city.

Ezekiel 14:9

And if the prophet is enticed to utter a prophecy, I the LORD have enticed that prophet, and I will stretch out my hand against him and destroy him from among my people Israel.

Ezekiel 18:4

Behold, all souls are mine; the soul of the father as well as the soul of the son is mine: the soul who sins shall die. (ESV)

Ezekiel 18:20

The soul who sins shall die. The son shall not suffer for the iniquity of the father, nor the father suffer for the iniquity of the son. The righteousness of the righteous shall be upon himself, and the wickedness of the wicked shall be upon himself. (ESV)

Ezekiel 28:18

By the multitude of your iniquities, in the unrighteousness of your trade you profaned your sanctuaries; so I brought fire out from your midst;

it consumed you, and I turned you to ashes on the earth in the sight of all who saw you. (ESV)

Ezekiel 32:5–7

I will spread your flesh on the mountains and fill the valleys with your remains. I will drench the land with your flowing blood all the way to the mountains, and the ravines will be filled with your flesh. When I snuff you out, I will cover the heavens and darken their stars; I will cover the sun with a cloud, and the moon will not give its light.

✱✱✱

Genesis 2:17

But you must not eat from the tree of the knowledge of good and evil, for when you eat from it you will certainly die.

Genesis 7:20–23

The waters rose and covered the mountains to a depth of more than fifteen cubits. Every living thing that moved on the earth perished—birds, livestock, wild animals, all the creatures that swarm over the earth, and all mankind. Everything on dry land that had the breath of life in its nostrils died. Every living thing on the face of the earth was wiped out; people and animals and the creatures that move along the ground and the birds were wiped from the earth. Only Noah was left, and those with him in the ark.

Genesis 19:24

Then the LORD rained on Sodom and Gomorrah sulfur and fire from the LORD out of heaven.

Genesis 38:9–10

But Onan knew that the child would not be his; so whenever he slept with his brother's wife, he spilled his semen on the ground to keep from providing offspring for his brother. What he did was wicked in the LORD's sight; so the LORD put him to death also.

***

Isaiah 13:9

See, the day of the LORD is coming—a cruel day, with wrath and fierce anger—to make the land desolate and destroy the sinners within it.

Isaiah 13:11–12

I will punish the world for its evil, the wicked for their sins. I will put an end to the arrogance of the haughty and will humble the pride of the ruthless. I will make people scarcer than pure gold, more rare than the gold of Ophir.

Isaiah 13:15–16

Whoever is captured will be thrust through; all who are caught will fall by the sword. Their infants will be dashed to pieces before their eyes; their houses will be looted and their wives violated.

Isaiah 13:18–19

Their bows will strike down the young men; they will have no mercy on infants, nor will they look with compassion on children. Babylon, the jewel of kingdoms, the pride and glory of the Babylonians, will be overthrown by God like Sodom and Gomorrah.

Isaiah 14:21

Prepare a place to slaughter his children for the sins of their ancestors; they are not to rise to inherit the land and cover the earth with their cities.

Isaiah 34:9

And the streams of Edom shall be turned into pitch, and her soil into sulfur; her land shall become burning pitch. (ESV)

Isaiah 66:24

And they shall go out and look on the dead bodies of the men who have rebelled against me. For their worm shall not die, their fire shall not be quenched, and they shall be an abhorrence to all flesh. (ESV)

***

Jeremiah 17:27
But if you do not listen to me, to keep the Sabbath day holy, and not to bear a burden and enter by the gates of Jerusalem on the Sabbath day, then I will kindle a fire in its gates, and it shall devour the palaces of Jerusalem and shall not be quenched.

Jeremiah 25:33
At that time those slain by the LORD will be everywhere—from one end of the earth to the other. They will not be mourned or gathered up or buried, but they will be like dung lying on the ground.

Jeremiah 25:34–38
Weep and moan, you evil shepherds! Roll in the dust, you leaders of the flock! The time of your slaughter has arrived; you will fall and shatter like a fragile vase. You will find no place to hide; there will be no way to escape. Listen to the frantic cries of the shepherds, The leaders of the flock are wailing in despair, for the LORD is ruining their pastures. Peaceful meadows will be turned into a wasteland by the LORD's fierce anger. He has left his den like a strong lion seeking its prey, and their land will be made desolate by the sword of the enemy and the LORD's fierce anger. (NLT)

***

Job 4:8–9
As I have observed, those who plow evil and those who sow trouble reap it. At the breath of God they are no more; at the blast of his anger they perished.

***

John 15:6
If a man abide not in me, he is cast forth as a branch, and is withered; and men gather them, and cast them into the fire, and they are burned. (KJV)

***

Joshua 6:20–21

When the people heard the sound of the rams' horns, they shouted as loud as they could. Suddenly, the walls of Jericho collapsed, and the Israelites charged straight into the town and captured it. They completely destroyed everything in it with their swords—men and women, young and old, cattle, sheep, goats, and donkeys. (NLT)

Joshua 7:24–25

Then Joshua, together with all Israel, took Achan son of Zerah, the silver, the robe, the gold bar, his sons and daughters, his cattle, donkeys and sheep, his tent and all that he had, to the Valley of Achor. . . . Then all Israel stoned him, and after they had stoned the rest [of his family], they burned them.

Joshua 8:24–25

When Israel had finished killing all the men of Ai in the fields and in the wilderness where they had chased them, and when every one of them had been put to the sword, all the Israelites returned to Ai and killed those who were in it. Twelve thousand men and women fell that day—all the people of Ai.

Joshua 10:40

So Joshua subdued the whole region, including the hill country, the Negev, the western foothills and the mountain slopes, together with all their kings. He left no survivors. He totally destroyed all who breathed, just as the LORD, the God of Israel, had commanded.

Joshua 11:11

Everyone in it they put to the sword. They totally destroyed them, not sparing anything that breathed, and he burned Hazor itself.

Joshua 11:14

The Israelites carried off for themselves all the plunder and livestock of these cities, but all the people they put to the sword until they completely destroyed them, not sparing anyone that breathed.

***

1 Kings 15:28–30

Baasha killed Nadab in the third year of Asa king of Judah and succeeded him as king. As soon as he began to reign, he killed Jeroboam's whole family. He did not leave Jeroboam anyone that breathed, but destroyed them all, according to the word of the LORD given through his servant Ahijah the Shilonite, This happened because of the sins Jeroboam had committed and had caused Israel to commit, and because he aroused the anger of the LORD, the God of Israel.

1 Kings 20:35–36

By the word of the LORD one of the company of the prophets said to his companion, "Strike me with your weapon," but he refused. So the prophet said, "Because you have not obeyed the LORD, as soon as you leave me a lion will kill you." And after the man went away, a lion found him and killed him.

***

2 Kings 19:35

That night the angel of the LORD went out and put to death a hundred and eighty-five thousand in the Assyrian camp. When the people got up the next morning—there were all the dead bodies!

***

Leviticus 10:1–2

Aaron's sons Nadab and Abihu took their censers, put fire in them and added incense; and they offered unauthorized fire before the LORD, contrary to his command. So fire came out from the presence of the LORD and consumed them, and they died before the LORD.

Leviticus 20:9

Anyone who curses their father or mother is to be put to death. Because they have cursed their father or mother, their blood will be on their own head.

Leviticus 20:10

If a man commits adultery with another man's wife—with the wife of his neighbor—both the adulterer and the adulteress are to be put to death.

Leviticus 20:11

If a man has sexual relations with his father's wife, he has dishonored his father. Both the man and the woman are to be put to death; their blood will be on their own heads.

Leviticus 20:12

If a man has sexual relations with his daughter-in-law, both of them are to be put to death. What they have done is a perversion; their blood will be on their own heads.

Leviticus 20:13

If a man has sexual relations with a man as one does with a woman, both of them have done what is detestable. They are to be put to death; their blood will be on their own heads.

Leviticus 20:14

If a man marries both a woman and her mother, it is wicked. Both he and they must be burned in the fire, so that no wickedness will be among you.

Leviticus 20:15

If a man has sexual relations with an animal, he is to be put to death, and you must kill the animal.

Leviticus 20:16

If a woman approaches an animal to have sexual relations with it, kill both the woman and the animal. They are to be put to death; their blood will be on their own heads.

Leviticus 20:27

A man or woman who is a medium or spiritist among you must be put to death. You are to stone them; their blood will be on their own heads.

Leviticus 21:9

If a priest's daughter defiles herself by becoming a prostitute, she disgraces her father; she must be burned in the fire.

Leviticus 24:16

Anyone who blasphemes the name of the LORD is to be put to death. The entire assembly must stone them. Whether foreigner or native-born, when they blaspheme the Name, they are to be put to death.

Leviticus 24:17

Anyone who takes the life of a human being is to be put to death.

Leviticus 24:21

Whoever kills an animal must make restitution, but whoever kills a human being is to be put to death.

Leviticus 27:29

No person devoted to destruction may be ransomed; they are to be put to death.

***

Malachi 4:1

For behold, the day is coming, burning like an oven, when all the arrogant and all evildoers will be stubble. The day that is coming shall set them ablaze, says the LORD of hosts, so that it will leave them neither root nor branch. (ESV)

Malachi 4:3

And you shall tread down the wicked, for they will be ashes under the soles of your feet, on the day when I act, says the LORD of hosts. (ESV)

✳✳✳

Matthew 10:28

And do not fear those who kill the body but cannot kill the soul. Rather fear him who can destroy both soul and body in hell. (ESV)

Matthew 15:4 (Jesus repeating Moses's admonishment, who was speaking for God)

"For God said, 'Honor your father and mother' and 'Anyone who curses their father or mother is to be put to death.'"

Matthew 25:41

"Then he will say to those on his left, 'Depart from me, you who are cursed, into the eternal fire prepared for the devil and his angels.'"

✳✳✳

Mark 7:10 (Jesus repeating Moses's admonishment)

"For Moses said, 'Honor your father and your mother,' and, 'Anyone who curses their father or mother is to be put to death.'"

✳✳✳

Numbers 11:1

Now when the people complained, it displeased the LORD; for the LORD heard it, and His anger was aroused. So the fire of the LORD burned among them, and consumed some in the outskirts of the camp. (NKJV)

Numbers 15:32–36

While the Israelites were in the wilderness, a man was found gathering wood on the Sabbath day. Those who found him gathering wood brought him to Moses and Aaron and the whole assembly, and they kept him in custody, because it was not clear what should be done to him. Then the LORD said to Moses, "The man must die. The whole assembly must stone him outside the camp." So the whole assembly took him outside the camp and stoned him to death, as the LORD commanded Moses.

Numbers 31:7
They fought against Midian, as the LORD commanded Moses, and killed every man.

Numbers 31:15–18
"Have you allowed all the women to live?" [Moses] asked them. "They were the ones who followed Balaam's advice and enticed the Israelites to be unfaithful to the LORD in the Peor incident, so that a plague struck the LORD's people. Now kill all the boys. And kill every woman who has slept with a man, but save for yourselves every girl who has never slept with a man."

Numbers 35:16–18
But if he struck him down with an instrument of iron, so that he died, he is a murderer; the murderer shall be put to death. And if he struck him down with a stone in the hand, by which a man may die, and he died, he is a murderer; the murderer shall be put to death. Or if he struck him down with a weapon of wood in the hand, by which a man may die, and he died, he is a murderer; the murderer shall be put to death. (RSV)

Numbers 35:20–21
And if he stabbed him from hatred, or hurled at him, lying in wait, so that he died, or in enmity struck him down with his hand so that he died, then he who struck the blow shall be put to death; he is a murderer; the avenger of blood shall put the murderer to death, when he meets him. (RSV)

*✶✶

Psalm 110:5–6

The LORD is at your right hand; he will crush kings on the day of his wrath. He will judge the nations, heaping up the dead and crushing the rulers of the whole earth.

✱✱✱

Revelation 2:22–23

So I will cast her on a bed of suffering, and I will make those who commit adultery with her suffer intensely, unless they repent of her ways. I will strike her children dead. Then all the churches will know that I am he who searches hearts and minds, and I will repay each of you according to your deeds.

Revelation 9:15

And the four angels who had been kept ready for this very hour and day and month and year were released to kill a third of mankind.

Revelation 9:18

A third of mankind was killed by the three plagues of fire, smoke and sulfur that came out of their mouths.

Revelation 13:10

He that killeth with the sword must be killed with the sword.(KJV)

Revelation 18:21

And a mighty angel took up a stone like a great millstone, and cast it into the sea, saying, "Thus with violence shall that great city Babylon be thrown down, and shall be found no more at all." (KJV)

✱✱✱

Romans 1:26–32

For this cause God gave them up unto vile affections: for even their women did change the natural use into that which is against nature: And likewise also the men, leaving the natural use of the woman, burned in their lust one toward another; men with men working that which is unseemly, and receiving in themselves that recompense of their error which was meet. And even as they did not like to retain God in their knowledge, God gave them over to a reprobate mind, to do those things which are not convenient; Being filled with all unrighteousness, fornication, wickedness, covetousness, maliciousness; full of envy, murder, debate, deceit, malignity; whisperers, Backbiters, haters of God, despiteful, proud, boasters, inventors of evil things, disobedient to parents, Without understanding, covenant breakers, without natural affection, implacable, unmerciful: Who knowing the judgment of God, that they which commit such things are worthy of death, not only do the same, but have pleasure in them that do them. (KJV)

Romans 1:29–32
They have become filled with every kind of wickedness, evil, greed and depravity. They are full of envy, murder, strife, deceit and malice. They are gossips, slanderers, God-haters, insolent, arrogant and boastful; they invent ways of doing evil; they disobey their parents; they have no understanding, no fidelity, no love, no mercy. Although they know God's righteous decree that those who do such things deserve death, they not only continue to do these very things but also approve of those who practice them.

✱✱✱

1 Samuel 15:3
"Now go and smite Amalek, and utterly destroy all that they have, and spare them not; but slay both man and woman, infant and suckling, ox and sheep, camel and ass." (KJV)

1 Samuel 18:27
Wherefore David arose and went, he and his men, and slew of the Philistines two hundred men; and David brought their foreskins, and they

gave them in full tale to the king, that he might be the king's son in law. And Saul gave him Michal his daughter to wife. (KJV)

✳✳✳

Zechariah 13:2–3

"I will remove both the prophets and the spirit of impurity from the land. And if anyone still prophesies, their father and mother, to whom they were born, will say to them, 'You must die, because you have told lies in the LORD's name.' Then their own parents will stab the one who prophesies."

✳✳✳

Zephaniah 1:2–3

I will sweep away everything from the face of the earth," declares the LORD. "I will sweep away both man and beast; I will sweep away the birds in the sky and the fish in the sea—and the idols that cause the wicked to stumble. When I destroy all mankind on the face of the earth," declares the LORD.

✳✳✳

In Jeremiah 48:10, God says, "Cursed be he who does the Lord's work remissly, cursed he who holds back his sword from blood." (NAB) There is not a lot of holding back in the Bible, and though the majority of these verses were drawn from the Old Testament, there are quite a few from the New Testament, as well. Christian apologists often call foul when the Old Testament is used to illustrate the Bible as violent and awful, but they are missing a point made several times in the New Testament: Jesus explicitly says that the old laws still apply, effectively giving his seal of approval to the Old Testament. Matthew 5:17–20 lays this out pretty explicitly:

> Do not think that I have come to abolish the Law or the Prophets; I have not come to abolish them but to fulfill them. For truly I tell you, until

heaven and earth disappear, not the smallest letter, not the least stroke of a pen, will by any means disappear from the Law until everything is accomplished. Therefore anyone who sets aside one of the least of these commands and teaches others accordingly will be called least in the kingdom of heaven, but whoever practices and teaches these commands will be called great in the kingdom of heaven. For I tell you that unless your righteousness surpasses that of the Pharisees and the teachers of the law, you will certainly not enter the kingdom of heaven.[7]

The Old Testament is not abrogated by Jesus at any point in the New Testament, and there are similar reminders of this in other parts of the Gospel. As such, Christians are stuck with it as half of the Bible, despite the fact that it is often difficult to explain, and, indeed, justify. Further, many bedrock beliefs of Christian nationalists—creationism, that homosexuality is a sin, and that the death penalty is based on biblical principles, for example—come directly from the Old Testament, along with a strong ethos of judgment and punishment that are central to their worldview (and difficult to support using only the New Testament). Relativism is evil, and relativism is used to describe anything that weakens the black-and-white assertions about sin in the Old Testament—some of them, anyway.

It is interesting, really: The Old Testament fits far more easily with Christian nationalism but is so problematic to defend that they often retreat from it when pressed. For example, you might have noticed in Leviticus that the wording for the verse condemning homosexuality is almost identical to those condemning cursing or attacking one's parents and adultery. The wages of those sins are death, and the sinner is held responsible for that outcome. But a significant number of Christians commit these sins, including many clergy members (at least, it would seem, when it comes to adultery), so it is very difficult to hide the hypocrisy inherent in strongly enforcing one rule while taking a relatively understanding stance on the others. In some cases, the rules are deemed historical artifacts to sidestep troublesome challenges. The Bible is the literal Word of God . . . but Christians see no problem in wearing clothing woven of two materials, wearing gold, pearls, and expensive clothing, cutting their hair and beards, and getting tattoos.[8] Those commands are deemed no longer relevant, while, inexplicably, other very similar proscriptions are still thought to apply to modern life.

In terms of the New Testament, it is far less violent than the Old Testament, despite the violent passages from Matthew, Mark, Acts, Romans, John, and Revelations included in the preceding list. The problem is that it is still violent, the Old Testament is still half the Bible, and that extremely violent half of the Bible is used extensively by Christian nationalists and fundamentalist Christians to provide significant underpinnings for their belief systems. We will now focus on a few specific populations who experience violent victimization as the result of specific biblical tenets of this belief system.

WOMEN AS WICKED AND SUBHUMAN

I will use a quote from former President Jimmy Carter to open a discussion of the violence directed at women as a result of Christian nationalist beliefs:

> The truth is that male religious leaders have had—and still have—an option to interpret holy teachings either to exalt or subjugate women. They have, for their own selfish ends, overwhelmingly chosen the latter. Their continuing choice provides the foundation or justification for much of the pervasive persecution and abuse of women throughout the world.[9]

Christianity has treated women terribly since its creation, beginning with the actual story of creation, in which Eve is made as a subservient helper to Adam, and then is used as the scapegoat for the expulsion of humans from the Garden into a world of pain, toil, and death. Feminist scholars have subjected the story of Eve to tremendous efforts of interpretation and reinterpretation to address this apparent indication that men are superior to women, but I see no need to enter that particular fray,[10] since it seems clear that it is fiction written by men with a vested interest in keeping women subservient.

Entire books—and many of them—have been written on the topic of women's maltreatment under the auspices of Christianity, and that task is clearly beyond the scope of this endeavor. What is germane is that the Bible serves as an accomplice in a lot of violence perpetrated against women, mainly because women are cast as something less than men, weak and evil, and as existing in the service of men.[11] When you assign a role such as this, there are consequences, and I think those consequences are particularly easy to see in the case of domestic violence and rape, though not exclusive to these offenses.[12] When a type of person is demeaned and degraded, it makes victimizing them that much easier. When that type of person is characterized as property whose duty it is to submit to you, it becomes almost inevitable. Here again, I will let the scripture make my point regarding the dim view of women present in Christian doctrine:

Colossians 3:18 (Paul)
Wives, submit to your husbands, as is fitting in the Lord. (ESV)

✳✳✳

1 Corinthians 11:3 (Paul)
I would have you know, that the head of every man is Christ; and the head of the woman is the man; and the head of Christ is God. (KJV)

1 Corinthians 11:8–10 (Paul again)
For man did not come from woman, but woman from man; neither was man created for woman, but woman for man. It is for this reason that a woman ought to have authority over her own head, because of the angels. . .

1 Corinthians 14:34–35 (Paul)
Let your women keep silence in the churches: for it is not permitted unto them to speak; but they are commanded to be under obedience, as also saith the law. And if they will learn anything, let them ask their husbands at home: for it is a shame for women to speak in the church. (KJV)

✳✳✳

Deuteronomy 21:11–14

If you notice among the captives a beautiful woman and are attracted
to her, you may take her as your wife. Bring her into your home and have
her shave her head, trim her nails and put aside the clothes she was wearing
when captured. After she has lived in your house and mourned her father
and mother for a full month, then you may go to her and be her husband
and she shall be your wife. If you are not pleased with her, let her go wherever she wishes. You must not sell her or treat her as a slave, since you
have dishonored her.

Deuteronomy 22:20–21

If, however, the charge is true and no proof of the young woman's virginity can be found, she shall be brought to the door of her father's house
and there the men of her town shall stone her to death. She has done an
outrageous thing in Israel by being promiscuous while still in her father's
house. You must purge the evil from among you.

Deuteronomy 22:23–24

If a damsel that is a virgin be betrothed unto an husband, and a man
find her in the city, and lie with her; Then ye shall bring them both out unto
the gate of the city, and ye shall stone them with stones that they die; the
damsel, because she cried not, being in the city; and the man, because he
hath humbled his neighbor's wife: so thou shalt put away evil from among
you. (KJV)

Deuteronomy 22:28–29

If a man happens to meet a virgin who is not pledged to be married
and rapes her and they are discovered, he shall pay her father fifty shekels
of silver. He must marry the young woman, for he has violated her. He can
never divorce her as long as he lives.

✲✲✲

Ecclesiastes 7:26
And I find more bitter than death the woman, whose heart is snares and nets, and her hands as bands: whoso pleaseth God shall escape from her; but the sinner shall be taken by her. (KJV)

Ecclesiastes 7:27–28
"Look," says the Teacher, "this is what I have discovered: Adding one thing to another to discover the scheme of things—while I was still searching but not finding—I found one upright man among a thousand, but not one upright woman among them all."

✳✳✳

Ephesians 5:22–24 (Paul)
Wives, submit yourselves to your own husbands as you do to the Lord. For the husband is the head of the wife as Christ is the head of the church, his body, of which he is the Savior. Now as the church submits to Christ, so also wives should submit to their husbands in everything.

✳✳✳

Genesis 3:16
To the woman he said, "I will make your pains in childbearing very severe; with painful labor you will give birth to children. Your desire will be for your husband, and he will rule over you."[13]

Genesis 19:31–36
One day the older daughter said to the younger, "Our father is old, and there is no man around to give us children—as is the custom all over the earth. Let's get our father to drink wine and then sleep with him to preserve our family line through our father."

That night they got their father to drink wine, and the older daughter went in and slept with him. He was not aware of it when she lay down or when she got up.

The next day the older daughter said to the younger, "Last night I slept with my father. Let's get him to drink wine again tonight, and you go in and sleep with him so we can preserve our family line through our father." So they got their father to drink wine that night also, and the younger daughter went in and slept with him. Again he was not aware of it when she lay down or when she got up.

So both of Lot's daughters became pregnant by their father.

Genesis 39: 7–20

And after a while his master's wife took notice of Joseph and said, "Come to bed with me!"

But he refused, "With me in charge," he told her, "my master does not concern himself with anything in the house; everything he owns he has entrusted to my care. No one is greater in this house than I am. My master has withheld nothing from me except you, because you are his wife. How then could I do such a wicked thing and sin against God?" And though she spoke to Joseph day after day, he refused to go to bed with her or even be with her.

One day he went into the house to attend to his duties, and none of the household servants was inside. She caught him by his cloak and said, "Come to bed with me!" But he left his cloak in her hand and ran out of the house.

When she saw that he had left his cloak in her hand and had run out of the house, she called her household servants. "Look," she said to them, "this Hebrew has been brought to us to make sport of us! He came in here to sleep with me, but I screamed. When he heard me scream for help, he left his cloak beside me and ran out of the house."

She kept his cloak beside her until his master came home. Then she told him this story: "That Hebrew slave you brought us came to me to make sport of me. But as soon as I screamed for help, he left his cloak beside me and ran out of the house."

When his master heart the story his wife told him, saying, "This is how your slave treated me," he burned with anger. Joseph's master took him and put him in prison, the place where the king's prisoners were confined.[14]

✱✱✱

Judges 16:1–5, 15–21

One day Samson went to Gaza, where he saw a prostitute. He went in to spend the night with her. The people of Gaza were told, "Samson is here!" So they surrounded the place and lay in wait for him all night at the city gate. They made no move during the night, saying, "At dawn, we'll kill him."

But Samson lay there only until the middle of the night. Then he got up and took hold of the doors of the city gate, together with the two posts, and tore them loose, bar and all. He lifted them to his shoulders and carried them to the top of the hill that faces Hebron.

Some time later, he fell in love with a woman in the Valley of Sorek whose name was Delilah. The rulers of the Philistines went to her and said, "See if you can lure him into showing you the secret of his great strength and how we can overpower him so we may tie him up and subdue him. Each one of us will give you eleven hundred shekels of silver."

[Delilah asks Samson three times what his secret is, and he lies to her each time.]

Then she said to him, "How can you say, 'I love you,' when you won't confide in me? This is the third time you have made a fool of me and haven't told me the secret of your great strength." With such nagging she prodded him day after day until he was sick to death of it.

So he told her everything. "No razor has ever been used on my head," he said, "because I have been a Nazirite dedicated to God from my mother's womb. If my head were shaved, my strength would leave me, and I would become as weak as any other man."

When Delilah saw that he had told her everything, she sent word to the rulers of the Philistines, "Come back once more; he has told me everything." So the rulers of the Philistines returned with the silver in their hands. After putting him to sleep on her lap, she called for someone to shave off the seven braids of his hair, and so began to subdue him. And his strength left him.

Then she called, "Samson, the Philistines are upon you!"

He awoke from his sleep and thought, "I'll go out as before and shake myself free." But he did not know that the LORD had left him.

Then the Philistines seized him, gouged out his eyes and took him down to Gaza. Binding him with bronze shackles, they set him to grinding grain in the prison.

***

1 Kings 11:3–6; 9

[Solomon] had seven hundred wives of royal birth and three hundred concubines, and his wives led him astray. As Solomon grew old, his wives turned his heart after other gods, and his heart was not fully devoted to the LORD his God, as the heart of David his father had been. He followed Ashtoreth the goddess of the Sidonians, and Molek the detestable god of the Ammonites. So Solomon did evil in the eyes of the LORD; he did not follow the LORD completely, as David his father had done. . . .

The LORD became angry with Solomon because his heart had turned away from the LORD, the God of Israel, who had appeared to him twice. [*And punished him by taking all of his kingdom, save one tribe, from his son.*]

***

Leviticus 12:2, 5

If a woman conceives and bears a male child, she shall be ceremonially unclean seven days; as at the time of her menstruation, she shall be unclean. . . . If she bears a female child, she shall be unclean two weeks, as in her menstruation; her time of blood purification shall be sixty-six days. (NRSV)

Leviticus 15:19–21

When a woman has a discharge that is her regular discharge from her body, she shall be in her impurity for seven days, and whoever touches her shall be unclean until the evening. Everything upon which she lies during her impurity shall be unclean; everything also upon which she sits shall be unclean. Whoever touches her bed shall wash his clothes, and bathe in water, and be unclean until the evening. (NRSV)

Leviticus 18:19
You shall not approach a woman to uncover her nakedness while she is in her menstrual uncleanness. (NRSV)

Leviticus 21:9
If a priest's daughter defiles herself by becoming a prostitute, she disgraces her father; she must be burned in the fire.

✳✳✳

Numbers 5:17–22, 29–31
Then he shall take some holy water in a clay jar and put some dust from the tabernacle floor into the water. After the priest has had the woman stand before the LORD, he shall loosen her hair and place in her hands the reminder-offering, the grain offering for jealousy, while he himself holds the bitter water that brings a curse. Then the priest shall put the woman under oath and say to her, "If no other man has had sexual relations with you and you have not gone astray and become impure while married to your husband, may this bitter water that brings a curse not harm you. But if you have gone astray while married to your husband and you have made yourself impure by having sexual relations with a man other than your husband"—here the priest is to put the woman under this curse—"may the LORD cause you to become a curse among your people when he makes your womb miscarry and your abdomen swell. May this water that brings a curse enter your body so that your abdomen swells or your womb miscarries."

Then the woman is to say, "Amen. So be it."

. . . This, then, is the law of jealousy when a woman goes astray and makes herself impure while married to her husband, or when feelings of jealousy come over a man because he suspects his wife. The priest is to have her stand before the LORD and is to apply this entire law to her. The husband will be innocent of any wrongdoing, but the woman will bear the consequences of her sin.

Numbers 31:15–18

"Have you allowed all the women to live?" [Moses] asked them. "They were the ones who followed Balaam's advice and enticed the Israelites to be unfaithful to the LORD in the Peor incident, so that a plague struck the LORD's people. Now kill all the boys. And kill every woman who has slept with a man, but save for yourselves every girl who has never slept with a man."

Numbers 31:25–35

And the LORD said to Moses, "You and Eleazar the priest and the family leaders of each tribe are to make a list of all the plunder taken in the battle, including the people and animals. Then divide the plunder into two parts, and give half to the men who fought the battle and half to the rest of the people. From the army's portion, first give the LORD his share of the plunder—one of every 500 of the prisoners and of the cattle, donkeys, sheep, and goats. Give this share of the army's half to Eleazar the priest as an offering to the LORD. From the half that belongs to the people of Israel take one of every fifty of the prisoners and of the cattle, donkeys, sheep, goats, and other animals. Give this share to the Levites in charge of maintaining the LORD's Tabernacle." So Moses and Eleazar the priest did as the LORD commanded Moses. The plunder remaining from everything the fighting men had taken totaled 675,000 sheep and goats, 72,000 cattle, 61,000 donkeys, and 32,000 virgin girls. (NLT)

✳✳✳

1 Peter 3:1–3 (Peter)

Wives, in the same way submit yourselves to your own husbands so that, if any of them do not believe the word, they may be won over without words by the behavior of their wives, when they see the purity and reverence of your lives. Your beauty should not come from outward adornment, such as elaborate hairstyles and the wearing of gold jewelry or fine clothes.

***

Revelation 2:20–23

You tolerate that woman Jezebel, who calls herself a prophet. By her teaching she misleads my servants into sexual immorality and the eating of food sacrificed to idols. I have given her time to repent of her immorality, but she is unwilling. So I will cast her on a bed of suffering, and I will make those who commit adultery with her suffer intensely, unless they repent of her ways. I will strike her children dead.

Revelation 14:4

These are those who do not defile themselves with women, for they remained virgins. They follow the Lamb wherever he goes. . . .

***

1 Timothy 2:11–15 (Paul)

"A woman should learn [from men] in quietness and full submission. I do not permit a woman to teach or to have authority over a man; she must be quiet. For Adam was formed first, then Eve. And Adam was not the one deceived; it was the woman who was deceived and became a sinner. But women will be saved through childbearing—if they continue in faith, love and holiness with propriety."

Women are viewed variously as deceitful, untrustworthy, sexual predators, unclean, the cause of the fall of mankind, spoils of war, and above all, subordinate and inferior to men. The doctrine of creationism in Genesis actually renders women subhuman, since they were created from part of a man. Women are admonished to submit to men in all things, and there are consequences when they do not, since such behavior is not pleasing to God.[15] This belief system bears an obvious connection to both rape and domestic violence, and it is my contention that these ideas, which permeate American culture through Christianity, increase the rate of violence against women. If women are as evil as the Bible portrays them, it is not surprising that men sometimes feel the need to take them, literally, in hand.

Contrary to a common misperception, the Bible does not explicitly advocate husbands beating their wives at any point, and, in fact, contains several passages admonishing men to treat their wives well; but there is an undercurrent featuring the concepts of property, misogyny, and violence between men and women in the Bible that is palpable.[16] For example, in keeping with the cultural values of the time, rape is a property offense, and the woman's father is the victim.[17] The father is paid fifty shekels of silver for his injury, and the woman ends up married to her rapist forever. Women are treated as chattel in the Bible because that was their role in the social order at the time. The problem is that the Bible has not changed in this respect, whereas the world has, and Christian nationalists still cling to the obvious antiquities in the Bible, including this interpretation of women's roles.

In Ephesians 5:33, men are told to love their wives as they love themselves; at the same time, wives are told to respect their husbands. But in terms of domestic violence, what might a man feel justified in doing if he perceives that his wife does not respect him? If a wife does not love, honor, and obey to the husband's satisfaction, the Bible certainly sets the stage for a man to punish his wife. Punishing women is a ubiquitous theme in the scriptures—why would punishment not be okay in the home?

Domestic violence is among the greatest criminal threats women face—nearly a third of all female homicide victims are killed by an intimate partner,[18] and in 70–80 percent of all domestic homicides—regardless of which partner ends up as the victim—the male physically abused the female prior to the murder.[19] Moreover, an estimated 30–60 percent of intimate partner violence perpetrators also abuse children living in the home, creating a kind of hostage situation for the rest of the family members.[20] It is an extremely serious problem in the form of personalized terrorism that often bleeds over into public violence, as well.[21] While men can certainly be abused, the incidence is fairly low, and the injuries are rarely serious enough to result in hospital visits; while female-perpetrated violence certainly happens, this is largely a problem in which the violence is perpetrated by men against women.[22]

But where does the Bible come into this, if it never explicitly condones wife beating? The Bible does explicitly sanction beating children and "stupid people," and abusive spouses are skilled at finding fault with their partners to justify their violence.[23] Proverbs 10:13 states that: "Wisdom is found on the lips of the discerning, but a rod is for the back of one who has no sense." Given how often women are portrayed as feckless and devious in the Bible, it would require no stretch for this to serve as a justification for an abuser to beat a woman. Coupled with the idea that women are their husbands' property, and that it is okay for men to punish women, this is all the approval a perpetrator would likely need.

Like anyone else reading the Bible, perpetrators will be particularly attracted to the passages that make them feel better about what they do, and disregard the rest. Even if an abuser does not read the Bible, he is significantly more likely than nonabusers to prefer a cultural system in which women hold a traditional, submissive role in the family, and the Bible goes far in providing the justification for this structure.[24] Traditional patriarchal families increase the likelihood that women and children will experience violence in all three major religions (Christianity, Judaism, and Islam).[25]

Ephesians 5:22–24 is a perfect example of what the Bible has to say about being a good wife: "Wives, submit yourselves to your own husbands as you do to the Lord. For the husband is the head of the wife as Christ is the head of the church, his body, of which he is the Savior. Now as the church submits to Christ, so also wives should submit to their husbands in everything." In a passage in Numbers, wives are held responsible for their husband's feelings of jealousy and required to prove their fidelity with the assistance of the religious community.[26] These messages are a dangerous mix of ideas to send to both abusers and their victims.

Abusers use these traditional roles and expectations to justify perpetrating violence against their partners, and victims are more likely to submit having been told that they should acquiesce to their husbands. In fact, in one large sample of domestic violence victims, 85 percent identified themselves as "Christian" but only 8 percent reported their abuse to their clergy.[27] In another study, 54 percent of religious and 38 percent of nonreligious victims requested help and guidance from a clergy member. Among these victims, 30 percent reported that the contact was satisfactory or very satisfactory, 29 percent reported it as unsatisfactory, and 42 percent said it was very unsatisfactory. Dissatisfied respondents recounted that they had been told such things as, "try harder not to provoke him," and, "Hope for the best. God will change him."[28]

Even without direct intervention by clergy, biblical narratives contribute greatly to the learned helplessness that women experience in such violent situations. There are a host of secular reasons why women stay in violent domestic situations—children, shame, lack of money and alternatives—but research has shown that, in the case of religious women, religion serves as both a justification and a coping mechanism that keeps them in violent relationships.[29] The Bible is rife with stories in which faith is tested through adversity, in addition to the direct messages regarding the subservient role of women in marriage; suffering is often rewarded with miraculous gifts from God when the adherent remains steadfast in their beliefs through the ordeal. Learned helplessness in the abusive marriage becomes something of a sacred mandate, replete with prayers that God will change the heart and mind of the violent offender.[30]

When it comes to rape, women are portrayed in a variety of negative ways, including a story featuring a woman lying about being sexually assaulted out of spite.[31] Any lust men feel is the fault of women in the scriptures, who are often portrayed as cunning temptresses manipulating innocent men into sexual acts and behaviors that anger God.[32] It is easy to see the impact the sexual portrayal of women has on men's conceptions about rape, which is treated as a common and somewhat mundane offense in the Bible. Research shows that clergy members practicing in fundamentalist Protestant denominations are far more likely to believe rape myths, have considerably sexist ideologies, and to place the responsibility and blame for rape on victims.[33] If the leadership of fundamentalist churches hold such views, it is unlikely that they are not communicated. Another study found a positive relationship for Protestant fundamentalists between both domestic violence and approval for violence as a means of solving personal problems.[34] Yet another scholar noted that hierarchical structures rendering women subordinate in the family system are almost universally supported by religious belief systems.[35]

The Bible is flat depressing on the issue. In another biblical passage, men are admonished to stone women to death if they do not yell loudly enough to prove that a rape was occurring rather than a consensual liaison.[36] Almost every rape myth can be linked back to passages in the Bible, from the idea that women lie about rape to get men in trouble, to the idea that women are promiscuous and tempt men into raping them, to the idea that it is not really violence, to the idea that men cannot control themselves when they desire a woman, to the idea that women actually want it, to the idea that women are capable of preventing rape, to the idea that men are entitled to sex with their wives.[37] In case the messages in the Bible were not clear enough, in 1998, the Southern Baptist Convention amended its essential statement of beliefs to include a declaration that a wife should "submit herself graciously" to her husband's leadership.[38]

Anyone who says the Bible is not disdainful of women either has an extremely dim view of women, or has not actually spent much time reading the Bible. It is paternalistic in the best case and contemptuous at worst. The whole notion of priests and holy men avoiding as much contact as possible with women speaks volumes to this derision. Revelation 14:4 served as a great justification for a celibate priesthood, as well as a clear statement about the biblical attitude toward women: "These are those who do not defile themselves with women, for they remained virgins. They follow the Lamb wherever he goes. . . ."[39]

Christians often attempt to mitigate the slur toward women in this verse by claiming that it refers only to prostitutes. Again, I am no theologian, but prostitutes are mentioned explicitly many times over in the Bible. If the intent of this verse is directed at prostitutes, why would that not be explicit here, as well? The most damning evidence against this explanation is the rest of the Bible itself, which bristles with references of scorn and condescension toward women, with only a few exceptions. The bottom line for women can be summed up through Paul's admonishment in 1 Timothy 2:11–15: "A woman should learn [from men] in quietness and full submission. I do not permit a woman to teach or to have authority over a man; she must be quiet. For Adam was formed first, then Eve. And Adam was not the one deceived; it was the woman who was deceived and became a sinner."

Clearly, women are not well-served by the Bible, and Christian nationalists embrace these biblical teachings. Such attitudes toward women can be tested, though the instrument will need to be subtle in order to measure real attitudes rather than societal expectations or religious defensiveness. Perpetrators can and should be tested on these beliefs, as well as their origins. While women are victimized less often than men, the care they take to protect themselves from victimization relative to men suggests that they should be victimized far less often than they are. I have included women as a special population here because I believe Christian nationalist ideology, and the culture it influences in the United States, explains much of the violence perpetrated against them.

GOD HATES HOMOSEXUALS

Christian nationalists make no secret of their contempt for LGBT people and almost invariably use the Bible to justify their position of intolerance. As public opinion has shifted in the United States to a point where more than half of all Americans now support gay marriage, and the Supreme Court has ruled it unconstitutional to deny this right, their rhetoric has shifted toward a more apologetic tone—"we do not make the rules, we are just compelled by our faith to follow them"—but is still just as strident in its opposition. In 1973, Pat Robertson said that, "The acceptance of homosexuality is the last step in the decline of Gentile Christianity."[40] Indeed, the Christian right views the battle against gay rights and acceptance as something of a watershed issue, to the extent that in 2011 the New International Version translation of the Bible was rewritten to make verses related to homosexuality clearer in their denunciation.[41] While many sympathetic theologians and commentators have tried to address and dismiss the biblical prohibition against homosexuality, a look at the relevant verses makes this a difficult view to support:

1 Corinthians 6:9–10
Or do you not know that wrongdoers will not inherit the kingdom of God? Do not be deceived: Neither the sexually immoral nor idolaters nor adulterers nor men who have sex with men nor thieves nor the greedy nor drunkards nor slanderers nor swindlers will inherit the kingdom of God.

✷✷✷

Leviticus 18:22
Do not have sexual relations with a man as one does with a woman; that is detestable.

Leviticus 20:13
If a man has sexual relations with a man as one does with a woman, both of them have done what is detestable. They are to be put to death; their blood will be on their own heads.

✷✷✷

Romans 1:26–27
Because of this, God gave them over to shameful lusts. Even their women exchanged natural sexual relations for unnatural ones. In the same way the men also abandoned natural relations with women and were inflamed with lust for one another. Men committed shameful acts with other men, and received in themselves the due penalty for their error.

✷✷✷

1 Timothy 1:10
. . . for the sexually immoral, for those practicing homosexuality, for slave traders and liars and perjurers—and for whatever else is contrary to the sound doctrine.

As painful as this might be to Christian LGBT people, the Bible is crystal clear on the issue. I did not include the tale of Sodom and Gomorrah, because it is arguably addressing the issue of hospitality more so than homosexuality, but its exclusion from the list of passages devoted to gay people does not mitigate the clarity of the Bible in this case: Gay people are sinners, and the penalty for this particular sin is death. The issue of LGBT people existing, let alone wanting the right to be married, spurs a far stronger reaction among Christian nationalists than many other "sins" for a few reasons.

First, the open acceptance of homosexuality contradicts the Christian nationalist veneration of an idealized view of the "traditional family," and the idea that things used to be both hunky and dory when nuclear families went to church together, had picnics, and went fishing. This glowing, romanticized past—which tends to look a lot like the 1950s—does not feature people trapped in miserable marriages, domestic violence, child molestation, or openly gay people. Those features were present, of course, but hidden beneath the veneer of social expectations, and that is how Christian nationalists prefer it.

Second, because the Bible is so clear in its reproach of gay sexuality, advances in LGBT rights signal the declining influence of Christian nationalism. They cannot even keep gay people in the closet anymore, and, worse, many Americans are not in the least bothered by that fact. Homosexuality serves as a sort of canary in the coal mine of Christian influence, and the bird appears to be terminally ill by this measure. It is impossible to mark progress in hate crime victimization rates over the years, both because hate crime legislation is so new and because LGBT victims would have been understandably reluctant to report attacks in the past—or at least to report them honestly as stemming from their sexual orientation. Moreover, many LGBT people were able to escape notice as LGBT when hate crime legislation was first enacted, and were inclined to do so when this belief system held more sway over public opinion. All of these factors make increased reporting over time very likely, reducing the value of longitudinal comparisons.

Third, homosexuals serve as an excellent out-group for Christian nationalists to focus their efforts on to retain and expand their social, political, and cultural influence in the United States. This group has the added benefit of committing a sin they are not likely to commit themselves (if they are heterosexual), making it easier to target them from a self-righteous position. The cohesion of the movement is enhanced through their juxtaposition with LGBT people, a group that angers God. Divorce and remarriage is a pretty big sin in the Bible, too, but given the numbers of conservative Christians who do just that, you do not hear much of anything on the topic.[42] LGBT people do not present the same hypocrisy problem, aside from a few notable instances with church leaders such as Ted Haggard.[43] If you are not gay or lesbian, you are probably not tempted, so resisting temptation is not an issue. All of these reasons account for why homosexuality has become "the mobilizing passion for much of the religious right."[44] This antagonism goes far beyond simple opposition to gay marriage, including actively fighting against a variety of LGBT people's civil liberties and rights, such as the ability to share health insurance coverage, adopt and foster children, serve in the military, and be legally protected from employment and housing discrimination.

The impact of this doctrine is violence against gay people—and gay men, in particular, who account for 53 percent of all hate crimes motivated by a sexual orientation bias.[45] In light of this, it is interesting that gay male sex is explicitly mentioned in the Bible numerous times, while lesbian sex is only mentioned once. Christian nationalist enmity for LGBT people, the notion that LGBT people receive that enmity directly from God through the teachings of the Bible, and the idea that LGBT people essentially do not deserve to live because of their sexual orientation certainly exacerbates the problem. Even the suggestion that someone is gay has likely resulted in many honor killings among straight men due to the stigma attached, and the root of that stigma can be found in the Bible.[46]

SPARE THE ROD AND SPOIL THE CHILD

Children are on the receiving end of a tremendous amount of violence in the Bible, just as children are far too often abused and victimized in modern life. Bible passages dealing with children (where they are not being slaughtered) tend to portray them as either completely innocent or inherently bad, but the preponderance of Christian child-rearing advice is markedly skewed toward the latter view. Here again, I will let the scriptures speak for themselves on the matter:

Deuteronomy 8:5
Know then in your heart that as a man disciplines his son, so the LORD your God disciplines you.

Deuteronomy 20:13–14
When the LORD your God delivers [a city] into your hand, put to the sword all the men in it. As for the women, the children, the livestock and everything else in the city, you may take these as plunder for yourselves.

Deuteronomy 21:18–21
If someone has a stubborn and rebellious son who does not obey his father and mother and will not listen to them when they discipline him, his father and mother shall take hold of him and bring him to the elders at the gate of his town. They shall say to the elders, "This son of ours is stubborn and rebellious. He will not obey us. He is a glutton and a drunkard." Then all the men of his town are to stone him to death.

Deuteronomy 23:2
A bastard shall not enter into the congregation of the LORD; even to his tenth generation shall he not enter into the congregation of the LORD. (KJV)

✳✳✳

Ephesians 6:1
Children, obey your parents in the LORD, for this is right.

Ephesians 6:2–4
"Honor your father and mother . . . that it may go well with you and that you may live long in the land." Fathers, do not provoke your children

to anger, but bring them up in the discipline and instruction of the Lord. (ESV)

✷✷✷

Exodus 20:5
". . . for I the LORD thy God am a jealous God, visiting the iniquity of the fathers upon the children unto the third and fourth generation of them that hate me." (ESV)

Exodus 21:15
"Anyone who attacks their father or mother is to be put to death."

Exodus 21:17
"Anyone who curses their father or mother is to be put to death."

Exodus 22:29–30
"You must give me the firstborn of your sons. Do the same with your cattle and your sheep. Let them stay with their mothers for seven days, but give them to me on the eighth day."

Exodus 34:6–7
The LORD, the LORD, the compassionate and gracious God, slow to anger, abounding in love and faithfulness, maintaining love to thousands, and forgiving wickedness, rebellion and sin. Yet he does not leave the guilty unpunished; he punishes the children and their children for the sin of the parents to the third and fourth generation.

✷✷✷

Ezekiel 20:26
"I defiled them through their gifts—the sacrifice of every firstborn— that I might fill them with horror so they would know that I am the LORD."

✷✷✷

Genesis 22:2
Then God said, "Take your son, your only son, whom you love—
Isaac—and go to the region of Moriah. Sacrifice him there as a burnt
offering on a mountain I will show you."

Genesis 38:7
But Er, Judah's firstborn, was wicked in the LORD's sight; so the
LORD put him to death.

***

Hebrews 12:6–7
For the Lord disciplines the one he loves, and chastises every son
whom he receives." It is for discipline that you have to endure. God is
treating you as sons. For what son is there whom his father does not discipline? (ESV)

***

Hosea 9:12
Even if they rear children, I will bereave them of every one.

Hosea 9:16
Ephraim is blighted, their root is withered, they yield no fruit. Even if
they bear children, I will slay their cherished offspring.

Hosea 13:16
. . . because they have rebelled against their God. They will fall by the
sword; their little ones will be dashed to the ground, their pregnant women
ripped open.

***

Isaiah 13:16
Their infants will be dashed to pieces before their eyes; their houses
will be looted and their wives violated.

Isaiah 13:18
Their bows will strike down the young men; they will have no mercy on infants, nor will they look with compassion on children.

Isaiah 14:21
Prepare a place to slaughter his children for the sins of their ancestors; they are not to rise to inherit the land and cover the earth with their cities.

✲✲✲

Judges 11:30–31
And Jephthah made a vow to the LORD: "If you give the Ammonites into my hands, whatever comes out of the door of my house to meet me when I return in triumph from the Ammonites will be the LORD's, and I will sacrifice it as a burnt offering." [*Spoiler alert: Jephthah's daughter winds up being the burnt offering.*]

✲✲✲

2 Kings 2:23–24
From there Elisha went up to Bethel. As he was walking along the road, some boys came out of the town and jeered at him. "Get out of here, Baldy!" they said. "Get out of here, Baldy!" He turned around, looked at them and called down a curse on them in the name of the LORD. Then two bears came out of the woods and mauled forty-two of the boys.

✲✲✲

Leviticus 20:9
For everyone who curses his father or his mother shall surely be put to death. He has cursed his father or his mother. His blood shall be upon him. (NKJV)

Leviticus 26:21–22
"If even then you remain hostile toward me and refuse to obey,

I will inflict you with seven more disasters for your sins. I will release wild animals that will kill your children and destroy your cattle, so your numbers will dwindle and your roads will be deserted." (NLT)

✱✱✱

Mark 9:43
And if your hand causes you to sin, cut it off. It is better for you to enter life crippled than with two hands to go to hell, to the unquenchable fire. (ESV)

✱✱✱

Proverbs 13:24 (King Solomon)
Whoever spares the rod hates their children, but the one who loves their children is careful to discipline them.

Proverbs 19:18–19 (King Solomon)
Discipline your children, for in that there is hope; do not be a willing party to their death. A hot-tempered person must pay the penalty; rescue them, and you will have to do it again.

Proverbs 20:30 (King Solomon)
Blows and wounds scrub away evil, and beatings purge the inmost being.

Proverbs 22:15 (King Solomon)
Foolishness is bound in the heart of a child; but the rod of correction shall drive it far from him. (KJV)

Proverbs 23:13–14
Do not withhold discipline from a child; if you punish them with the rod, they will not die. Punish them with the rod and save them from death.

Proverbs 29:15 (King Solomon)

The rod and a reprimand imparts wisdom, but a child left undisciplined disgraces its mother.

Proverbs 29:17

Discipline your son, and he will give you rest; he will give delight to your heart. (ESV)

***

Psalm 109:9–13

May his children be fatherless and his wife a widow. May his children be wandering beggars; may they be driven from their ruined homes. May a creditor seize all he has; may strangers plunder the fruits of his labor. May no one extend kindness to him or take pity on his fatherless children. May his descendants be cut off, their names blotted out from the next generation.

Psalm 137:8–9

O daughter of Babylon, who art to be destroyed; happy shall he be, that rewardeth thee as thou hast served us. Happy shall he be, that taketh and dasheth thy little ones against the stones. (KJV)

***

2 Samuel 12:13–14

Then David said to Nathan, "I have sinned against the LORD." Nathan replied, "The LORD has taken away your sin. You are not going to die. But because by doing this you have shown utter contempt for the LORD, the son born to you will die." [*The child dies seven days later.*]

The treatment of children in the Bible seems particularly bleak even in a time when life was shorter and quite a lot harder. When parents are not being cautioned to beat them with a rod and indoctrinate them into the faith,

God seems to use them as instruments of revenge against their parents, a way to punish his enemies, or as pawns through which their parents can prove the sincerity of their faith in God. And in all of these cases, children are killed. Child abuse is a serious and often hidden problem in the United States, and the fact that the Bible encourages hitting children to bring them to heel can only reinforce the beliefs of abusive parents. In fact, abusive parents are more closely adhering to the literal Word of God than parents who do not hit their children. As a result of this theology, the idea that children require corporal punishment has become deeply engrained in our societal norms.

Results from the National Survey of Families and Households showed that fundamentalist Protestant parents were far more likely than other parents to use corporal punishment in the form of spanking.[47] In another study, nearly a third (29 percent) of conservative Protestant parents reported spanking their children three or more times a week, compared with 3 percent of Roman Catholic and none of the parents who were unaffiliated with a particular denomination.[48] Of particular interest is a finding that religious beliefs are more salient predictors of aggression within families than religious affiliation alone.[49] In the National Survey of Families and Households, the level of agreement with measures such as fundamentalism ("I regard myself as a religious fundamentalist") was significantly and positively correlated with a parent's reliance on corporal punishment.[50] This finding is not unusual: In another study, parents who believed the Bible is the literal and inerrant Word of God that provides answers to all earthly problems used corporal punishment on their preschool and elementary school children far more often than parents with less conservative religious views.[51]

Other studies confirm that religiosity alone is not as powerful a predictor of corporal punishment as parents having a literal interpretation of the Bible. Criminologists Grasmick, Bursik, and Kimpel found that a literal belief in the Bible accounted for nearly all of the difference between religious groups in advocacy of corporal punishment, controlling for socioeconomic and demographic variables.[52] Similarly, another study found that mothers and fathers who reported believing in a literal interpretation of the

Bible were more likely to agree more strongly with items such as: "Children should always be spanked when they misbehave" and "Parents spoil their children by picking them up and comforting them when they cry."[53]

Recent challenges to corporal punishment have been met with a wave of resistance from the right, who tread a thin line in couching spanking as a good, old-fashioned child-rearing technique ("I was spanked, and I turned out okay"). The problem is the lack of understanding that this belief likely enables more abuse to occur where the hitting is not purely instructional. It is a difficult topic, but I believe this is an area for research in criminology that has been sorely neglected, or shunted off to other fields such as social work. But the physical abuse of a child is a crime, and the only difference between an assault and abuse is the age of the victim relative to the offender, which should be viewed as an aggravating rather than mitigating factor in the offense. At the very least, we need to study the impact of this belief system on physical punishment to see whether it is, indeed, playing a part in the abuse of children.[54] Another area for further research might be the impact of corporal punishment on future violent behavior.

Of course, there are a lot of loving passages in the Bible, as well, but I have not included them here because they do not define the belief system of the Christian right so much as these passages do. Christian nationalism is only about love and forgiveness where adherents and potential adherents are concerned (with the possible exception of children and fetuses): for everyone else, it is largely about hate, judgment, and exclusion.[55] It is a belief system that does not play well with other belief systems because a central theme in its doctrine is that it should be the *only* belief system.

The more innocuous parts of Christian doctrine get a tremendous amount of play, at any rate, so I do not feel terribly bad about using the Bible cafeteria-style to make my points here through picking and choosing relevant verses, particularly as my use is not designed to support hurting anyone. Christian nationalists tend to use these verses both as the premise and justification for their belief systems, but fall back on the sweeter passages when cornered. My point is that these horrible, destructive, and violent aspects of the Bible have a significant impact on the Christian nationalist belief system—and that belief system has permeated American culture far beyond the confines of the movement. Further, since Christian nationalists believe the Bible is the "infallible truth," I see no need to apologize for bringing these passages to your attention.[56] If one cares to claim that these passages are the literal Word of God, or even God-inspired, then all of these passages are fair game for attention. And in the United States, 30 percent report believing that the Bible is the literal Word of God, with 49 percent reporting that they believe it is the inspired Word of God (but should not be taken literally), and only 17 percent saying they believe it is a book of ancient stories written by man.[57]

God's "eye for an eye" might have given way to "turn the other cheek" in the New Testament, but Christian nationalist behavior and speech give little indication of this shift. In the final chapter, I discuss the intractable nature of much of this influence from a Christian nationalist standpoint, but I also offer some suggestions going forward for the rest of the country if my theory proves correct. Jesus's message was overwhelmingly one of altruism and peace, but if Christian nationalists do not embrace and extend that message to others, they remain a force perpetuating violence. How, then, do we address this social problem, while maintaining the freedoms we enjoy?

CHAPTER SIX

THE LION OR THE LAMB—
THE FUTURE OF CRIME
AND JUSTICE IN AMERICA

Mark my word, if and when these preachers get control of the party, and they're sure trying to do so, it's going to be a terrible damn problem. Frankly, these people frighten me. Politics and government require compromise, but these Christians believe they are acting in the name of God, so they can't and won't compromise.
—Barry Goldwater, quoted in
Conservatives Without Conscience, by John W. Dean

The problem with the world is that the intelligent people are full of doubts, while the stupid ones are full of confidence.
—Charles Bukowski, quoted in *Sunlight Here I Am*,
by David S. Calonne

Everyone is entitled to his own opinion, but not his own facts.
—Daniel Patrick Moynihan, quoted in
"Facts Are Facts," by Timothy J. Penny

Fix reason firmly in her seat, and call to her tribunal every fact, every opinion. Question with boldness even the existence of a God; because, if there is one, he must more approve of the homage of reason, than that of blindfolded fear.
—Thomas Jefferson to Peter Carr, 1787,
The Papers of Thomas Jefferson

One of the great strengths of the United States is . . . we have a very large Christian population—we do not consider ourselves a Christian nation or a Jewish nation or a Muslim nation. We consider ourselves a nation of citizens who are bound by ideals and a set of values.
—President Barack Obama, in a press conference,
April 6, 2009

FROM THEORY TO RESEARCH TO IMPROVEMENT

A s with most social problems, the impact of Christian nationalism is easier to identify than address. In this chapter, I will discuss the major problems in reducing the criminogenic influence of this movement, suggest some ways to at least ameliorate that influence, and offer some ideas for rational responses to Christian nationalism. The aim is necessarily to reduce violent crime in the United States through reducing the influence of Christian nationalism. The movement has such strong built-in resistance to change that it is likely a fool's errand—not to mention un-American—to suggest trying to attenuate their beliefs in order to reduce their impact on violence, but there are still actions that will at least ease the negative impact.

One of the problems in dealing with Christian nationalism is that criminologists (and politicians) have addressed the impact of religion in a very narrow way, almost invariably assuming that religion serves as a social control that helps bind people to conventional society in a manner that will reduce criminality.[1] According to such a view, Christian nationalist influence will encourage participation in noncriminal, pro-social activities and expose young people to law-abiding role models, which will reduce delinquency.[2] In this manner, the body of criminological work focuses on a narrow social aspect of religious life—the participation in the activities of the institution—rather than theological or cultural aspects of religious life that might impact criminality. They rarely even discern between religious denominations or even religions in their analyses, much less delve into the impact of religious beliefs on criminal behavior, or compare religious belief systems to one another, because religion has been viewed solely through the lens of social control. The last facet in the assumptions underlying most criminological work on religion is the presumption that fear of spending an eternity in hell will serve to deter adherents from committing criminal acts. But what if all this research misses the forest for the trees due to this emphasis on religion purely as a form of social control?

The idea behind theories of social control is that people need to be controlled to prevent them from committing crime because the tendency to commit crime is universal. Interestingly, this idea could be viewed as biblical in its orientation. Control theories assume a consensus view—the idea that a society has a common set of noncriminal beliefs and norms. Thus, people who are more tightly bonded to mainstream society and beliefs will be less likely to commit crime. There are different elements of social bonds—for example, attachment, the genuine, emotional affection one might feel for one's parents or friends, and the extent to which one cares about their opinions.[3] This facet of a social bond makes it more likely that we will adopt the beliefs of people with whom we have an emotional attachment.

Additionally, commitment, or having a stake in conformity and thus something to lose if one offends, involvement in conventional activities that keep one too busy to engage in crime and delinquency, and a belief that crime is wrong all serve to strengthen the bonds that keep people from offending. It is a sound idea with a lot of support—but it might not give us the whole picture when it comes to crime and religion. The body of research on religious belief and behavior generally shows an inconsistent but modest reduction in criminality (mostly low-level delinquency), but this leaves far too much crime unaccounted for.

In his book, *Crime and Nature*, Marcus Felson provides an elegant explanation for the difficulty in predicting criminal actions due to the variety of responses people have to situations, pointing out that "living things might respond in varied ways to the exact same challenge."[4] This is the simplest explanation for the difficulties associated with explaining criminality that I have ever heard, and it nails the point. While some people grow up in poverty and never commit a crime, many do. While some people who grew up in extremely religious families might commit crimes, or add to the societal features that increase crime generally, some do not. Determining exact causes for criminal behavior theoretically is thus a tricky—if not doomed—endeavor.

Of course, most theorists do not aim to explain all crime, or even all of a particular type of crime—they simply try to make sense of factors that make certain crimes more likely to occur. But Felson is on to something in noting that human behavior tends to be a moving target, which often blurs the lines of prediction and explanation to a maddening degree. The case of preachers' kids, or PKs, as they are often called, is a great example of this. PKs are notorious in church circles, as they are often the exact definition of irony in terms of their behavior. Drinking, early sexual encounters, and other types of mischief are commonly ascribed to them at greater rates than kids not sporting a parent in the clergy.

I know of no studies to confirm this widely held perception that borders on an axiom, but anecdotal evidence of PK misdeeds abound. In a sense, PKs likely provide an example of my theory in miniature: Though it seems counterintuitive to many that fundamentalist Christians might have a perceptible aggravating effect on levels of criminality, it may well be the case. Of course, it might also be the case that it is simply a misperception—who knows if PKs are as bad as people think, or if it is simply that people are more likely to notice when PKs behave badly because it runs counter to expectations (in much the same manner that people tend to notice psychologists with messy personal lives). Sometimes perceptions are such that you would bet your house that they are correct, and, yet, you would be wrong.

Conversely, a great number of Christians tend to believe that the absence of religious beliefs creates a moral and ethical vacuum—and that the opposite is true for those with religious beliefs. Survey research shows that the majority of Americans would concur with Dostoyevsky in saying, "Where there is no God, all is permitted": Remember, more than half say they would not vote for a well-qualified atheist candidate.[5] Indeed, when psychological researchers Azim Shariff and Ara Norenzayan primed research subjects with words like God or divine, they tended to behave more generously toward others and be less likely to cheat than control groups.[6] However, the research team noted that this may well be due to an evolutionary imperative to protect one's reputation: The same results were achieved when subjects were placed in rooms with posters featuring eyes on them.

People tend to behave better when they think people are watching them, and it appears that there is an effect when Christians are reminded that God is watching. But is this the stuff of true morality—or simply the result of an omnipotent panopticon effect?[7] When people take care not to commit crimes within the range of security cameras, it seems likely that self-preservation might be at play more so than morality. Without priming people to recall their belief that God is watching them, what would the results show for Christian nationalists versus people of a more secular bent? Christian nationalists have a fairly antagonistic belief system when it comes to the poor, who are often portrayed in this belief system as undeserving of help. It seems likely that their generosity would be curbed in the absence of an audience. Further, research has demonstrated that they are far less generous—and, in fact, hostile to members of other groups—when they are reminded of their own mortality.[8]

Even the presence of a spiritual chaperone causing people to behave more charitably toward one another makes little sense in light of what we know about the least religious nations, Sweden and Denmark—both of which have extremely low crime rates.[9] In fact, a study of eighteen democracies revealed that less religious societies tend to have lower rates of both murder and suicide across the board.[10]. We will not know the impact of religiosity with certainty until more research is conducted on the effect, and that research should not start with an assumption that religiosity inhibits criminality simply because the act of participating in religious institutions brings with it a measure of social control. This concept essentially turns religiosity into an activity, such as participating in school-sponsored sports and other after-school programs, which show a pretty consistent impact in reducing delinquency.[11] But the influence is far wider than this.

It is, at the very least, fair to say that the impact of religion on criminality is still an open question in the field of criminology. The moderate support we see for religion's reduction of some very specific types of nonserious delinquency far from settles the question, and it is remarkable that so few criminologists have addressed this intriguing relationship with respect to violence. This may be, at least in part, a manifestation of the greater difficulty in truly measuring the effect. Pallid variables such as church attendance simply will not capture the variations in religious beliefs. For example, this approach fails to discern between liberal forms of Christianity and conservative and Christian nationalistic forms of Christianity. It is possible, and even likely, that liberal Christianity, with its nearly exclusive focus on the more redemptive, social justice precepts of the New Testament, has a positive impact on reducing criminal behavior. If that is the case, and if these differences were fleshed out by researchers, it is possible that even the modest gains in deterrence shown in previous research might vanish, or indeed, be reversed, in the case of Christian nationalism.

Another factor rarely taken into account in studies of religion and crime is the environment in which a religious person lives. Studies have found that the prosocial influence of religiosity dissipates in situations where the religious individual is not surrounded by a like-minded community of believers.[12] The influence of this mainstream, Christian community apparently buttresses the anticriminal effect through strengthening and supporting good behavior. It seems likely that it also provides an audience who would disapprove of bad behavior, along with positively reinforcing good behavior. But quite a lot of crime—especially more serious and violent crime—does not take place in this context. Few researchers have taken this joint consideration into account with respect to religion.[13]

Another difficulty in measuring phenomena such as religion is hypocrisy and dishonesty. For example, it is unlikely that a survey of PKs would be of much use in getting to the bottom of the idea that they are less "moral" than other kids, as they would be keenly aware of the answers they should be giving on such measures. Actions speak louder than words, and with respect to testing this theory, that is especially true. Divorce is a great example of this: Christians profess a strong belief in the sanctity of marriage, but divorce rates do not support the idea that this belief is consistent with action. In fact, divorce rates for born-again and evangelical Christians are pretty much identical to that of the general population.[14] Divorce is clearly the biggest threat to marriage in the United States and elsewhere, but you do not see Christians picketing divorce courts or going on Fox News to talk about how divorce is ruining the sacred institution of marriage.[15] All this is to say that researchers will need to take care in ensuring that they are digging a little deeper, particularly where survey instruments are employed.

Finally, I would encourage the use of qualitative methodology, where researchers observe their subjects directly—particularly through work with active offenders—as a tool to explore the impact of religiosity in a deeper way and within the context in which much violence occurs. In a recent qualitative study of serious and violent active street offenders, criminologists Volkan Topalli, Timothy Brezina, and Mindy Bernhardt discovered that religion plays a significant role in offending. In their sample of forty-eight offenders, forty-four reported that they were Christians, with one Muslim and three atheists. In the study, they found that many offenders had an inaccurate or incomplete understanding of religion and used religious theology selectively in order to justify or excuse their offending.[16] This ignorance about, and selective application of scripture is not confined to offenders; there is considerable evidence that noncriminal Christian fundamentalists frequently use the Bible in this way as well.[17] The qualitative researchers concluded that:

> Offenders in our study overwhelmingly professed a belief in God and identified themselves with a particular religion, but also regularly engaged in serious criminality. Even more interesting however, our data further suggest a possible criminogenic role for religious beliefs among our sample of hardcore street offenders; these offenders actively referenced religious doctrine to justify past offenses and to excuse the continuation of serious criminal conduct.[18]

If my theory is correct, religion serves as just this sort of mechanism in a significant portion of violent crime, not just serious and persistent offending—just as it serves as the underpinning for a significant amount of terroristic violence.

Finally, in keeping with my prediction that rates of violence will be higher where Christian nationalism has a greater foothold, we turn to the South, where both violence and Christian nationalism thrive. Researchers have found a positive relationship between the percentage of conservative Protestants and the rate of homicide that is significant in Southern cities, but not in other regions of the country.[19] This provides some support for my theory, but further examination specific to the nationalistic aspect of this brand of conservative Christianity is warranted.

FREEDOM FROM RELIGIOUS TYRANNY

So how do you address a population that is extremely resistant to even hearing information that runs counter to their belief system? To a certain extent, this is true of everyone, due to confirmation bias and a number of other innate short-comings in our ability to rationally assess evidence contrary to our beliefs, but in the case of Christian nationalists, the resistance is likely to be far stronger for a couple of reasons. First, the Bible warns Christians of trickery designed to test or destroy their faith, so they are primed to react with suspicion and anger when presented with information that challenges their worldview. This started in Genesis with the devil disguised as a serpent tempting Eve with knowledge, and it is a theme echoed elsewhere in the Bible and in Christian nationalist circles. Second, because religion and patriotism serve as insulators from fear of death, the reaction to a threat to these protective ideologies will be more aggressively negative, particularly where awareness of one's inevitable death has been triggered in some manner.

The truth is that it is probably foolish to suggest that any sort of constructive discourse will change hearts or minds on this front. I am sure this will be viewed as a controversial statement, since it essentially removes the possibility of a dialogue with Christian nationalists in order to address crime more effectively. But while it might not be a popular suggestion, it is based on solid research in the neurosciences, psychology, and sociology— all of which suggest that their minds are so unlikely to change as to render attempts a wasted effort.[20]

People who base their opinions on facts do not tend to understand Christian nationalists and thus tend to engage them in ways that would be unconvincing to them, such as citing research findings. The futility of suggesting that we continue to try to do this is unsustainable as a suggestion based on this theory. Take the death penalty as an example. If I told you that death penalty costs far more than life in prison without parole when we are in serious economic trouble in the United States, that it goes against a UN resolution calling for a moratorium on its use,[21] that the United States is the only Western democracy still employing it as a punishment,[22] that it has no general deterrent effect, that it is fraught with inequality in its application, that states that employ it have higher homicide rates, and that it occasionally results in the death of someone who is innocent, what would your reaction be? If, as a criminologist, I explained all of these facts, you would likely at least consider them.

If you were a Christian nationalist, however, you would likely find yourself thinking about the biblical support for the practice, and probably start doubting me, and my motivation, immediately. Christian nationalists are not confused by facts. As such, presenting them over and over again, expecting them to compel a change in thinking is, to borrow an old cliché, the definition of insanity.

Christian nationalism has created a hegemonic ideology that both promotes and justifies a rigid, punishment-oriented worldview.[23] While Christian nationalists howl about religious persecution, claiming Christianity is the last acceptable target for discrimination, the truth is that modern religious tyranny takes another form: Christian nationalists bullying the rest of the population into silence about the impact of their belief system by accusing those who protest of religious persecution. You would face dire consequences as a public figure, for example, if you were to point out that the ideology of conservative religiosity is flawed, antiquated, and harmful, even though you wouldn't hesitate to talk about any other belief with negative consequences for the country.

Freedom of speech and belief are central tenets in our national identity, but they do not work both ways when it comes to Christian nationalists. The adherents of this movement loudly criticize social developments that offend them, and the rest of the country simply takes it.[24] It is acceptable to disagree with their positions, but it is not acceptable to question those positions, because they are cloaked in the veil of religion and thus out-of-bounds. This is a harmful state of affairs akin to reason fighting superstition with hands tied. Our whole system of government is based on the free and open exchange of ideas, premised on the notion that the best ideas will be put into practice. This cannot happen when one set of ideas is off-limits for discussion and yet has significant representation in what passes for debate. We must start examining and discussing the impact of religion in the United States like grown-ups.

THE TEN COMMANDMENTS IN ACTION

Christian nationalists would like to see the Ten Commandments (listed in Exodus 20 and recounted again in Deuteronomy 5) and other biblical principles serve as the basis for law in the United States, but few people even know them all—and the number who cannot list the commandments rises significantly among Christian nationalists themselves.[25] The Ten Commandments[26] are:

1. "I am the LORD your God, who brought you out of the land of Egypt, out of the house of bondage. You shall have no other gods before Me."

2. "You shall not make for yourself a carved image—any likeness of anything that is in heaven above, or that is in the earth beneath, or that is in the water under the earth; you shall not bow down to them or serve them. For I, the LORD your God, am a jealous God, visiting the iniquity of the fathers upon the children to the third and fourth generations of those who hate Me, but showing mercy to thousands, to those who love Me and keep My commandments."

3. "You shall not take the name of the LORD your God in vain, for the LORD will not hold him guiltless who takes His name in vain."

4. "Remember the Sabbath day, to keep it holy. Six days you shall labor and do all your work, but the seventh day is the Sabbath of the LORD your God. In it you shall do no work: you, nor your son, nor your daughter, nor your male servant, nor your female servant, nor your cattle, nor your stranger who is within your gates. For in six days the LORD made the heavens and the earth, the sea, and all that is in them, and rested the seventh day. Therefore the LORD blessed the Sabbath day and hallowed it."

5. "Honor your father and your mother, that your days may be long upon the land which the LORD your God is giving you."

6. "You shall not murder."

7. "You shall not commit adultery."

8. "You shall not steal."

9. "You shall not bear false witness against your neighbor."
10. "You shall not covet your neighbor's house; you shall not covet your neighbor's wife, nor his male servant, nor his female servant, nor his ox, nor his donkey, nor anything that is your neighbor's."[27]

While Christian nationalists very much want to see the Ten Commandments play a larger role in the United States, they—and the majority of Americans (60 percent)—cannot name even five of the Ten Commandments.[28] Surprisingly, research revealed that only 60 percent of American adults could even identify "thou shalt not kill" as a commandment.[29] Given this, it should not be surprising that most people do not realize the number of commandments that would create an exclusively Judeo-Christian orientation for the government, and that they constitute almost half of God's decrees from the Mount, making the wish for a biblical justice system less than promising for religious freedom in the United States. The goal of Christian nationalism is not religious freedom, however: It is Christian supremacy, as specified in the first commandment.

The fight over a 2.6-ton Ten Commandments statue installed in the Montgomery, Alabama, judicial building highlights the symbolic value of Christianity's hold over public life to the Christian nationalist movement. The chief justice of the Alabama Supreme Court, Roy Moore, had installed the statue, and was dismissed from his position after defying a judge's order to remove it. He instantly became a martyr and hero in the Christian nationalist movement, for his defense of the Christian faith. The irony of the battle in light of the second commandment was, apparently, lost on Moore and his supporters.

Roy Moore is an excellent example of Christian nationalist values, having fought against teaching evolution and removing segregationist language from the state constitution (aside from the deeds I will discuss here), so I will use him as something of a poster child for the movement in order to highlight some of its features. Moore's Ten Commandment statue fight was not his first foray into the Christian nationalist spotlight. In 1995, Moore was sued by the ACLU when he was still a circuit judge for both a Ten Commandments plaque he hung in his courtroom and for leading his juries in prayer prior to hearing cases. Things heated up when then governor Fob James announced that he would call in "the National Guard, state troopers, and the Alabama and Auburn football teams to keep Moore's tablets on the wall."[30] Michelle Goldberg, author of *Kingdom Coming*, described what happened next:

> That case reached an ambiguous conclusion in 1998, when the state supreme court threw out the lawsuit on technical grounds. By then, Moore had become a star of the right. Televangelist D. James Kennedy's Coral Ridge Ministries raised more than $100,000 for his legal defense fund, and Moore spoke at a series of rallies that drew thousands. His right-wing fame helped catapult him to victory in the 2000 race for chief justice of the state supreme court.[31]

Moore then used his new platform to take three children from their lesbian mother and award custody to their allegedly abusive father. In his decision, he made the following statements about homosexuality and the power of the state:

> [Homosexuality is] abhorrent, immoral, detestable, a crime against nature, and a violation of the laws of nature and of nature's God upon which this Nation and our laws are predicated. The State carries the power of the sword, that is, the power to prohibit conduct with physical penalties, such as confinement and even execution. It must use that power to prevent the subversion of children toward this lifestyle, to not encourage a criminal lifestyle.[32]

Most recently, Moore made news by ordering Alabama's probate judges not to issue marriage licenses to LGBT couples in the wake of positive same-sex marriage decisions in the state. But Moore is not a solitary crank: He is the tip of the iceberg.[33] The encroachment of religion into these public realms is the goal of the Christian nationalist movement, and they are often successful in their efforts, as seen in the recent Supreme Court Hobby Lobby decision, in which the Religious Freedom Restoration Act (RFRA) was extended to a corporation that successfully argued insuring employees for four types of birth control they considered abortifacients placed a substantial burden on their religious beliefs. It should be noted that the FDA does not define any of these drugs as abortifacients, but the Court ruled it sufficient that these drugs were considered such according to the religious beliefs of the plaintiffs. Given this, if a religious employer claims IUDs or Tylenol cause abortions, the decision supports an employer avoiding Affordable Care Act insurance coverage for them, without any scientific support for the belief.

The United States is not a particularly hospitable place for people with religious beliefs other than Christianity (or those with no theistic leanings). In the United States, the assumption in many areas of public life is that people are Christians, from using the Bible to swear in witnesses and prospective jurors in courtrooms to opening public meetings with explicitly Christian prayers. These assumptions, unchallenged, make the environment in the United States less comfortable for citizens who are not Christian, and they are an area in which Christian nationalists battle to retain the upper hand. The rest of Americans would do well to take note of areas in social life where Christian nationalism has a grip and do more than chuckle at such exploits.

There are clauses in the constitutions of eight states—Arkansas, Maryland, Mississippi, North Carolina, Pennsylvania, South Carolina, Tennessee, and Texas—banning atheists from holding public office. While this is a moot point legally, due to the 1961 Supreme Court decision in *Torasco v. Watkins*, which unanimously held that the no religious test clause in the US Constitution prohibits such a litmus test for serving in a public office, these clauses remain in these eight state constitutions and are indicative of Christian nationalist influence. Unapologetically addressing issues such as this to further delineate the line between Christian nationalism and the workings of government is an important step in reducing its influence.

WHAT WOULD JESUS REALLY DO?

For starters, Jesus would never hang out with Christian nationalists. They would have nothing in common, and he would likely find them annoying.

They are modern day Pharisees: judgmental rather than understanding, capitalistic rather than socialistic, hateful rather than loving, and militant rather than peaceful. In short, they are the antithesis of everything that Jesus stood for. Dan Wakefield, author of *The Hijacking of Jesus: How the Religious Right Distorts Christianity and Promotes Prejudice and Hate,* speaks to the warlike culture of the movement, which is totally at odds with the teachings of Jesus Christ:

> In our topsy-turvy society, the leaders of the religious right are more open and aggressive in using the terminology of war than are their political counterparts; these ministers are more comfortable with the rhetoric of battle than are senators and generals. Jerry Falwell assures the faithful that "God is Prowar." Recruiters of the religious right are enlisting "soldiers" and "warriors" to the ranks of their "army." Their language is military, from the World Prayer Center in Colorado Springs, which is proudly known as "a spiritual NORAD" to the "Commanders" of the Royal Rangers, the religious right version of the Boy Scouts, whose training for manhood includes pistol, shotgun, and muzzle-loading rifle training, beginning in the "subjunior" category of ages eleven to thirteen, and a merit badge in "atomic energy," which requires constructing "a Bohr model of the Hydrogen Atom model of the atom."[34]

Christian nationalists are fighting a war in this country, and they are winning a lot of battles because the other side is largely absent from the field. In part, this is because most of their natural opposition does not even know they exist. If all of this sounds hyperbolic to you, consider this exhortation from George Grant, the former executive director of D. James Kennedy's Coral Ridge Ministries:

> Christians have an obligation, a mandate, a commission, a holy responsibility to reclaim the land for Jesus Christ—to have dominion in civil structures, just as in every other aspect of life and godliness.
> But it is dominion we are after. Not just a voice.
> It is dominion we are after. Not just influence.
> It is dominion we are after. Not just equal time.
> It is dominion we are after.

World conquest. That is what Christ has commissioned us to accomplish. We must win the world with the power of the Gospel. And we must never settle for anything less. . . . Thus, Christian politics has as its primary intent the conquest of the land—of men, families, institutions, bureaucracies, courts, and the governments for the Kingdom of Christ.[35]

White supremacist groups use Christianity as a justification for violence against members of other races, ethnicities, sexual orientations, and religion affiliations because it is perfectly suited to the task.[36] The violence and judgment of Christian doctrine also serves as a powerful reinforcement for the ideology of white supremacy.[37] We see the same effect in the case of domestic terrorism, which is also strengthened by an emphasis on the eschatological theology of apocalyptic doctrine.[38] This spiritual war encourages violence through elevating "true believers" and demonizing other groups and religions to serve as the foil for these divine warriors, who are viewed as having God's approval for such violence.[39]

If I have done the job I have set out to do, by now you can see that this justification and support for violence is not simply a matter of ignorant—or willfully ignorant—people bastardizing the Bible for their own purposes. The Bible contains loving passages, certainly, but it also houses no small amount of hatred and vengeance to serve this purpose. Nor are prejudices hard to serve using the Bible, which has been used to justify slavery, objections to interracial and gay marriage, anti-Semitism, and sexism, among other human rights violations. Interestingly, a review of research on the Southern subculture of violence revealed that racial prejudice had a significant relationship with both support for the death penalty and for aggressive acts of violence, as does religious fundamentalism. The review concluded that racial prejudice and religious fundamentalism work together to create both violent and punitive worldviews in the South.[40] Organizing and identifying through hatred for out-groups plays a criminogenic role in this brand of Christian nationalist religiosity that should be explored further.

The antigovernmental aspect of these extremist groups warrants further investigation, as well. At the far end of the spectrum, where white supremacists and domestic terrorists tend to hang out, the antigovernment sentiment is explicit and central, but a less virulent form of this sentiment is a feature of more mainstream Christian nationalism, as well. This feeling is simply directed more specifically at forces in government viewed as working against their progress and beliefs. The current tendency toward gridlock in Congress serves as a good example of the Christian nationalist attitude in this regard. Christian nationalists are extremely patriotic and supportive when a conservative administration is in place but will fight tooth and nail against any other command structure, regardless of the impact on the country, because they are playing a longer game than their opponents.

The conflict Christian nationalists see themselves as engaging in is eternal and much larger than the sum of its individual members. They fight against the tide of what they view as sin and decay, but ultimately their reward will be in heaven, and others will come behind them to continue the fight for God. Realizing that they are unlikely to "win" the war for America in their lifetime, they are engaged in a timeless struggle of good against evil. This conception of a perpetual war has great utility in maintaining allegiance to the cause; it is the focal point around which this community of people is organized, and that organization makes them stronger through making the boundaries of their group more clearly delineated.[41] You are either for God or against God and on precisely their terms. The demands of the movement for "complete loyalty, unwavering belief, and rigid adherence to a distinctive lifestyle"[42] are comforting to people looking for the reassurance of this kind of structure, insulation, and certainty.

An enemy helps solidify the movement further, and enemies abound. Governments, lifestyles, individuals, policies, social movements, and the like all serve as excellent enemies, and one of the underlying motivations in fighting them is to exert power. Look at the example of fights over creationism versus evolution through this lens:

> Learning creationism rather than evolution does not prepare a person for a career in the global economy, but it might make a person feel more existentially secure, and certainly provides the authority of self-righteousness. The increasing popularity of fundamentalism arises from personal insecurity, which results from social decline—both economic and status decline. Fundamentalist movements, especially at the grassroots

level (creationism in schools, for example), has nothing to do with facts or logic, but with power. The believer willfully disregards logic and evidence, and instead embraces a belief, which he or she then attempts to force on the school board. The believer receives emotional gratification from this because it feels good to force the school board and the intelligentsia more generally to submit. It provides emotional gratification in place of real personal and social improvement. Creationism in science classes will not improve education, but it will make some parents feel more important.[43]

And this is comforting in terms of combating existential fears regarding death, as well. That is a lot of emotional bang for the buck that more moderate and liberal people rarely consider, but it is important to understand this in order to combat the negative consequences of Christian nationalism, including violence. I do not know what Jesus would do, but I would feel fairly comfortable placing a fat bet on the notion that he would not support the Christian nationalist agenda and would be appalled by the warlike language and adversarial behavior they engage in over social issues.[44] Finally, I have serious doubts that Jesus would be thrilled to see the Bible as a justification and rationalization for violence.

I hope this book spurs a slew of research and interest on the impact of Christian nationalism on crime, and I hope those investigations are nuanced and dig deeply into the effect of the theology, rather than simply attributing a positive effect to religion that is more likely due to structural and situational factors inherent in participating in any group espousing mainstream social values.[45] In the next section, I will briefly discuss ten ideas to address the negative impact of Christian nationalism, and, hopefully, its criminogenic effect.

TEN SUGGESTIONS FOR COMBATING RELIGIOUS VIOLENCE IN THE UNITED STATES

These suggestions for reducing the criminogenic influence of Christian nationalism are based on the research conducted for this book and the theory I have posited here, which I hope will be greatly expanded and improved upon through further research on the topic. Many of these propositions are aimed at reducing the influence of Christian nationalism overall, but I believe they are necessary to reduce its violent impact, since the movement itself is generating this criminogenic influence on American culture. That said, I offer these proscriptions as a starting point:

1. Talk about religion—and its influence in public life.

People need to know about Christian nationalists, including some Christian nationalists and their allies, who are not even familiar with the term Christian nationalist. You cannot respond to something you have not identified, and far too many people do not even know this movement and belief system exists. Further, some people passively support the movement without realizing its aims, and they might think better of that support if they were more informed. The basic theology is aggressive and seeks dominion over the lives of all Americans—not just Christians. Shed light on this fact.

2. Do not expend resources trying to educate Christian nationalists —they cannot hear you.

In chapter four, I discussed the reasons why Christian nationalists are extremely resistant to information that threatens their belief system. Keep that in mind, and do not waste resources trying to effect change through changing their minds about their beliefs. This belief system is deeply engrained and brings about a pattern of thought that is markedly different from secular notions of rationality, logic, and proof. Recent research confirms that religious instruction even has a significant impact on the thought process surrounding what is real and fictional in children.[46] With adults, that same instruction and exposure is coupled with a strong social identity that is not likely to change. Save your strength for conversations that might make a difference.

3. Apply social, political, and economic pressure wherever possible to combat the more negative and criminogenic messages from Christian nationalists.

In particular, women, children, LGBT, atheists, and people of minority faiths are all in need of greater protection, as they are singled out for especially harmful treatment from Christian nationalists. Do whatever you can to protect groups and individuals who are marginalized or targeted by Christian nationalism. Who knows—if they are unsuccessful in their goals with respect to these groups, it might lessen their zeal for this type of aggressiveness.

Marriage equality will be an interesting case to watch in this regard. Christian nationalists and their allies have all but lost the fight against marriage equality as of this writing. On July 26, 2015, the Supreme Court ruled, in *Obergefell v. Hodges*, that states cannot ban same-sex couples from marrying. It is unlikely that even losing this crucial battle will result in their retiring from such efforts in the future, but as LGBT people gain more and more mainstream acceptance, the impact on Christian nationalists will likely be greater acceptance as well, albeit at a slower rate than their less conservative and religious counterparts. This is the type of progress that has been lowering rates of violence over time—and will continue to do so, if my theory is correct. The less of a hold conservative Christianity has over American society, the less violent crime we should experience.

4. Do not fight intolerance with intolerance.

Two wrongs really do not make a right, so it is important to avoid becoming the thing you are fighting. There is a fine line between trying to reduce the influence of Christian nationalism and assuming the characteristics they embody in trying to do so. Holding Christian nationalism responsible for the harm it causes and working to reduce that harm is not the same as stamping it out. Adherents to this movement thrive on adversity and are quick to see persecution against them everywhere. There is no need to allow the belief system to go unchecked for fear of inciting these feelings, but it is quite another thing to actually lend weight to them.

Religion can have positive effects—I am not suggesting that it does not, nor that is should be in any manner viewed as an enemy, to borrow a page from their playbook. If there is an enemy, it is violent and destructive doctrines in religion—not the religions themselves:

> It is easy to look at religious conflicts and quickly propose that if we take religion out of the picture we would no longer have conflict. Take religion out of the Kosovo, out of the Kashmir, out of Ireland, out of Palestine and Israel, and there would be no conflicts in those parts of the world. This line of thought, however, overlooks the potential of religion to dissolve the very tensions it "creates." People are passionate about religion. We cannot simply erase it out of their lives and existence. An even better approach may be to invest in religion as a solution. This approach takes courage and creativity. It embarks those up to the challenge on an arduous adventure, a bumpy but rewarding ride.[47]

The goal is to help shape religious beliefs into a positive social force where they are not currently functioning as such, rather than to curb true religious freedom.

5. Encourage Christian nationalists and their allies—witting and unwitting—to draw their theology from the more loving passages in the New Testament, through bringing attention to the atrocities and violence in the Old, as well as some found in the New.

Question and confront Old Testament belief systems. If you see Christian nationalists using Old Testament passages to justify violent attitudes or actions, while claiming to do so out of love, call them on their use of that doctrine. Point out hypocrisy and messages that are not loving and redemptive. Make it as difficult as possible for this belief system to maintain social support.

6. Protect the division between church and state.

Eliminating the division between church and state is a central goal of Christian nationalists that would mean an end, or at least a serious erosion, of many of the rights that Americans treasure. Shed light on inappropriate religious encroachments into the realm of government. Fight the presumption of Christianity in the public forum. Many of the areas where Christianity appears innate in public life are simply leftovers from the McCarthy era, when Christian nationalism had something of a heyday embedding symbols and rituals of the movement into the everyday lives of American citizens. It is best for secular areas of social life to remain secular in order to reduce negative Christian nationalist influence.

7. Fight for a less punitive, more just criminal justice system.

Our criminal justice system is broken, and fixing it requires public support. We incarcerate far too many people for nonviolent offenses. We still use the death penalty, despite its obvious moral, legal, and economic drawbacks. We have allowed imprisoning people to become a business where profit is the bottom line. We have cut spending in areas that are essential to reducing recidivism rates, such as drug and alcohol treatment, job training, and prisoner reintegration programs. We are so tough on crime that we are losing respect on the world stage.

Christian nationalists will vote for politicians promising to be tough on crime regardless of the social consequences. Be sure to cancel their votes, and make it clear that you think it is time we get smart on crime, instead.

8. Draw attention to the criminogenic impact of religion when you see it.

In the United States, the media has a tendency to shy away from calling attention to religious motivations in crime where that religion is Christianity, allowing a lot of the impact of Christian nationalism to go unnoticed. Do what you can to highlight this impact on social media outlets, in editorials, and through making calls to media outlets. If you are a criminologist or other professional asked for opinions in the news media, make the connection to Christian fundamentalism explicit in your commentary when it is present.

9. Educate yourself about the amount of government money flowing into these faith-based institutions.

If we are to use the Christian nationalists' war metaphors, you should know that we are paying for too much of the cost for the other side of the conflict. Government spending for faith-based initiatives that do little more than spout propaganda for conservative Christian values need to be curtailed. Similarly, when you see tax-exempt, faith-based organizations engaging in political activism, call foul and loudly. Support strengthening the laws against blending these purposes without paying taxes and for tougher penalties when such laws are violated.

10. If you are a criminologist, research the connection between Christian nationalism and violence.

Go on—you have got work to do, and it is a fascinating topic.

NOTES

CHAPTER ONE: WHEN DID CHRISTIANS
GET SO MEAN (AGAIN)?

1. Wendy Kaminer, "The Last Taboo: Why America Needs Atheism," *New Republic*, Oct. 14, 1996, 27.

2. For a great discussion of this phenomenon, see Jean Hardisty, *Mobilizing Resentment: Conservative Resurgence from the John Birch Society to the Promise Keepers* (Boston: Beacon Press, 1999).

3. Matt. 5:10–12.

4. Unfortunately, the ideology of the American religious right often ignores most of Jesus's sermon from this mountain near Capernaum—particularly the first seven teachings in the Beatitudes: blessed are the poor in spirit, those who mourn, the meek, those who hunger for righteousness, the merciful, the pure in heart, and the peacemakers.

5. In fact, as I write, King Abdullah has just introduced a series of new laws defining atheists as terrorists in Saudi Arabia. See Adam Whithnall, "Saudi Arabia Declares All Atheists Are Terrorists in New Law to Crack Down on Political Dissidents," *Independent*, April 1, 2014, http://www.independent.co.uk/news/world/middle-east/saudi-arabia-declares-all-atheists-are-terrorists-in-new-law-to-crack-down-on-political-dissidents-9228389.html (accessed April 2, 2014).

6. See Scott Atran, *Talking to the Enemy: Faith, Brotherhood, and the (Un)Making of Terrorists* (New York: HarperCollins, 2010); Albert Bandura, "Mechanisms of Moral Disengagement," in *Origins of Terrorism: Psychologies, Ideologies, Theologies, States of Mind*, ed. Walter Reich (Washington, DC: Woodrow Wilson Center, 1998), 161–91; Benjamin Barber, *Fear's Empire: War, Terrorism, and Democracy* (New York: Norton, 2003); Martha Crenshaw, "An Organizational Approach to the Analysis of Political Terrorism," *Orbis* 29 (1985): 465–89; Martha Crenshaw, "The Psychology of Political Terrorism," in *Political Psychology: Contemporary Problems and Issues*, ed. Margaret Hermann (San Francisco, CA: Jossey-Bass, 1986), 379–413; Bruce Hoffman, *Holy Terror: The*

Implications of Terrorism Motivated by a Religious Imperative (Santa Monica, CA: Rand, 1993); Magnus Ranstorp, "Terrorism in the Name of Religion," *Journal of International Affairs* 50 (1996): 41–63; and David C. Rapaport, "Fear and Trembling: Terrorism in Three Religious Traditions," *American Political Science Review* 78 (1984): 658–76.

7. Though the latter two topics are beyond the scope of this book, the impact in these areas is easy to discern vis-à-vis the biblical concept of dominion over the earth.

8. I will address the specific statistics on American incarceration rates and capital punishment later in the book. For now, suffice it to say that buying the idea that we are soft on crime is akin to believing that President Obama is not a US citizen. For an overview, see Stuart Banner, *The Death Penalty: An American History* (Cambridge, MA: Harvard University Press, 2003); James O. Finckenauer, "Public Support for the Death Penalty: Retribution as Just Deserts or Retribution as Revenge," *Justice Quarterly* 5 (1988): 81–100; Harold G. Grasmick et al., "Religion, Punitive Justice, and Support for the Death Penalty," *Justice Quarterly* 10 (1993): 289–314; David Garland, *Peculiar Institution: America's Death Penalty in an Age of Abolition* (New York: Oxford University Press, 2010); Roger Hood and Carolyn Hoyle, *The Death Penalty: A Worldwide Perspective* (New York: Oxford University Press, 2008); Daniel S. Nagin and John V. Pepper, eds., *Deterrence and the Death Penalty* (Washington, DC: National Academies Press, 2012); and Matthew B. Robinson, *Death Nation: The Experts Explain American Capital Punishment* (Upper Saddle River, NJ: Prentice Hall, 2007).

9. A theology that holds that the second coming will not occur until Christians rule the earth for a thousand years. Incidentally, Rousas J. Rushdoony was a real charmer, calling for the "the death penalty for gay people, blasphemers, and unchaste women, among other sinners" (Michelle Goldberg, *Kingdom Coming: The Rise of Christian Nationalism* [New York: Norton, 2007], 37). The list of attributes of Christian nationalism are credited to Michelle Goldberg as well.

10. Gen. 1:28: "And God blessed them, and God said unto them, Be fruitful, and multiply, and replenish the earth, and subdue it: and have dominion over the fish of the sea, and over the fowl of the air, and over every living thing that moveth upon the earth" (King James Version). While this passage is central to Christian nationalist ideology, common interpretations of this passage also have harmful environmental implications.

11. In fact, the John Birch Society launched a campaign against the retail secularization of Christmas in 1959 that was strikingly similar to that which

began in earnest in 2004, though it drew far less attention the first time around. In the more recent incarnation, Fox News runs yearly "Christmas Under Siege" segments about this conspiracy perpetrated by "secular progressives," and Fox news anchor John Gibson even wrote a book charging that the secularization of department stores was nothing short of a "war on Christianity" (John Gibson, *The War on Christmas: How the Liberal Plot to Ban the Sacred Christian Holiday Is Worse Than You Thought* [New York: Sentinel Press, 2005]. Compare this to the earlier version: Hubert Kregeloh, *There Goes Christmas?!* [Belmont, MA: American Opinion, 1959].) For an interesting discussion of the political aspect of this issue and its wider implications, see Bill Press, *How the Republicans Stole Christmas: The Republican Party's Declared Monopoly on Religion and What Democrats Can Do to Take it Back* (New York: Doubleday, 2005).

12. To say that this list of organizations is the tip of the iceberg is a huge understatement. For an incredibly thorough treatment of the Christian nationalism movement, see Goldberg, *Kingdom Coming*. For a closer look at just one of these organizations, see Ken Abraham, *Who Are the Promise Keepers? Understanding the Christian Men's Movement* (New York: Doubleday, 1997); Bryan W. Brickner, *The Promise Keepers: Politics and Promises* (Lanham, MD: Lexington Books, 1999); and Nancy Novosad, "God Squad: The Promise Keepers Fight for a Man's World," *Progressive* 60 (1996): 25–30.

13. Thomas Jefferson, "First Inaugural Address," March 4, 1801, *Avalon Project*, Yale Law School, http://avalon.law.yale.edu/19th_century/jefinau1.asp.

14. The 35 percent finding represents all people who are "born again" Christians—a group with a very wide spectrum of beliefs, ranging from ultraconservative to moderate. As such, it is unlikely that the upper end of this spread accurately captures the percentage of Americans who are both conservative and Christian. According to Barna, in 2006 and 2007, respectively, there were 101 million "born again" Christians and 18 million evangelical Christians in the ranks of the religious in the United States—a good number of which are Christian nationalists, whether they know it or not.

15. It is difficult to argue with the electoral weight of evangelical Christians, which will receive attention in chapter four as it relates to influencing public policy.

16. Robert T. Schatz, Ervin Staub, and Howard Lavine, "On the Varieties of National Attachment: Blind versus Constructive Patriotism," *Political Psychology* 20 (1999): 151–74.

17. Paul Bell, "Would You Believe It?" *Mensa Magazine*, February 11, 2007,

12–13. See also Richard Lynn, John Harvey, and Helmuth Nyborg, "Average Intelligence Predicts Atheism Rates across 137 Nations," *Intelligence* 37 (2009): 11–15. I had to think about whether to put this information in, as it seems like sort of a nasty thing to point out, but then realized that this flavor of Christianity prides itself on its anti-intellectualism. As such, perhaps it will be viewed as a compliment. At the same time, I know many other Christians who are extremely intelligent, so bear in mind that we are talking about larger statistical patterns here.

18.   Kathleen C. Leonard et al., "Parent-Child Dynamics and Emerging Adult Religiosity: Attachment, Parental Beliefs, and Faith Support," *Psychology of Religion and Spirituality* 5 (2013): 5–14.

19.   Richard Dawkins, *The God Delusion* (New York: Houghton Mifflin, 2006).

20.   2 Tim 2:15.

21.   On *The 700 Club* in 2006, Pat Robertson offered this demure commentary about "liberal" professors: "They are racists, murderers, sexual deviants, and supporters of al Qaeda—and they could be teaching your kids!" (James B. Twitchell, *Shopping for God: How Christians Went from in Your Heart to in Your Face* [New York: Simon and Schuster, 2007].)

22.   Apparently, aside from suggesting that a literal interpretation of the Bible is problematic, some of the uproar over evolution stems from the idea that a world that is millions of years old fails to sufficiently inspire a sense of urgency in believers with respect to the "end times," as changes come too gradually in this paradigm. (This courtesy of Ken Ham, CEO and president of the nonprofit ministry responsible for the Disneyland-esque Creation Museum in Petersburg, Kentucky.) (Gordy Slack, "Inside the Creation Museum," *Salon*, August 5, 2007, http://www.salon.com/news/feature/2007/05/31/creation_museum/index.html [accessed November 6, 2014].)

23.   Honestly, as someone who's made a few *Deliverance* cracks in my time, I was embarrassed to realize how snotty I had been—and, worse, how stupid and wrong. There are bigots and good people in every region of this country. If you make cracks about Southerners or Christians based on negative stereotypes you hold about them, well, congratulations: You are a bigot—and thus in a good position to understand bigotry and the ideas and feelings that drive it. All of the rationalizations you make to distinguish between mocking your preferred group for derision and people mocking other groups, such as blacks, women, Jewish people, gay and lesbian people, and the like?—racists, homophobes, and anti-Semites feel that same sense of justification.

24.   For a great discussion, see Stan L. Albrecht and Tim B. Heaton,

"Secularization, Higher Education, and Religiosity," *Review of Religious Research* 26 (1984): 43–58; Elaine H. Ecklund and Jerry Z. Park, "Conflict between Religion and Science among Academic Scientists?" *Journal for the Scientific Study of Religion* 48 (2009): 276–92; and Elaine H. Ecklund and Christopher P. Scheitle, "Religion among Academic Scientists: Distinctions, Disciplines, and Demographics," *Social Forces* 54 (2007): 289–307.

25. This may sound extreme, but if you look at the recipe for fascism, the ingredients are clearly present in many of the stated goals of conservative Christianity: nationalism, corporatism, and militarism, among others. Similarly, the conservative Christian movement in the United States lists among their enemies many common to fascist movements: communism, liberalism, and international socialism, among others. For a comprehensive discussion of fascism both historically and ideologically, see Roger Griffin, *The Nature of Fascism* (New York: Routledge, 2003); and Roger Griffin, ed., *Fascism* (New York: Oxford University Press, 1995). For a discussion of fascism specific to conservative Christianity in the present-day United States, see Chris Hedges, *American Fascism: The Christian Right and the War on America* (New York: Free Press, 2007). I do not mean to imply that full-frontal fascism is imminent in the United States, or, indeed, likely. I am simply pointing out a structural similarity between Christian reconstructionism and fascism. You have to admit—it is at least fascist-esque.

26. There is a biological basis for resistance and animosity in the face of beliefs that challenge our own worldviews; for an accessible overview, I recommend Daniel Gardner, *The Science of Fear: How the Culture of Fear Manipulates Your Brain* (New York: Plume, 2008).

CHAPTER TWO: JESUS LOVES YOU, BUT WE'RE HIS FAVORITES

1. Thanks to ReligiousTolerance.org for noting that "A case can be made that Christianity did not start in Palestine. According to Acts 11, the followers of Jesus were first called Christians in Antioch. Also, the Romans imposed the name "Palestine" on the Holy Land only circa 135 CE, long after most of the books of the Christian scriptures (New Testament) were written. Finally, the first followers of Yeshua of Nazareth considered themselves a new sect within Judaism not the followers of a new religion" (Religious Tolerance, "Christianity: The World's Largest Religion," http://www.religioustolerance.org/christ.htm [accessed May 16, 2013]).

2. And this should be particularly true where those religions are more closely tied to national governments.

3. See Steven F. Messner and Richard Rosenfeld, *Crime and the American Dream* (Belmont, CA: Wadsworth, 2007); and Franklin E. Zimring and Gordon Hawkins, *Crime Is Not the Problem: Lethal Violence in America* (New York: Oxford University Press, 1997).

4. Though we only lost that title last year, and only by 1 percent. Incidentally, I am not making that up to be funny, since, well, it isn't. Mexico is number one. We are number two. (Food and Agriculture Organization of the United Nations, *The State of Food and Agriculture*, 2013, http://www.fao.org/docrep/018/i3300e/i3300e.pdf [accessed February 1, 2014].)

5. US Department of the Treasury, "History of 'In God We Trust,'" http://www.treasury.gov/about/education/Pages/in-god-we-trust.aspx (accessed December 27, 2013). The House Un-American Activities Committee (HUAC) was actually borne of Christian Nationalist sentiment from its inception in 1937, when chairman Martin Dies received a congratulatory telegram from the Ku Klux Klan for the formation of the committee, which read: "Every true American, and that includes every Klansman, is behind you and your committee in its effort to turn the country back to the honest, freedom-loving, God-fearing American to whom it belongs." Later, Dies—who was a Klan supporter and had even spoken at Klan rallies—refused to investigate the KKK organization, saying it represented an American custom akin to running whiskey. For an interesting history of HUAC, see Frank J. Donner, *The Un-Americans* (New York, NY: Ballantine, 1961).

6. And I will say right up front that I am a criminologist, not a trained historian, and that this discussion will be necessarily brief, as it is not the focus of this book. All I am attempting to do here is provide a *Reader's Digest* version of what appears to be the consensus of the vast majority of trained historians on the single issue of the role of religion in government. I will provide a quote or two from each founding father to illustrate this consensus view (and the quotes are admittedly cherry-picked to reflect what their overall attitudes seemed to be). I hope that my characterizations are more than fair and that most scholars in American history and political science will be satisfied that I captured the essence of their beliefs pretty well. For a criminologist.

7. David L. Holmes, *The Faiths of the Founding Fathers* (New York: Oxford University Press, 2006). Incidentally, since the term doesn't get bandied about much these days: Deists are people who believe that God created the world and then minded his own business, essentially. This conception would not involve

God getting all up in the affairs of humans, no matter how hard they prayed for intervention.

8. Richard B. Morris, *Seven Who Shaped Our Destiny: The Founding Fathers as Revolutionaries* (New York: HarperCollins, 1973). This is, by the way, a great, readable work by a historian who knows how to keep history as interesting as it is and deserves to be.

9. John Adams, *The Quotable John Adams* (Guilford, CT: Lyons, 2008), 150.

10. "The Barbary Treaties, 1786–1816: Treaty of Peace and Friendship, Signed at Tripoli, November 4, 1796," *Treaties and Other International Acts of the United States of America, Volume 2*, ed. Hunter Miller (Washington, DC: Government Printing Office, 1931). Available online through the Avalon Project of Yale Law School, avalon.law.yale.edu/18th_century/bar1796t.asp.

11. John Adams, "A Defence of the Constitutions of Government of the United States of America (1787–1788)," in *The American Enlightenment: The Shaping of the American Experiment and a Free Society*, ed. by Adrienne Koch (New York: George Braziller Press, 1965), 258.

12. Carl Van Doran, *Benjamin Franklin* (1938; repr., New York: Viking Press, 2002), 777–78.

13. Benjamin Franklin, *Poor Richard's Almanack*, 1758, 52.

14. Ron Chernow, *Alexander Hamilton* (New York: Penguin Press, 2004).

15. Alexander Hamilton, Federalist No. 1, "General Introduction," *Independent Journal*, October 27, 1787.

16. Richard B. Morris, ed., *John Jay: The Winning of the Peace; Unpublished Papers, 1780–1784* (New York: Harper & Row Publishers, 1980), 709. See also Walter Stahr, *John Jay: Founding Father* (London: Hambledon Continuum Press, 2005); and Patricia U. Bonomi, "John Jay, Religion, and the State," *New York History* 81 (2000): 8–18.

17. John Jay, *The Correspondence and Public Papers of John Jay, Vol. 4 (1794–1826)*, ed. Henry P. Johnston (New York: G. P. Putnam's Sons, 1893).

18. James H. Hutson, ed. *The Founders on Religion: A Book of Quotations* (Princeton, NJ: Princeton University Press, 2005).

19. Holmes, *Faiths of the Founding Fathers*.

20. John Ferling, *Adams vs. Jefferson: The Tumultuous Election of 1800* (New York: Oxford University Press, 2004), 154. See also, Isaac Kramnick and R. Laurence Moore, *The Godless Constitution: The Case against Religious Correctness* (New York: Norton, 1997); and Charles B. Sanford, *The Religious Life of Thomas Jefferson* (Charlotte, NC: University of North Carolina Press, 1987).

21. Gregg L. Frazer, *The Religious Beliefs of America's Founders: Reason, Revelation, Revolution* (Lawrence, KS: University Press of Kansas, 2012).

22. Sanford, *Religious Life of Thomas Jefferson.*

23. James H. Hutson, ed., *The Founders on Religion* (Princeton, NJ: Princeton University Press, 2007), 64.

24. James Madison, *James Madison: Writings, 1772–1836* (Des Moines, IA: Library of America, 1999), 33.

25. Irving Brant, *James Madison the Nationalist, 1780–1787* (Morgantown, PA: Sullivan Press, 2008). See also James Madison, *James Madison on Religious Liberty*, ed. Robert S. Alley (Amherst, NY: Prometheus Books, 1985). Madison also warned against endorsing Christianity, in his *Memorial and Remonstrance against Religious Assessments* in 1785: "Who does not see that the same authority which can establish Christianity, in exclusion of all other Religions, may establish with the same ease any particular sect of Christians, in exclusion of all other Sects?"

26. David Barton, *The Myth of Separation: What Is the Correct Relationship between Church and State?* (Aledo, TX: WallBuilders Press, 1992).

27. For some examples of this, see Chris Rodda, *Liars for Jesus: The Religious Right's Alternate Version of American History* (North Charleston, SC: CreateSpace Publishing, 2006).

28. Barton, *Myth of Separation.*

29. Though I am not impugning information from such sources, I tend to be cautious in sourcing information from any end of the spectrum where bias is concerned. In fact, I am especially diligent when the information supports my views, as that is where we are all—liberal and conservative—most susceptible to forgetting our healthy skepticism.

30. Rob Boston, interview by Keith Olbermann, *Countdown with Keith Olbermann*, MSNBC, February 10, 2010, http://www.nbcnews.com/id/35347645/ns/msnbc-countdown_with_keith_olbermann/t/countdown-keith-olbermann-wednesday-february-th/#.VgwMzPlViko. Rob Boston is a senior policy analyst and director of communications for the nonprofit organization Americans United for the Separation of Church and State.

31. At some point after I wrote this section, WallBuilders changed their website to intimate that Barton had always accepted responsibility for these problems, as a Christian should, in the context of slamming secular scholars for harping on about it. My earlier research—and even the tone of the current discussion on WallBuilders—suggests that this is a stretch.

32. "Unconfirmed Quotations," *WallBuilders*, http://www.wallbuilders.com/libissuesarticles.asp?id=138585, January 2000 (accessed December 2012). The article reads as though it was written by someone other than Barton, particularly in the sections about the criticisms directed at him, but no author is identified. The page was updated on February 19, 2013 to include several quotes reported to have been found in original sources along with many that are still questionable, though I do not know if the claim to validation is accurate.

33. Ibid.

34. Ibid. This section has since been removed from the WallBuilders website.

35. Eckholm, Erik, "History Buff Sets a Course for the Right," *New York Times*, May 5, 2011, A1. That "history buff" description is accurate reporting, incidentally: Barton's degree, from Oral Roberts University, is in Christian education. He also holds an honorary doctorate from Pensacola Christian College.

36. Jeff Huett, "2012 Shurden Lectures Explore American History," *Baptist Joint Committee for Religious Liberty*, May 14, 2012, http://bjconline.org/2012-shurden-lectures-explore-american-history/ (accessed May 26, 2013).

37. David Barton, *The Jefferson Lies: Exposing the Myths You've Always Believed about Thomas Jefferson* (New York: Thomas Nelson, 2012).

38. Jennifer Schuessler, "And the Worst Book of History Is . . . ," *New York Times*, July 16, 2012, http://artsbeat.blogs.nytimes.com/2012/07/16/and-the-worst-book-of-history-is/?_r=0 (accessed July 10, 2013); and "About David Barton," *Southern Poverty Law Center*, https://www.splcenter.org/fighting-hate/extremist-files/individual/david-barton (accessed August 12, 2015). See also Chris Rodda, "Debunking David Barton's *Jefferson's Lies* (Because They Still Need to Be Debunked)," *Huffington Post*, September 16, 2013, http://www.huffingtonpost.com/chris-rodda/debunking-david-bartons-j_b_3936810.html.

39. Stephen E. Lucas, ed., *The Quotable George Washington: The Wisdom of an American Patriot* (Madison, WI: Madison House, 1999).

40. The full text of this section of the Bill of Rights reads: "Congress shall make no law respecting an establishment of religion, or prohibiting the free exercise thereof; or abridging the freedom of speech, or of the press; or the right of the people peaceably to assemble, and to petition the government for a redress of grievances."

41. For great discussions about American brands of Christianity and culture, see Stephen Prothero, *American Jesus: How the Son of God Became a National Icon* (New York: Farrar, Straus, and Giroux, 2003); and James G. Moseley, *A Cultural History of Religion in America* (Westport, CT: Greenwood Press, 1981).

42. Pew Research Center, "The American-Western European Values Gap: American Exceptionalism Subsides," *Pew Global Attitudes Project*, November 17, 2011, http://www.pewglobal.org/2011/11/17/the-american-western-european -values-gap/ (accessed June 6, 2013).

43. Alexis de Tocqueville, *Democracy in America*, trans. by Henry Reeve (London: Saunders and Otley, 2007).

44. James B. Twitchell, *Shopping for God: How Christianity Went from in Your Heart to in Your Face* (New York: Simon and Schuster, 2007). Excellent book, by the way.

45. As with many topics in this book, this single issue of Christian nationalist influence on American politics is too broad to do justice here, but if you are interested in learning more, I recommend the following books: Michelle Goldberg, *Kingdom Coming: The Rise of Christian Nationalism* (New York: Norton, 2007); Jeff Sharlet, *The Family: The Secret Fundamentalism at the Heart of American Power* (New York: HarperCollins, 2008); Clint Willis and Nate Hardcastle, eds., *Jesus Is Not a Republican: The Religious Right's War on America* (New York: Thunder's Mouth Press, 2005); Garry Wills, *Under God: Religion and American Politics* (New York: Simon and Schuster, 1990); Thomas B. Edsall, *Building Red America: The New Conservative Coalition and the Drive for Permanent Power* (New York: Basic Books, 2006); Ray Suarez, *The Holy Vote: The Politics of Faith in America* (New York: Harper Collins, 2006); Betty Clermont, *The Neo-Catholics: Implementing Christian Nationalism in America* (Atlanta: Clarity Press, 2009); and Chris Hedges, *American Fascism: The Christian Right and the War on America* (New York: Free Press, 2007).

46. Edsall, *Building Red America*, 8. See also Alan I. Abramowitz and Kyle L. Saunders, "Is Polarization a Myth?" *Journal of Politics* 70 (2008): 542–55; and Jeffrey Alexander, "Citizen and Enemy as Symbolic Classification: On the Polarizing Discourse of Civil Society," in *Cultivating Differences: Symbolic Boundaries and the Making of Inequality*, ed. Michèle Lamont and Marcel Fournier (Chicago, IL: University of Chicago Press, 1992), 289–308.

47. The Pew Forum on Religion and Public Life, "Global Christianity—A Report on the Size and Distribution of the World's Christian Population," *Pew Research Center*, December 19, 2011, http://www.pewforum.org/2011/12/19/ global-christianity-exec/ (accessed February 2, 2013). This study consists of a country-by-country analysis of about 2,400 data sources, including censuses and nationally representative population surveys.

48. Drawn from a representative sample of more than 35,000 adults in

the United States, with additional oversamples of Eastern Orthodox Christians, Buddhists, and Hindus. Pew Forum, "U.S. Religious Landscape Survey, 2012," *Pew Center on Religion & Public Life*, 2013, http://religions.pewforum.org/reports (accessed April 6, 2014).

49. Frank Newport, "In US, 42% Believe Creationist View of Human Origins," *Gallup Politics*, 2014, http://www.gallup.com/poll/170822/believe-creationist-view-human-origins.aspx (accessed October 5, 2015). Drawn from a random sample of 1,028 adults living in the United States. A 95 percent confidence interval that the maximum margin of sampling error was ±4 percentage points was achieved.

50. Pew Forum on Religion and Public Life, "Global Christianity: A Report on the Size and Distribution of the World's Christian Population," *Pew Research Center*, December 19, 2011, http://www.pewforum.org/2011/12/19/global-christianity-exec/ (accessed October 1, 2015). Interesting fact: the Southern Baptist Convention is the largest specific Protestant denomination in the United States—a fact that likely plays a big role in the context of regional differences in crime rates in America.

51. In fact, for a look at this belief system at work in Catholicism, check out Clermont, *The Neo-Catholics*.

52. I am not arguing that Christians do not face discrimination and even persecution for their faith globally, particularly in North Korea and many Muslim countries. But in the United States, Christian persecution often amounts more to fetishizing martyrdom. This likely springs from 2 Tim. 3:12 and the idea that good Christians will suffer for following Christ. If suffering is a tenet of your faith, persecution narratives are sought to legitimize that faith. In the United States, this often amounts to creating and exaggerating slights in the absence of real persecution. There is even compelling and credible evidence that much of the narrative about the persecution of early Christians is not historically accurate. See Candida Moss, *The Myth of Persecution: How Early Christians Invented a Story of Martyrdom* (New York: HarperOne, 2014).

53. Candida Moss, "The Myth of Christian Persecution," *HuffPost Religion*, August 9, 2014, http://www.huffingtonpost.com/candida-moss/the-myth-of-christian-persecution_b_2901880.html (accessed August 9, 2014).

54. Randall Balmer, *Mine Eyes Have Seen the Glory: A Journey into the Evangelical Subculture in America* (New York: Oxford University Press, 1989).

55. Penny Edgell, Joseph Gerteis, and Douglas Hartmann, "Atheists as 'Other': Moral Boundaries and Cultural Membership in American Society," *American Sociological Review* 71 (2006): 211–34.

56. Ibid., 212.

57. Ibid., 230.

58. Jeffrey M. Jones, "Atheists, Muslims see Most Bias as Presidential Candidates," *Gallup*, June 21, 2012, http://www.gallup.com/poll/155285/atheists-muslims-bias-presidential-candidates.aspx (accessed June 23, 2012). Results were based on telephone interviews conducted June 7–10, 2012, with a random sample of 1,004 adults, aged eighteen and older, living in all fifty states and the District of Columbia. A 95 percent confidence interval that the maximum margin of sampling error was ±4 percentage points was achieved.

59. As prejudices have become less overt, and thus even more difficult to measure, the gist of the problem has grown more pronounced over time. See Brent B. Benda and Robert F. Corwyn, "Are the Effects of Religion on Crime Mediated, Moderated, and Misrepresented by Inappropriate Measures?" *Journal of Social Service Research* 27 (2001): 57–86; Manuela Barreto and Naomi Ellemers, "The Perils of Political Correctness: Men's and Women's Responses to Old-Fashioned and Modern Sexist Views," *Social Psychology Quarterly* 68 (2005): 75–88; Markus Brauer, Wolfgang Wasel, and Paula Niedenthal, "Implicit and Explicit Components of Prejudice," *Review of General Psychology* 4 (2000): 79–101; Douglas P. Crowne and David Marlowe, *The Approval Motive* (New York: Wiley, 1964); William A. Cunningham, Kristopher J. Preacher, and Mahzarin R. Banaji, "Implicit Attitude Measures: Consistency, Stability, and Convergent Validity," *Psychological Science* 12 (2001): 163–170; John F. Dovidio et al., "On the Nature of Prejudice: Automatic and Controlled Processes," *Journal of Experimental Social Psychology* 33 (1997): 510–40; Freiderike Eyssel and Gerd Bohner, "The Rating of Sexist Humor Under Time Pressure as an Indicator of Spontaneous Sexist Attitudes," *Sex Roles* 57 (2007): 651–60; Donald R. Kinder and Howard Schuman, "Racial Attitudes: Developments and Divisions in Survey Research," in *A Telescope on Society: Survey Research and Social Science at the University of Michigan and Beyond*, ed. James S. House et al. (Ann Arbor, MI: University of Michigan Press, 2004), 365–92; Melanie A. Morrison et al., "An Investigation of Measures of Modern and Old-Fashioned Sexism," *Social Indicators Research* 48 (1999): 39–50; Michael A. Olson and Robert H. Fazio, "Relations Between Implicit Measures of Prejudice: What Are We Measuring?" *Psychological Science* 14 (2003): 636–39; and Laurie A. Rudman and Richard D. Ashmore, "Discrimination and the Implicit Association Test," *Group Processes & Intergroup Relations* 10 (2007): 359–72.

60. Darrin Grinder and Steve Shaw, *Presidents and Their Faith: From George Washington to Barack Obama* (Boise, ID: Russell Media, 2012).

61. Randall Balmer, *God in the White House: How Faith Shaped the Presidency from John F. Kennedy to George W. Bush* (New York: HarperOne, 2008).

62. John Blake, "Why a President's Faith May Not Matter," *CNN*, June 30, 2012, http://religion.blogs.cnn.com/2012/06/30/why-a-presidents-faith-may-not-matter/ (accessed August 10, 2014).

63. Richard Reeves, *President Nixon: Alone in the White House* (New York: Simon & Schuster, 2002); and Don Fulsom, *Nixon's Darkest Secrets: The Inside Story of America's Most Troubled President* (New York: Thomas Dunne Books, 2012).

64. Stephen Mansfield, *The Faith of George W. Bush* (New York: Tarcher, 2003). It is unlikely he would have won even a first term, of course, as conservative voters probably would have taken issue with his cocaine use, drinking problem, DWI, and dubious military record if Jesus had not stepped in to wipe his sins away. When you think about it, it is flat amazing what people on the right are willing to overlook when a candidate's religious resume meets with their approval.

65. This is a conservative estimate taken from Hannah Fischer, "Iraq Casualties: U.S. Military Forces and Iraqi Civilians, Police, and Security Forces," *Congressional Research Service. Report for Members and Committees of Congress*, 2010, https://www.fas.org/sgp/crs/mideast/R40824.pdf.

66. Robert A. Caro, *The Passage of Power: The Years of Lyndon Johnson* (New York: Knopf, 2012).

67. Grinder and Shaw, *Presidents and Their Faith*.

68. Jimmy Carter, *Living Faith* (New York: Broadway Books, 1998).

69. Stephen Mansfield, *The Faith of Barack Obama* (Nashville, TN: Thomas Nelson, 2008). Mansfield is a conservative author, who received "angry emails" and had speaking engagements canceled in response to writing this book, according to an interview in John Blake, "Why a President's Faith May Not Matter," *CNN*, June 30, 2012, http://religion.blogs.cnn.com/2012/06/30/why-a-presidents-faith-may-not-matter/ (accessed August 10, 2014).

70. Not that you probably need references for this statement, but just in case . . . in no particular order: Helen Ellerbe, *The Dark Side of Christian History* (Orlando, FL: Morningstar & Lark, 1995); Jeff Sharlet, *The Family: The Secret Fundamentalism at the Heart of American Power* (New York: Harper, 2008); Mark Juergensmeyer, *Terror in the Mind of God: The Global Rise of Religious Violence* (Berkeley, CA: University of California Press, 2000); Hector Avalos, *Fighting Words: The Origins of Religious Violence* (Amherst, NY: Prometheus Books, 2005); Regina Schwartz, *The Curse of Cain: The Violent Legacy of Monotheism* (Chicago: The University of Chicago Press, 1997); Sam Harris, *Letter to*

a Christian Nation (New York: Knopf, 2006); Charles Selengut, *Sacred Fury: Understanding Religious Violence* (Berkeley, CA: Altamira Press, 2004); John Teehan, *In the Name of God: The Evolutionary Origins of Religious Ethics and Violence*, 5th ed. (New York: Wiley-Blackwell, 2010); Peter Jenkins, *Jesus Wars: How Four Patriarchs, Three Queens, and Two Emperors Decided What Christians Would Believe for the Next 1,500 years* (New York: HarperOne, 2011); Arthur Grenke, *God, Greed, and Genocide: The Holocaust through the Centuries* (Washington, DC: New Academia Publishing, 2005); Jack D. Eller, *Cruel Creeds, Virtuous Violence: Religious Violence across Culture and History* (Amherst, NY: Prometheus Books, 2010); and Mark J. Allman, *Who Would Jesus Kill?: War, Peace, and the Christian Tradition* (Winona, MN: Anselm Academic, 2008). I could go on and on, but this is a fair smattering of the sources I used on this particular issue in my research in case you need them. See the bibliography for more on this topic, due to the overlap in many sources.

71. While nobody expects the Spanish Inquisition . . . the first time . . . Christian nationalists still do not see such persecution in their aims. Most are unaware of this history, at any rate, and ethnocentrism and nationalism would render warnings moot.

I gave a lot of thought to including a discussion of religious nationalism in the context of the Holocaust but opted not to since it is such a charged topic and seems so over the top (and overused in the negative), but it is the focus of much revisionist history on the religious right. In case you were not aware of this, Darwin is the cause of the Holocaust, not anti-Semitism, and several intelligent-design (AKA creationism) textbooks cite this example of the evils of natural selection. Fleshing out the role of eugenics, Darwinism, and religion is too far astray from my task here, but see Robert J. Richards, *Was Hitler a Darwinian? Disputed Questions in the History of Evolutionary Theory* (Chicago, IL: University of Chicago Press, 2013); and Richard A. Koenigsberg, *Nations Have the Right to Kill: Hitler, the Holocaust and War* (New York: Library of Social Science, 2009).

72. Carl F. H. Henry, *The Uneasy Conscience of Modern Fundamentalism* (Grand Rapids, MI: William B. Eerdmans Publishing, 2003).

73. For a thoughtful discussion about the tensions in "coming out" as an atheist or agnostic, see Richard Dawkins, *The God Delusion* (New York: Houghton Mifflin, 2006).

74. Pew Forum on Religion & Public Life, "U.S. Religious Landscape Survey, 2012," *Pew Research Center*, 2013, http://religions.pewforum.org/reports (accessed April 6, 2014).

75. Pew Forum on Religion & Public Life, "Not All Nonbelievers Call Themselves Atheists," *Pew Research Center*, April 2, 2009, http://www.pewforum.org/2009/04/02/not-all-nonbelievers-call-themselves-atheists/ (accessed January 9, 2014).

76. Pew Forum on Religion & Public Life, "Who Knows What about Religion," *Pew Research Center,* September 28, 2010. http://www.pewforum.org/2010/09/28/u-s-religious-knowledge-survey-who-knows-what-about-religion/ (accessed October 5, 2015).

77. Dave Silverman, "It's No Surprise that Atheists Know More about Religion than Most Americans," *Fox News*, September 28, 2010, http://www.foxnews.com/opinion/2010/09/28/dave-silverman-pew-survey-atheists-Bible-preacher-god-islam-holy-american.html (accessed May 14, 2014).

78. See also Stan L. Albrecht and Tim B. Heaton, "Secularization, Higher Education, and Religiosity," *Review of Religious Research* 26 (1984): 43–58.

79. Gen. 2:16–17 (NIV): "And the Lord God commanded the man, 'You are free to eat from any tree in the garden; but you must not eat from the tree of the knowledge of good and evil, for when you eat from it you will certainly die.'"

CHAPTER THREE: WHY PICK ON CHRISTIAN NATIONALISTS?

1. Colin J. Baier and Bradley R. E. Wright, "'If You Love Me, Keep My Commandments': A Meta-Analysis of the Effect of Religion on Crime," *Journal of Research in Crime and Delinquency* 38 (2001): 3–21.

2. Edward M. Adlaf and Reginald G. Smart, "Drug Use and Religious Affiliation, Feelings and Behavior," *British Journal of Addiction* 80 (1985): 163–171; Acheampong Y. Amoeteng and Stephen J. Bahr, "Religion, Family, and Adolescent Drug Use," *Sociological Perspectives* 29 (1986): 53–76; Stephen J. Bahr and John P. Hoffman, "Religiosity, Peers, and Adolescent Drug Use," *Journal of Drug Issues* 38 (2008): 743–70; Brent B. Benda, "The Effect of Religion on Adolescent Delinquency Revisited," *Journal of Research in Crime and Delinquency* 32 (1995): 446–65; Brent B. Benda and Robert F. Corwyn, "Religion and Delinquency: The Relationship after Considering Family and Peer Influences," *Journal for the Scientific Study of Religion* 36 (1997): 81–92; Brent B. Benda, Sandra K. Pope, and Kelly J. Kelleher, "Church Attendance and Religiosity: Their Relationship to Adolescents' Use of Alcohol, Other Drugs, and

Delinquency," *Alcoholism Treatment Quarterly* 24 (2006): 75–87; and Stephen K. Bliss and Cynthia L. Crown, "Concern for Appropriateness, Religiosity, and Gender as Predictors of Alcohol and Marijuana Use," *Social Behavior and Personality* 22 (1994): 227–38. For a near comprehensive list of this research, see the bibliography section. Overall, the results of all of this research are mixed.

3. The notion of patriotism I use in this underlying assumption is culled from ideals of loyal and responsible citizenship set out by the founders of our country. While this definition will differ somewhat from notions of patriotism in modern, popular discourse on the part of Christian nationalists, here again, I am not addressing this issue on Christian nationalists' terms.

4. Jeff Sharlet, "Through a Glass Darkly: How the Christian Right is Reimagining U.S. History," *Harper's* , December 2006, http://jeffsharlet.com/content/wp-content/uploads/2008/09/through_a_glass.pdf (accessed October 12, 2014).

5. The United States government spends more than $200 million annually on abstinence-only education; the results for these programs and virginity pledges are anything but encouraging, according to the bulk of research on the topic. They generally result in little, if any, change in the frequency of teen sex, but are strongly correlated with teens not taking precautions when they do have sex. See Pamela K. Kohler et al., "Abstinence-Only and Comprehensive Sex Education and the Initiation of Sexual Activity and Teen Pregnancy," *Journal of Adolescent Health* 42 (2008): 344–51; Janet E. Rosenbaum, "Patient Teenagers? A Comparison of the Sexual Behavior of Virginity Pledgers and Matched Nonpledgers," *Pediatrics* 123 (2009): e110–e120; Janet E. Rosenbaum, "Reborn a Virgin: Adolescents' Retracting of Virginity Pledges and Sexual Histories," *American Journal of Public Health* 96 (2006): 1098–1103; and John Santelli et al., "Abstinence-Only Education Policies and Programs: A Position Paper of the Society for Adolescent Medicine," *Journal of Adolescent Health* 38 (2006): 83–87.

6. "Therefore go and make disciples of all nations, baptizing them in the name of the Father and of the Son and of the Holy Spirit" (Matt. 28:19, NIV). There are too many passages related to this issue to list here, but suffice it to say that there is a definite edict to bring Christianity to others and to acknowledge that one is a Christian. The semantics of many of these passages are interesting, in that Christians are to avoid being prideful with respect to their faith but face consequences if they are ashamed of their faith in God (see, for example, Mark 8:38, "If anyone is ashamed of me and my words in this adulterous and sinful generation, the Son of Man will be ashamed of them when he comes in his Father's

glory with the holy angels" [NIV]). It is a tough line to walk for the average person, in fairness to those trying to walk it—and it is understandable that many err on the side of pride rather than have their belief called into question.

7. Such as denoting that they must show agreement with seven out of ten tenets, or in specifying what level of agreement is required (e.g. "strongly agree" versus "agree" or "somewhat agree" on a Likert scale). Such distinctions are necessarily arbitrary and better made by researchers informed by their findings. Suffice it to say that I believe any level of agreement with even three of these tenets will likely provide a reliable sample of Christian nationalists, though I suspect they will score far higher. There are existing measures of fundamentalism that might also be doctored to capture nationalistic components, and those components will be discussed later. See, for example, Bob Altemeyer and Bruce Hunsberger, "A Revised Religious Fundamentalism Scale: The Short and Sweet of It," *International Journal for the Psychology of Religion* 14 (2004): 47–54.

8. Though they give ample lip service to Jesus's love and forgiveness, it is generally in the context of believers and potential believers.

9. Jill Lepore, *The Whites of Their Eyes: The Tea Party's Revolution and the Battle over American History* (Princeton: Princeton University Press, 2010).

10. Gal. 6:7–8 (NIV): "Do not be deceived: God cannot be mocked. A man reaps what he sows. Whoever sows to please their flesh, from the flesh will reap destruction; whoever sows to please the Spirit, from the Spirit will reap eternal life."

11. See, for example, Albert Bandura, Bill Underwood, and Michael E. Fromson. "Disinhibition of Aggression through Diffusion of Responsibility and Dehumanization of Victims," *Journal of Research in Personality* 9 (1975): 253–69.

12. Sheldon Solomon, Jeff Greenberg, and Tom Pyszczynski are largely responsible for bringing this phenomenon to light, and authoring terror-management theory. It is based on the work of Earnest Becker and defines the mechanisms by which aggression, and even violence, are more likely to result in the wake of mortality reminders. Their work is fascinating and has been supported by much research on the topic, conducted by themselves and others. I am deeply indebted to their work: Earnest Becker, *The Denial of Death* (New York: Free Press, 1973); Abram Rosenblatt et al., "Evidence For Terror Management Theory: I. The Effects of Mortality Salience on Reactions to Those Who Violate or Uphold Cultural Values," *Journal of Personality and Social Psychology* 57 (1989): 681–90; Abram Rosenblatt et al., "Evidence for Terror Management Theory: II. The Effects

of Mortality Salience on Reactions to Those Who Threaten or Bolster the Cultural Worldview," *Journal of Personality and Social Psychology* 58 (1990): 308–18; Tom Pyszczynski, Sheldon Solomon, and Jeff Greenberg, *In the Wake of 9/11: The Psychology of Terror* (Washington DC: American Psychological Association, 2002); Jeff Greenberg, Tom Pyszczynski, and Sheldon Solomon. "The Causes and Consequences of a Need for Self-Esteem: A Terror Management Theory," in *Public Self and Private Self*, ed. Roy F. Baumeister, 189–212 (New York: Springer-Verlag, 1986); Abram Rosenblatt et al., "Evidence for Terror Management Theory: II. The Effects of Mortality Salience on Reactions to Those Who Threaten or Bolster the Cultural Worldview," *Journal of Personality and Social Psychology* 58 (1990): 308–18; Sheldon Soloman, Jeff Greenberg, and Tom Pyszczynski, "The Terror Management Theory of Social Behavior: Psychological Functions of Self Esteem and Cultural Worldviews," *Advances in Experimental Social Psychology* 24 (1991): 93–116; Victor Florian and Mario Mikulincer, "Fear of Death and the Judgment of Social Transgressions: A Multidimensional Test of Terror Management Theory," *Journal of Personality and Social Psychology* 73 (1997): 369–80; Eva Jonas and Peter Fischer, "Terror Management and Religion: Evidence that Intrinsic Religiousness Mitigates Worldview Defense Following Mortality Salience," *Journal of Personality and Social Psychology* 91 (2006): 553–67; Jamie L. Goldenberg et al., "Fleeing the Body: A Terror Management Perspective on the Problem of Human Corporeality," *Personality & Social Psychology Review* 4 (2000): 200–18; Jeff Greenberg et al., "Assessing the Terror Management Analysis of Self-Esteem: Converging Evidence of an Anxiety-Buffering Function," *Journal of Personality and Social Psychology* 63 (1992): 913–22; Jeff Greenberg, Sheldon Solomon, and Tom Pyszczynski, "Terror Management Theory of Self-Esteem and Cultural Worldviews: Empirical Assessments and Conceptual Refinements," in *Advances in Experimental Social Psychology*, ed. Mark Zanna (San Diego: Academic Press, 1997), 61–139; Jeff Greenberg et al., "Terror Management and Tolerance: Does Mortality Salience Always Intensify Negative Reactions to Others Who Threaten One's Worldview?" *Journal of Personality and Social Psychology* 63 (1992): 212–20; Jeff Greenberg et al., "Evidence of a Terror Management Function of Cultural Icons: The Effects of Mortality Salience on the Inappropriate Use of Cherished Cultural Symbols," *Personality and Social Psychology Bulletin* 21 (1995): 1221–28; and Tom Pyszczynski, Jeff Greenberg, and Sheldon Solomon, "A Dual-Process Model of Defense against Conscious and Unconscious Death-Related Thoughts: An Extension of Terror Management Theory," *Psychological Review* 106 (2007): 835–45.

13. For nonacademics, in lieu of reading hundreds of research articles on this topic, I highly recommend a brilliant documentary on the subject called *Flight from Death: The Quest for Immortality* (2006). Gabriel Byrne narrates this award-winning film, which will give you a pretty thorough understanding of the basics of this phenomenon.

14. Marsha L. Vanderford, "Vilifications and Social Movements: A Case Study of Pro-Life and Pro-Choice Rhetoric," *Quarterly Journal of Speech* 25 (1989): 166–82; Sharon Crowley, *Toward a Civil Discourse: Rhetoric and Fundamentalism* (Pittsburgh: University of Pittsburgh Press, 2006); Christopher B. Chapp, *Religious Rhetoric and American Politics: The Endurance of Civil Religion in Electoral Campaigns* (Ithaca, NY: Cornell University Press, 2012); and James Hitchcock, "The Enemies of Religious Liberty," *First Things* 140 (2004): 26–29.

15. James Robison, "The Enemy's Plan," *James Robison, A Weekly Commentary*, July 22, 2011, http://jamesrobison.net/?q=node/90 (accessed May 27, 2012).

16. Edwin Lemert, *Human Deviance, Social Problems and Social Control* (Englewood Cliffs, NJ: Prentice Hall, 1969); and Howard S. Becker, *Outsiders: Studies in the Sociology of Deviance* (New York: Free Press, 1963).

17. See the classic by Erving Goffman, *The Presentation of Self in Everyday Life* (New York: Anchor, 1959); Kathleen A. Ethier and Kay Deaux, "Negotiating Social Identity when Contexts Change: Maintaining Identification and Responding to Threat," *Journal of Personality and Social Psychology* 67 (1994): 243–51; Leonie Huddy, "From Social to Political Identity: A Critical Examination of Social Identity Theory," *Political Psychology* 22 (2001): 127–56; Marilynn B. Brewer and Joseph G. Weber, "Self-Evaluation Effects of Interpersonal versus Intergroup Social Comparison," *Journal of Personality and Social Psychology* 66 (1994): 268–75; Marilynn B. Brewer, "Social Identity, Distinctiveness, and In-Group Homogeneity," *Social Cognition*, 11 (1993): 150–64; Kay Deaux et al., "Parameters of Social Identity," *Journal of Personality and Social Psychology* 68 (1995): 280–91; Annette R. Flippen et al., "A Comparison of Similarity and Interdependence as Triggers for In-Group Formation," *Personality and Social Psychology Bulletin* 22 (1996): 882–93; Michael A. Hogg and Sarah C. Hains, "Intergroup Relations and Group Solidarity: Effects of Group Identification and Social Beliefs on Depersonalized Attraction," *Journal of Personality and Social Psychology* 70 (1996): 295–309; Michael A. Hogg and John C. Turner, "Interpersonal Attraction, Social Identification, and Psychological Group Formation," *European Journal of*

Social Psychology 15 (1985): 51–66; Linda A. Jackson et al., "Achieving Positive Social Identity: Social Mobility, Social Creativity, and Permeability of Group Boundaries," *Journal of Personality and Social Psychology* 70 (1996): 241–54; Amélie Mummendey et al., "Strategies to Cope with Negative Social Identity: Predictions by Social Identity Theory and Relative Deprivation Theory," *Journal of Personality and Social Psychology* 76 (1999): 229–45; Amélie Mummendey and Hans-Joachim Schreiber, "'Different' Just Means 'Better': Some Obvious and Some Hidden Pathways to In-Group Favouritism," *British Journal of Social Psychology* 23 (1984): 363–68; and Stéphane Perreault and Richard Y. Bourhis, "Ethnocentrism, Social Identification, and Discrimination," *Personality and Social Psychology Bulletin* 25 (1999): 92–103.

18. Lauren Markoe, "My Country 'Tis of Thee: Evangelicals Score Highest on Patriotism," Religion News Service, June 27, 2013, http://www.religionnews .com/2013/06/27/some-religious-groups-wave-the-flag-more-than-others/ (accessed March 13, 2014). Sample of 1,007 adults with a margin of error of ±3.1 percent.

19. Ibid.

20. Ibid.

21. Jim Sidanius et al., "Support for Harsh Criminal Sanctions and Criminal Justice Beliefs: A Social Dominance Perspective," *Social Justice Research* 19 (2006): 433–49.

22. Christopher D. Bader et al., "Divine Justice: The Relationship between Images of God and Attitudes toward Criminal Punishment," *Criminal Justice Review* 35 (2010): 90–106. Bader and his colleagues found that "angry and judgmental images of God are significant predictors of punitive attitudes regarding criminal punishment and the death penalty" (90).

23. Though there does seem to be one exception in this research—Mears found that conservative Protestantism did not have a statistically significant effect on support for punishing juvenile offenders more harshly. See Daniel P. Mears, "Getting Tough with Juvenile Offenders: Explaining Support for Sanctioning Youths as Adults." *Criminal Justice and Behavior* 28 (2001): 206–26. For a general discussion, see Neil Vidmar and Dale T. Miller, "Social Psychological Processes Underlying Attitudes toward Legal Punishment," *Law & Society Review* 14 (1980): 565–602.

24. See also Timothy R. Johnson and Andrew D. Martin, "The Public's Conditional Response to Supreme Court Decisions," *American Political Science Review* 92 (1998): 300–309. This research highlights the impact of Supreme Court decisions on public opinion, regardless of the issue.

25. See James O. Finckenauer, "Public Support for the Death Penalty: Retribution as Just Deserts or Retribution as Revenge," *Justice Quarterly* 5 (1988): 81–100. The consensus in the research is not surprising in light of Republican politics: conservative people are generally more punitive, perhaps in part because they are more prone to disgust.

While many people believe that fear of crime and a history of victimization lead to support for harsh punishments, criminologists find limited support for this relationship. See D. Garth Taylor, Kim L. Scheppele, and Arthur L. Stinchcombe, "Salience of Crime and Support for Harsher Criminal Sanctions," *Theory and Evidence in Criminology: Correlations and Contradictions* 26 (1979): 413–24; and Rick Seltzer and Joseph P. McCormick, "The Impact of Crime Victimization and Fear of Crime on Attitudes toward Death Penalty Defendants," *Violence & Victims* 2 (1987): 99–114.

26. Robert Martinson, "What Works?—Questions and Answers about Prison Reform," *Public Interest* 35 (1974): 22–54. ". . . with few and isolated exceptions, the rehabilitative efforts that have been reported so far have had no appreciable effect on recidivism" (25).

27. This is found in Exod. 21:24, Lev. 24:20, and again in Deut. 19:21 (and reiterated in Matt. 5:38). Additional Old Testament verses related to punishing murderers include Prov. 28:17, Exod. 20:13, and Num. 35:16–27, among others.

28. Prov. 24:25 and 20:26, respectively. See also Rom. 13:4 (NIV): "For the one in authority is God's servant for your good. But if you do wrong, be afraid, for rulers do not bear the sword for no reason. They are God's servants, agents of wrath to bring punishment on the wrongdoer."

29. Pew Research Center. "Continued Majority Support for Death Penalty," *Pew Research Center*, 2012. http://www.people-press.org/2012/01/06/continued -majority-support-for-death-penalty/ (accessed May 23, 2014).

30. Jean Hardisty. "Crime and Political Ideology," *Public Eye*, 2012, http:// www.publiceye.org/magazine/v18n3/hardisty_crime.html (accessed May 10, 2014).

31. International Centre for Prison Studies, "Prison Brief—Highest to Lowest Rates," *World Prison Brief* (London: King's College London School of Law, 2010), http://www.kcl.ac.uk/depsta/law/research/icps/worldbrief/wpb_stats .php?area=all&category=wb_poprate (accessed February 2013).

32. Ibid.

33. The resolution was adopted by an overwhelming majority: 104 UN member countries supported it, 54 opposed it (including the United States), with 29 abstentions.

34. Again, a quick look at the company we are keeping should give us pause: China, Iran, Pakistan, and Saudi Arabia share this top-five distinction with the United States.

35. For more information concerning international application of the death penalty, see Amnesty International, http://www.amnesty.org/en/death-penalty/international-law (accessed March 11, 2013).

36. Frank Newport, "In U.S., Support for Death Penalty Falls to 39-Year Low," *Gallup*, 2011, http://www.gallup.com/poll/150089/support-death-penalty-falls-year-low.aspx (accessed June 5, 2014). For a look at who ends up on death row, see also: John H. Blume, Theodore Eisenberg, and Martin T. Wells, "Explaining Death Row's Population and Racial Composition," *Journal of Empirical Legal Studies* 1 (2004): 165–207; Matthew B. Robinson, *Death Nation: The Experts Explain American Capital Punishment* (Upper Saddle River, NJ: Prentice Hall, 2007). Spoiler alert: This additional information does not make us look better.

37. Stephen Pinker, *The Better Angels of Our Nature: Why Violence Has Declined* (New York: Viking Press, 2011).

38. I am not going to present a ranking, as there are so many statistical pitfalls in doing so that it would be impossible to avoid criticism on a number of legitimate fronts, such as varying legal definitions for crimes in different countries and differences in reporting. Even issues such as the quality of medical care greatly impact the number of homicide victims in various countries, as it does in different regions and even neighborhoods in the United States. While it is something people do not give a lot of thought, the proximity and quality of medical care can easily mean the difference between an assault and a homicide. This is another factor that places us in an unflattering light with respect to our higher homicide rate; as compared to many countries ranking higher, we have better medical facilities and still boast higher rates of homicide.

39. You can assess this characterization for yourself through a variety of sources, such as the FBI and Department of Justice's Uniform Crime Reports (see, for example, "Crime in the United States by Volume and Rate per 100,000 Inhabitants, 1991–2010"). The United Nations' Survey of Crime Trends and Operations of Criminal Justice Systems is useful, as well. Take care that the data you employ for comparison is reported as a rate before you pack up and move to another country.

40. Michelle Goldberg, *Kingdom Coming: The Rise of Christian Nationalism* (New York: Norton, 2007).

41. The infamous Westboro Baptist Church might serve as an example of

a church enthusiastically and publicly adhering to many of the darker passages in the Bible at the expense of the entire New Testament. They are not wrong in many of their assertions from a biblical standpoint but embarrass even Christian nationalists in their unflinching and impolitic application of those beliefs.

42. Scott Shieman, "Socioeconomic Status and Beliefs about God's Influence in Everyday Life," *Sociology of Religion* 71 (2010): 25–51; and Stan L. Albrecht and Tim B. Heaton, "Secularization, Higher Education, and Religiosity," *Review of Religious Research* 26 (1984): 43–58. See also Pew Forum on Religion & Public Life, *Income Distribution within U.S. Religious Groups*, 2009, http://www. pewforum.org/Income-Distribution-Within-US-Religious-Groups.aspx (accessed April 6, 2014).

43. See also John E. Farley, *Majority-Minority Relations* (Upper Saddle River, NJ: Prentice Hall, 2010) for an overview of factors related to prejudice.

44. For more on social class and prejudices, see Bernard F. Whitley and Mary E. Kite, *The Psychology of Prejudice and Discrimination* (South Melbourne, Australia: Cengage Learning, 2010); Matthew Weeks and Michael B. Lupfer, "Complicating Race: The Relationship between Prejudice, Race, and Social Class Categorizations," *Personality and Social Psychology Bulletin* 30 (2004): 972–84; Thomas J. Pavlak, "Social Class, Ethnicity, and Racial Prejudice," *Public Opinion Quarterly* 37 (1973): 225–31; Naomi Struch and Shalom H. Schwartz, "Intergroup Aggression: Its Predictors and Distinctness from In-Group Bias," *Journal of Personality and Social Psychology* 56 (1989): 364–73; Charles M. Judd and Bernadette Park. "Out-Group Homogeneity: Judgments of Variability at the Individual and Group Levels," *Journal of Personality and Social Psychology* 54 (1988): 778–88; Marilynn B. Brewer, "Social Identity, Distinctiveness, and In-Group Homogeneity," *Social Cognition* 11 (1993): 150–64; Nilanjana Dasgupta, David DeSteno, and Matthew Hunsinger. "Fanning the Flames of Prejudice: The Influence of Specific Incidental Emotions on Implicit Prejudice," *American Psychological Association* 9 (2009): 585–91; and Brian Laythe et al., "Religious Fundamentalism as a Predictor of Prejudice: A Two-Component Model," *Journal for the Scientific Study of Religion* 41 (2002): 623–35.

45. Former French President Charles de Gaulle, as quoted in *Life* magazine, March 27, 1964.

46. For a discussion, see Kimberly D. Dodson, Leann N. Cabage, and Paul M. Klenowoski, "An Evidence Based Assessment of Faith-Based Programs: Do Faith-Based Programs 'Work' to Reduce Recidivism?" *Journal of Offender Rehabilitation* 50 (2011): 367–83. See also Laura Meckler, "U.S. Gave $1 Billion

in Faith-Based Funds," Associated Press, January 3, 2005, http://www.truth-out.
org/archive/component/k2/item/51552:ap-us-gave-1b-in-faithbased-funds
(accessed November 16, 2014).

47. See, for example, the Office of Juvenile Justice and Delinquency
Prevention's (OJJDP) faith-based and community initiatives page, http://www
.ojjdp.gov/fbci/programs.html (accessed March 14, 2013); the National Institute
of Justice's (NIJ) faith-based resources, https://www.ncjrs.gov/faithbased/
publications.html (accessed March 15, 2013); and the United States Department
of Justice's (DOJ) task force for faith-based and community initiative, http://
www.cops.usdoj.gov/Publications/Making_The_Match.pdf (accessed March 15,
2013), whose mission statement is: "The Task Force provides assistance to faith-
and community-based organizations in identifying funding opportunities within
the Federal government for which they are eligible to apply. The DOJ administers
programs to provide assistance to victims of crime, prisoners and ex-offenders,
and women who suffer domestic violence. In addition, the DOJ has initiatives
to target gang violence and at-risk youth" (http://www.justice.gov/archive/fbci/
index.html [accessed March 14, 2013]). The problem is that pressure has led these
agencies to realize that it is good PR to actively solicit proposals from faith-based
organizations, while it is risky business to fund programs that might be viewed as
"controversial" to these same groups.

48. NIV—You can, of course, easily see this respect in the Christian right's
treatment of President Obama.

49. Using abortion clinic violence as an example, from 1974 until 2012,
there have been at least eight murders, 17 attempted murders, 42 bombings, 181
acts of arson, 100 Butyric acid attacks, 198 assault and battery cases, and 428
death threats in the US, according to the National Abortion Federation violence
statistics. Not to mention kidnappings, burglaries, stalking, bioterrorism threats,
vandalism, invasions, trespassing. . . . The authority of secular law holds little
sway here. National Abortion Federation, https://www.prochoice.org/about_
abortion/violence/documents/Stats_Table_2013.pdf (accessed October 1, 2012).

50. Though this topic will be addressed further, if you are especially interested,
the damaging impact of dogmatism in public and private life are explored in
an excellent book on the topic, Judy J. Johnson, *What's So Wrong With Being
Absolutely Right: The Dangerous Nature of Dogmatic Beliefs* (Amherst, NY:
Prometheus Books, 2009). See also Al Gore, *The Assault on Reason* (New York:
Penguin Books, 2007). And speaking of assaults on reason, Al Gore never claimed
to have invented the internet or the Love Canal, and he did not lie in his comment

about *Love Story* having been reported in a Tennessee newspaper as being based on his and Tipper's relationship. This is a great example of the kind of shock and awe journalism promoted by the right-wing. See Scott Rosenberg, "Did Gore Invent the Internet?" *Salon*, October 5, 2000, http://www.salon.com/2000/10/05/gore_internet/ (accessed December 13, 2013). See also Evgenia Peretz, "Going After Gore," *Vanity Fair*, October, 14, 2007, http://www.vanityfair.com/politics/features/2007/10/gore200710 (accessed March 10, 2013). I digress, but it is such a good example of where the bar falls with respect to public information that I just had to include it. I will bet my house that there is a strong correlation between people who believe these stories and those still believing we found weapons of mass destruction in Saddam's panty drawer. Check out Jonathan Haidt, *The Righteous Mind: Why Good People Are Divided by Politics and Religion* (New York: Pantheon, 2012) while you're at it.

51. Most notably, marriage rights, which had been granted in thirty-seven states and the District of Columbia prior to the Supreme Court decision in *Obergefell v. Hodges* on June 26, 2015.

CHAPTER FOUR: A THEORY OF VIOLENT RELIGIOSITY

1. Richard Schickel, "Clint Eastwood on 'Baby,'" *Time*, February 20, 2005 (prior to his chat with the chair).

2. If you are not a criminologist, you can easily skip the last section of the chapter and purchase Ambien instead.

3. In a rather obvious deflection of skepticism on this count, church leaders often defend the integrity of the Jesus story against the existence of parallel myths by explaining that the devil planted this early history in order to test the faith of Christians. And no, I am not making that up to be funny.

4. There are a number of good books about the original sources for biblical stories, and Christ in particular. See Kersey Graves, *The World's Sixteen Crucified Saviors* (New York: Cosimo Classics, 1875); and John G. Jackson, *Christianity Before Christ* (Parsippany, NJ: American Atheist Press, 2002).

5. This is thought to be the basis for the resurrection story, in which the Son (sun) dies for three days and then is resurrected, literally bringing light to the world.

6. With good reason, in fairness—if you want to believe in Christianity, my advice is to steer clear of my entire reference section, as well as the Bible.

7. Mark 3:29 (NIV): "But whoever blasphemes against the Holy Spirit will never be forgiven; he is guilty of an eternal sin"; Luke 12:9–10 (NIV): "But he who disowns me before men will be disowned before the angels of God. And everyone who speaks a word against the Son of Man will be forgiven, but anyone who blasphemes against the Holy Spirit will not be forgiven."

8. In case you do not know exactly what smiting someone means . . . it refers to striking someone down, injuring or slaying them. In the Bible, the references almost exclusively refer to cases of lethal smiting.

9. There were too many punishments to hope to create a complete list, so these should be viewed as a representative sample. Moreover, since I do not wish to write the longest footnote in history, I will not list every verse in which some of these violent punishments, such as death or being thrown into a lake of fire, are mentioned. These punishments are found in the following passages and many others: Gen. 2:17; Exod. 21:20–21; Exod. 32:27; Num. 25:4; Num. 31:15–18; Deut. 21:11–14; Deut. 21:18–21; Judg. 19:25; 2 Sam. 4:12; 2 Kings 15:16; Ezek. 18:4; Ezek. 24: 9–10; Ps. 68:21; Ps. 89:23; Ps. 137: 9; Ps. 145:20; Isa. 13:9, 15, 16; Mal. 2:3; Matt. 18:9; Matt. 25:41; Rom. 1:32; Rom. 5:12; Rom. 6:23; 2 Cor. 7:10; 2 Thess. 1:9; James 1:15; Rev. 20:10; and Rev. 20:14–15.

10. Rom. 12:19 (KJV).

11. Lev. 19:19: "Keep my decrees. Do not mate different kinds of animals. Do not plant your field with two kinds of seed. Do not wear clothing woven of two kinds of material" (NIV).

12. Donald Black, "Crime as Social Control," *American Sociological Review* 48 (1983): 34–45.

13. English Standard Version.

14. Black, "Crime as Social Control."

15. This also occurs in the context of nonviolent crime, as anyone who has ever "egged" the house of an enemy knows. People steal from, spread rumors about, and vandalize the property of people they see as having wronged them. For this reason, if you own a business, it is a good idea to treat your employees well, as stealing is a common way of responding to managerial affronts.

16. Lynn A. Curtis, "Victim Precipitation and Violent Crime," *Social Problems* 21 (1974): 594–612; and Doug A. Timmer and William H. Norman, "The Ideology of Victim Precipitation," *Criminal Justice Review* 9 (1984): 63–68.

17. If you are a non-criminologist reading this book, you read that right: Men are at greater risk for victimization than women. This only seems counterintuitive because women are taught to be especially fearful of victimization due to their

relative size and strength, while men rarely concern themselves with fears about crime victimization. The reasons for men's greater risk are complicated, but while our protective attitude toward women and the care women take to avoid being victimized certainly come into play in that explanation, this is far from the whole story. Suffice it to say that we should be worrying about our sons far more than we do relative to our daughters.

18. We have Marcus Felson to thank for this simple and elegant model, which holds that in order for a crime to occur there must be a motivated offender, a suitable target, and the absence of capable guardianship. If you want to understand the reality of crime more than anyone on your block, I highly recommend Marcus Felson and Rachel Boba, *Crime & Everyday Life* (Thousand Oaks, CA: Sage, 2009).

19. See, for example, Richard E. Nisbitt and Dov Cohen, *Culture of Honor: The Psychology of Violence in the South* (Boulder, CO: Westview, 1996).

20. Obviously, I am not referring to the consequences, which can be awful, of course. I simply mean that they often involve somewhat petty squabbling gone bad. The lethal resolution rarely seems logical in light of the trivial nature of the initial affront unless it is viewed through the lens of honor or, as I am suggesting, the concept of punishment.

21. See Dan. 12:2, 3; Matt. 25:46, 13:41, 50; John 5:28; and Rev. 20:11–15, 21:8. It is interesting that this tenet is so central and frequently discussed that it no longer even occurs to us that it is violent to burn people alive for failing to believe in Jesus Christ as the Son of God. Note, too, that this is the cuddly New Testament we are talking about here.

22. See Matt. 13:50 for the furnace and weeping and gnashing of teeth and Rev. 14:11 for getting no rest. For other noteworthy descriptions of hell, see Mark 9:48 and Rev. 14:10, 20:14–15.

23. Rom. 2:11 (God is just) and Rom. 1:18, 21, 25 (it is a choice). Incidentally, even people who have not heard of Jesus are held accountable because God is revealed in nature and seeks those who seek him. See Rom. 1:20, Matt. 7:7, and Luke 19:10.

24. The second death refers to hell.

25. Randa Morris, "War on Christianity? FBI Hate Crime Statistics Utterly Destroy FOX News Lies," *Addicting Info*, February 20. 2015, http://www .addictinginfo.org/2015/02/20/war-on-christianity-fbi-hate-crime-statistics-utterly -destroy-fox-news-lies/ (accessed October 25, 2015). This article offers an illuminating rebuke to the claim that this "war" exists, using FBI statistics (and the statistics are correct).

26. Federal Bureau of Investigation, "Latest Hate Crime Statistics Report Released: Publication Includes New Data Collected Under Shepard/Byrd Act," December 8, 2014, https://www.fbi.gov/news/stories/2014/December/latest-hate -crime-statistics-report-released (accessed October 25, 2015).

27. John McKiggan, "Supreme Court of Canada Rules on Hate Speech vs. Free Speech: Saskatchewan v. Whatcott," *Legal Examiner*, March 4, 2013, http://atlanticcanada.legalexaminer.com/miscellaneous/supreme-court-of-canada -rules-on-hate-speech-vs-free-speech-saskatchewan-human-rights-commission -v-whatcott/ (accessed October 25, 2015).

28. While Christian nationalists have repeatedly distanced themselves from this association, the Ku Klux Klan is a textbook example of the belief system.

29. See, for example, Gen. 9:16; Lev. 24:17; Exod. 20:13, 21:12; Rom. 12:19, 13:1–14; Num. 35:30–31; and Matt. 5:21.

30. Matt. 26:52.

31. John 8:11—This is not a call to all Christians explicitly in the text, but it is taken as such (and it makes perfect sense that it is taken as such).

32. The loss of clergy alone would be problematic.

33. For a solid overview, see Jonneke Bekkenkamp and Yvonne Sherwood, *Sanctified Aggression: Legacies of Biblical and Post-Biblical Vocabularies of Violence* (New York: T & T Clark, 2004).

34. I do not know if I adhere to this belief personally, in that it is impossible for us to know if other animals are aware of their own eventual demise, but that is the standard line on the matter. And regardless of whether other animals are aware of their impending death or not, human beings definitely are, which is all we need to know for my purposes here.

35. "But, as it is written, 'What no eye has seen, nor ear heard, nor the heart of man imagined, what God has prepared for those who love him . . .'" (ESV).

36. "For here we have no lasting city, but we seek the city that is to come." (ESV)

37. John 14:2 (ESV): "In my Father's house are many rooms. If it were not so, would I have told you that I go to prepare a place for you?"

38. Neuroscientific research has revealed that conservatives tend to have a larger amygdala, which is the fear and anxiety center in the brain. Conversely, liberals tend to have more gray matter—at least in the anterior cingulate cortex— the region of the brain that assists people in coping with complexity. See Ryota Kanai et al., "Political Orientations Are Correlated with Brain Structure in Young Adults," *Current Biology* 21 (2011): 677–80. See also Holly A. McGregor et al.,

"Terror Management and Aggression: Evidence that Mortality Salience Motivates Aggression against Worldview-Threatening Others," *Journal of Personality and Social Psychology* 74 (1998): 590–605.

39. Michael H. Crowson, "Are All Conservatives Alike? A Study of the Psychological Correlates of Cultural and Economic Conservatism," *Journal of Psychology: Interdisciplinary and Applied* 143 (2009): 449–63.

40. We will be looking at Bob Altemeyer's research on right-wing authoritarianism (RWA) later in this chapter, but this quote from Altemeyer about people who are strongly RWA—such as Christian nationalists—speaks eloquently to this fear: "High RWAs stand about ten steps closer to the panic button than the rest of the population. They see the world as a more dangerous place than most others do, with civilization on the verge of collapse and the world of Mad Max looming just beyond." Bob Altemeyer, *The Authoritarian Specter* (Cambridge, MA: Harvard University Press, 1996), 100.

41. Tom Pyszczynski, Sheldon Solomon, and Jeff Greenberg, *In the Wake of 9/11: The Psychology of Terror* (Washington DC: American Psychological Association, 2002); and Mark J. Landau et al., "A Function of Form: Terror Management and Structuring the Social World," *Journal of Personality & Social Psychology* 87 (2004): 190–210.

42. See, for example, Abram Rosenblatt et al., "Evidence For Terror Management Theory: I. The Effects of Mortality Salience on Reactions to Those Who Violate or Uphold Cultural Values," *Journal of Personality and Social Psychology* 57 (1989): 681–90; Jeff Greenberg, Tom Pyszczynski, and Sheldon Solomon. "The Causes and Consequences of a Need for Self-Esteem: A Terror Management Theory," in *Public Self and Private Self*, ed. Roy F. Baumeister, 189–212 (New York: Springer-Verlag, 1986); Victor Florian and Mario Mikulincer, "Fear of Death and the Judgment of Social Transgressions: A Multidimensional Test of Terror Management Theory," *Journal of Personality and Social Psychology* 73 (1997): 369–80; Jeff Greenberg et al., "Assessing the Terror Management Analysis of Self-Esteem: Converging Evidence of an Anxiety-Buffering Function," *Journal of Personality and Social Psychology* 63 (1992): 913–22; and Tom Pyszczynski, Jeff Greenberg, and Sheldon Solomon, "A Dual-Process Model of Defense against Conscious and Unconscious Death-Related Thoughts: An Extension of Terror Management Theory," *Psychological Review* 106 (2007): 835–45.

43. Abram Rosenblatt et al., "Evidence for Terror Management Theory: II. The Effects of Mortality Salience on Reactions to Those Who Threaten or Bolster

the Cultural Worldview," *Journal of Personality and Social Psychology* 58 (1990): 308–18.

44. Eva Jonas and Peter Fischer, "Terror Management and Religion: Evidence that Intrinsic Religiousness Mitigates Worldview Defense Following Mortality Salience," *Journal of Personality and Social Psychology* 91 (2006): 553–67.

45. Sheldon Solomon, Jeff Greenberg, and Tom Pyszczynski, "The Terror Management Theory of Social Behavior: Psychological Functions of Self Esteem and Cultural Worldviews," *Advances in Experimental Social Psychology* 24 (1991): 93–116.

46. Jamie Goldenberg et al., "Fleeing the Body: A Terror Management Perspective on the Problem of Human Corporeality," *Personality & Social Psychology Review* 4 (2000): 200–18.

47. Greenberg, Pyszczynski, and Solomon, "The Causes and Consequences of a Need for Self-Esteem."

48. Compare that with the rancorous, nearly constant stream of hateful speech directed at President Obama—also in a time of war. It must drive the Dixie Chicks to drink (with Al Gore and Howard Dean, no doubt).

49. Holly A. McGregor et al., "Terror Management and Aggression: Evidence that Mortality Salience Motivates Aggression against Worldview-Threatening Others," *Journal of Personality and Social Psychology* 74 (1998): 590–605.

50. Mark J. Landau et al. "Deliver Us from Evil: The Effects of Mortality Salience and Reminders of 9/11 on Support for President George W. Bush," *Personality and Social Psychology Bulletin* 30 (2004): 1136–50.

51. Ernest Becker, *The Birth and Death of Meaning* (New York: Free Press, 1962), 161. Not incidentally, Ernest Becker's insights serve as the philosophical basis for this theoretical camp. Specifically, his 1962 book, *The Birth and Death of Meaning*, 1973 book, *The Denial of Death*, and his 1975 book, *Escape from Evil*.

52. To Joe Biden. See Joe Klein, "Why the 'War President' is Under Fire," *Time*, February 15, 2004, http://content.time.com/time/nation/article/0,8599,591270,00.html (accessed April 23, 2014).

53. The closest thing I could decipher with respect to God's plan regarding weed would be Genesis 1:29: "Then God said, 'I give you every seed-bearing plant on the face of the whole earth and every tree that has fruit with seed in it. They will be yours for food'" (NIV).

54. Altemeyer, *Authoritarian Specter*. See also Theodor W. Adorno et al., *The Authoritarian Personality* (New York: Harper and Bros, 1950).

55. Robert Altemeyer, *The Authoritarians* (Bob Altemeyer, 2006), 9, http://

members.shaw.ca/jeanaltemeyer/drbob/TheAuthoritarians.pdf (accessed April 14, 2013).

56. Altemeyer only refers to religion—this and other references to religion have been adapted for Christian nationalism, though they did not take much modification.

57. They uncritically believe that the other person is saying what they really feel and ignore contextual evidence that the person is pandering to their belief system. This plays a large part in their trust for unscrupulous leaders.

58. Altemeyer uses the top 25 percent on these measures as the cut-off for this category.

59. If you would like to explore the RWA scale yourself, it is available at http://members.shaw.ca/jeanaltemeyer/drbob/TheAuthoritarians.pdf.

60. Bob Altemeyer, *Enemies of Freedom: Understanding Right-Wing Authoritarianism* (San Francisco: Jossey-Bass, 1988), 222–24.

61. If you are a younger reader, Willie Horton was serving a life sentence without possibility of parole for murder when he became the beneficiary of a weekend furlough program in Massachusetts. He skipped furlough and eventually committed a rape, armed robbery, and assault. George H. W. Bush ran with the incident, which occurred under Dukakis's initiative, and Lee Atwater, then Bush's campaign manager, famously said, "By the time we're finished, they're going to wonder whether Willie Horton is Dukakis's running mate." Willie Horton was black, and ads featuring a menacing Horton in a mug shot prompted Jesse Jackson (and others) to charge that the ads were racist, which Bush denied. The ads became an infamous example of race and fear baiting that was ultimately successful.

62. Ronald Weitzer, "Racialized Policing: Residents' Perceptions in Three Neighborhoods," *Law & Society Review* 34 (2000): 129–55; and Ronald Weitzer and Steven A. Tuch, "Perceptions of Racial Profiling: Race, Class and Personal Experience," *Criminology* 50 (2002): 435–56.

63. Jeffrey Fagan and Garth Davies, "Street Stops and Broken Windows: Terry, Race, and Disorder in New York City," *Fordham Urban Law Journal* 28 (2000): 457–504; Jeffrey Fagan and Garth Davies, "Policing Guns: Order Maintenance and Crime Control in New York," in *Guns, Crime, and Punishment in America*, ed. by Bernard E. Harcourt (New York: University Press, 2003), 857–953; Jeffrey Fagan, Franklin E. Zimring, and June Kim, "Declining Homicide in New York: A Tale of Two Trends," *Journal of Criminal Law and Criminology* 88 (1998): 1277–1324. Geoffrey P. Alpert, John M. MacDonald, and Roger G. Dunham, "Police Suspicion and Discretionary Decision Making During Citizen

Stops," *Criminology* 43 (2005): 407–34; Jon B. Gould and Stephen D. Mastrofski, "Suspect Searches: Assessing Police Behavior under the U.S. Constitution," *Criminology and Public Policy* 3 (2004): 315–61; Samuel R. Gross and Debra Livingston, "Racial Profiling Under Attack," *Columbia Law Review* 102 (2002): 1413–1438; and Bernard E. Harcourt, *Illusion of Order: The False Promise of Broken Windows Policing* (Cambridge: Harvard University Press, 2001).

64. Douglas Savitsky, "Is Plea Bargaining a Rational Choice? Plea Bargaining as an Engine of Racial Stratification and Overcrowding in the United States Prison System," *Rationality and Society* 24 (2012): 131–67.

65. Bureau of Prisons, "A Storied Past," http://www.bop.gov/about/history/ (accessed May 14, 2012).

66. Ibid. See also Lauren E. Glaze and Laura M. Maruschak, *Parents in Prison and Their Minor Children*, Bureau of Justice Special Report, 2010, http://www.bjs.gov/content/pub/pdf/pptmc.pdf (accessed August 1, 2013). Over 1.7 million children had a parent in prison in the United States in 2010.

67. For blistering and accurate discussions about the state of the prison system in the United States, see Jeffrey H. Reiman, *The Rich Get Richer and the Poor Get Prison: Ideology, Class, and Criminal Justice*, 7th ed. (Boston: Allyn & Bacon, 2005); and Jens Soering, *An Expensive Way to Make Bad People Worse: An Essay on Prison Reform from an Insider's Perspective* (Lebanon, PA: Lantern Books, 2004).

68. Solomon Moore, "Prison Spending Outpaces All but Medicaid," *New York Times*, March 2, 2009, http://www.nytimes.com/2009/03/03/us/03prison.html?_r=0 (accessed April 10, 2013); Vicky Palaez, "The Prison Industry in the United States: Big Business or a New Form of Slavery?" *Centre for Research on Globalization*, 2008, http://www.globalresearch.ca/the-prison-industry-in-the-united-states-big-business-or-a-new-form-of-slavery/8289 (accessed June 14, 2014); and John W. Whitehead, "Jailing Americans for Profit: The Rise of the Prison Industrial Complex," *Huffington Post*, April 10, 2012, http://www.huffingtonpost.com/john-w-whitehead/prison-privatization_b_1414467.html (accessed May 5, 2013).

69. In Britain, Roman Catholics emerge as the most punitive group when judging those outside of their faith. L. B. Brown, "Aggression and Denominational Membership," *British Journal of Social and Clinical Psychology* 4 (2011): 175–78.

70. Committing more criminal acts.

71. The death penalty is to criminologists what climate change is to those in the various hard sciences who address global warming. The research is

overwhelming, but people who do not know anything about it will still argue with you about it as though it is a matter of opinion rather than one of fact.

72. The other two position statements were to endorse the Equal Rights Amendment in 1978, and, in 2007, to oppose media use of Uniform Crime Report data to deem cities as "dangerous" or "safe" because it is statistically incorrect and irresponsible to use the data in such a manner.

73. Kelly Phillips Erb, "Death and Taxes: The Real Cost of the Death Penalty," *Forbes*, September 22, 2011, http://www.forbes.com/sites/kellyphillipserb/2011/09/22/death-and-taxes-the-real-cost-of-the-death-penalty/ (accessed June 9, 2013). See also "Saving Lives and Money: States Plagued by Fiscal Woes Rethink their Stance on the Death Penalty," *Economist*, March 12, 2009, http://www.economist.com/node/13279051 (accessed March 30, 2013).

74. Ibid.

75. People who need to be "saved"—though I hate this terminology. In any other religion, the term conversion would apply, and I find the idea of "saving" someone revoltingly self-congratulatory. The term makes evangelicals feel great about what essentially amounts to advertising for Christianity.

76. For a look at the preference for funding faith-based programs, see National Criminal Justice Reference Service, "Faith-Based Resources: Grants and Funding," *Office of Justice Programs*, https://www.ncjrs.gov/faithbased/funding.html (accessed October 8, 2015).

77. However, there is evidence that black Americans view themselves as less patriotic than others: Pew Research Center for the People & the Press, "The Generation Gap and the 2012 Election, Section 4: Views of the Nation," 2011, http://www.people-press.org/2011/11/03/section-4-views-of-the-nation/ (accessed January 3, 2014).

78. I predict that there is also an impact on violence against women, children, people of differing faiths, and LGBT people, and I realize that all of these predictions are complex and difficult to test. For example, women are victimized at a lower rate than men, which would seem to run counter to my hypothesis. But women engage in less risky behavior than men, are more closely regulated, and are less aggressive. As such, their rates of violent victimization should be lower. The question is how much lower, and how much of that violence is the result of this belief system.

79. Barry A. Kosmin and Ariela Keysar, with Ryan Cragun and Juhem Navarro-Rivera, *American Nones: The Profile of the No Religion Population; A Report based on the American Religious Identification Survey, 2008* (Hartford, CT:

Trinity College, 2009), http://www.hartfordinfo.org/issues/wsd/FaithCommunity/ NONES_08.pdf (accessed October 9, 2015).

80. Ibid. For additional insight into the shifting realms of American faith, see Barry A. Kosmin and Seymour P. Lachman, *One Nation under God: Religion in Contemporary American Society* (New York: Random House, 1993). It is difficult to make reliable estimates about the prevalence of atheism in the contemporary world, but it is important work.

81. Pippa Norris and Ronald Inglehart, *Sacred and Secular: Religion and Politics Worldwide* (Cambridge, UK: Cambridge University Press, 2004).

82. Phil Zuckerman, "Atheism: Contemporary Numbers and Patterns," in *The Cambridge Companion to Atheism*, ed. Michael Martin (Cambridge: Cambridge University Press, 2007), 248–69.

83. Stephen Pinker, *The Better Angels of Our Nature: Why Violence Has Declined* (New York: Viking Press, 2011).

84. Paradoxically, Americans tend to overestimate their personal risk for homicide victimization, in large part due to the constant deluge of media attention focused on the most frightening of crimes. An interesting feature of this belief is that—generally speaking—those who are most fearful of victimization tend to have lower rates of actual victimization.

85. Pinker, *Better Angels of Our Nature*, 91–92.

86. Franklin E. Zimring and Gordon Hawkins, *Crime Is Not the Problem: Lethal Violence in America* (New York: Oxford University Press, 1997). And yes, I said France. French people have lots of guns and are not nearly as liberal as many people on both the left and right seem to think. They just manage not to kill and wound one another with their guns at nearly the rate that we do in the United States, save the recent Charlie Hebdo massacre. For credible findings that cast serious doubts on the notion that guns are the problem, see Gary Kleck, *Point Blank: Guns and Violence in America* (Piscataway, NJ: Aldine Transaction, 2005).

87. Steven F. Messner and Richard Rosenfeld, *Crime and the American Dream*, 4th ed. (Belmont, CA: Thomson Wadsworth, 2007).

88. Marcus Felson, "Predatory and Dispute-Related Violence: A Social Interactionist Approach," in *Advances in Criminological Theory*, vol. 5, ed. Ronald V. Clark and Marcus Felson (New Brunswick, NJ: Transaction, 1993), 103–25; M. Dwayne Smith and Margaret A. Zahn, eds., *Homicide: A Sourcebook for Social Research* (Thousand Oaks, CA: Sage, 1998); Marvin E. Wolfgang, *Patterns in Criminal Homicide* (Philadelphia: University of Pennsylvania Press, 1958); and Zimring and Hawkins, *Crime Is Not the Problem*.

89. Chris Mooney, "Scientists Are Beginning to Figure Out Why Conservatives Are . . . Conservative," *Mother Jones*, July 15, 2014, http://www.motherjones.com/politics/2014/07/biology-ideology-john-hibbing-negativity-bias (accessed July 15, 2014).

90. John R. Nibbing, Kevin B. Smith, and John R. Alford, "Differences in Negativity Bias Underlie Variations in Political Ideology," *Behavioral and Brain Sciences* 37 (2014): 297–350.

91. John T. Jost et al., "Political Conservatism as Motivated Social Cognition," *Psychological Bulletin* 129 (2003): 339–75. Incidentally, Jost drew acrid criticism for this finding from the conservative press, and particularly from hacks such as Ann Coulter and George Wills. Congressional Republicans even investigated their research grants, and, apparently, they received a fair amount of hate mail. I mention this because it is another example of it being de rigueur for the Christian right to present themselves as persecuted for their beliefs and opinions, while being the ones to dish it out. Note, too, that Jost's work was a well-respected review of a whole body of research by many scientists, not a theory. Talk about killing the messenger.

92. Mooney, "Scientists Are Beginning to Figure Out Why Conservatives Are . . . Conservative"; and Hulda Thórisdóttir and John T. Jost, "Motivated Closed-Mindedness Mediates the Effect of Threat on Political Conservatism," *Political Psychology* 32 (2011): 785–811.

93. Unless it is not controversial and pro-religion. See, for example, Byron B. Johnson, *More God, Less Crime: Why Faith Matters and How It Could Matter More* (West Conshohocken, PA: Templeton Press, 2011); Byron B. Johnson, David B. Larson, and Timothy C. Pitts, "Religious Programming, Institutional Adjustment and Recidivism among Former Inmates in Prison Fellowship Programs," *Justice Quarterly* 14 (1997): 145–66; Byron B. Johnson et al., "Escaping from the Crime of Inner Cities: Church Attendance and Religious Salience among Disadvantaged Youth," *Justice Quarterly* 17 (2000): 377–91; Byron B. Johnson et al., "The 'Invisible Institution' and Black Youth Crime: The Church as an Agency of Local Social Control," *Journal of Youth and Adolescence* 29 (2000): 479–98; Byron B. Johnson et al., "Does Adolescent Religious Commitment Matter? A Re-Examination of the Effects of Religiosity on Delinquency," *Journal of Research in Crime and Delinquency* 38 (2001): 22–44; Edward Adlaf and Reginald G. Smart, "Drug Use and Religious Affiliation, Feelings and Behavior," *British Journal of Addiction* 80 (1985): 163–71; Sung J. Jang and Byron R. Johnson. "Neighborhood Disorder, Individual Religiosity, and Adolescent Use of Illicit Drugs: A Test of Multilevel

Hypotheses," *Criminology* 39 (2001): 109–44; and Sung J. Jang, Christopher D. Bader, and Byron R. Johnson, "The Cumulative Advantage of Religiosity in Preventing Drug Abuse," *Journal of Drug Issues* 38 (2010): 771–98.

94. Such as the Heritage Foundation. American Enterprise Institute (AEI) president Arthur C. Brooks wrote the forward for Byron R. Johnson's book, *More God, Less Crime*. Conservative and Christian organizations front money for research showing the effectiveness of faith-based initiatives, then use those findings to lend credibility to garner funding for more faith-based initiatives.

CHAPTER FIVE: THE BIBLE, CAFETERIA STYLE

1. Raymond Ibrahim, "Are Judaism and Christianity as Violent as Islam?" *Middle East Quarterly* 16 (2009): 3–12. It should be noted that Ibrahim argues that Islam is more violent than Christianity and Judaism in this article.

2. For an interesting discussion on militaristic language in the New Testament, see chapter three of Davis Brown's *The Sword, the Cross, and the Eagle: The American Christian Just War Tradition* (New York: Rowman & Littlefield, 2008).

3. In his defense, this article was published in an academic journal, and thus was not intended for lay readers, and, if I had to put money on an interpretation, I would place my bet with his analysis of both Matthew and Revelations. However, I am not sure I would concur with his main thesis—that Islam has Christianity beat in explicit calls to violence. You could use this theory to predict high levels of violence where Islam is combined with nationalism, as well, and the patterns of violent criminality would provide support in the Middle East, just as it would in countries such as Israel, where nationalistic Judaism holds sway.

4. Peter Jenkins, "Dark Passages," *Boston Globe*, March 8, 2009.

5. All verses in this chapter are taken from the New International Version (NIV) of the Bible unless otherwise noted.

6. Exod. 34:6: "And he passed in front of Moses, proclaiming, 'The LORD, the LORD, the compassionate and gracious God, slow to anger, abounding in love and faithfulness.'" After reading these passages—even just the ones from Exodus—you might begin to wonder if this was not fear-induced obsequiousness. Or at least I did.

7. These passages do not tend to get a lot of attention from Christians, as

they also render the promise of eternal life a little more ambiguous than John 3:16 would suggest.

8. Though some conservative Christian parents might pull out Leviticus 19:28 to prevent their kids from getting tattoos. The prohibition on wearing clothing from two types of cloth comes from Lev. 19:19 and Deut. 22:11–12; braided hair, gold, pearls and expensive clothing are prohibited in 1 Tim. 2:9; and Lev. 19:27 prohibits cutting the hair on the side of your head and trimming your beard.

9. Jimmy Carter, *A Call to Action: Women, Religion, Violence and Power* (New York: Simon & Schuster, 2014). If you are interested in the plight of women in relation to religion, I cannot recommend this book highly enough.

10. I understand that someone who wants to retain their belief in God and the Bible has to engage in syntactical gymnastics if they do not care to accept that they are meant to be subservient to men, and I sympathize with the intent, but it is nearly impossible to do so. What emerges are analyses of words such as "helper" and "rule" and "woman" that defy logic. Starting with the point (Gen. 2:19–20) where God paraded all the animals past Adam to name but could not find a suitable helper among them, this story is difficult to salvage, though I have read painful machinations where the term "helper" is argued to mean a companion of equal status, among other attempts to ameliorate the damage done to women in this story.

11. I cannot resist this one example of the distain for women on the part of the Church, because it is so fundamental and representative: "As regards the individual nature, woman is defective and misbegotten, for the active power of the male seed tends to the production of a perfect likeness in the masculine sex; while the production of a woman comes from defect in the active power. . . ." (Thomas Aquinas, *Summa Theologica*, Q92, art. 1, Reply Obj. 1).

12. Jocelyn E. Anderson, *Woman Submit! Christians and Domestic Violence* (Auburndale, FL: One Way Press, 2007).

13. This is the New International Version. The Living Bible uses the term "master" instead of "rule," while the Modern Language Bible uses "dominate" in its stead.

14. The skepticism victims too often experience in the case of rape likely has its biblical roots here, but women are portrayed as conniving temptresses in so many passages that it is impossible to determine for certain.

15. See, for example, 1 Peter 3:1–2: "Likewise, you wives should be subordinate to your husbands so that, even if some disobey the word, they may be

won over without a word by their wives' conduct when they observe your reverent and chaste behavior" (NAB). See also 1 Tim. 2:11–15.

16. See, for example, Num. 31:25–35, in which women are inventoried after a war.

17. See Deut. 22:28–29: "If a man happens to meet a virgin who is not pledged to be married and rapes her and they are discovered, he shall pay her father fifty shekels of silver. He must marry the young woman, for he has violated her. He can never divorce her as long as he lives."

18. Federal Bureau of Investigation, *Uniform Crime Reports: Crime in the United States, 2012* (Washington, DC: United States Department of Justice, 2013), http://www.fbi.gov/about-us/cjis/ucr/ucr (accessed June 10, 2014).

19. Jacquelyn C. Campbell et al., "Assessing Risk Factors for Intimate Partner Homicide," *National Institute of Justice Journal* 250 (2003): 14–19. See also Lynn Langton, Michael Planty, and Jennifer Truman, *Criminal Victimization, 2012* (Washington, DC: Bureau of Justice Statistics, 2013), http://www.bjs.gov/index.cfm?ty=pbdetail&iid=4781 (accessed March 12, 2014).

20. Jeffrey L. Edelson, "The Overlap between Child Maltreatment and Woman Battering," *Violence Against Women* 5 (1990): 134–54.

21. A significant number of workplace shootings, hostage situations, and plain old public violence incidents are actually manifestations of intimate partner violence.

22. Kit Gruelle, a good friend and domestic violence advocate featured in the HBO documentary *Private Violence*, has the perfect response to the claim that men are abused by women to the same extent as the reverse: "Show me the bodies."

23. Prov. 20: 30 and 26: 3.

24. Michael P. Johnson, "Patriarchal Terrorism and Common Couple Violence: Two Forms of Violence against Women," *Journal of Marriage and the Family* 57 (1995): 283–94. Men are more likely to engage in abuse when these roles are violated (for example, when the wife is employed where the husband is not). See Heidi M. Levitt and Kimberly Ware, "'Anything with Two Heads is a Monster': Religious Leaders' Perspective on Marital Equality and Domestic Violence," *Violence Against Women* 12 (2006): 1169–90.

25. Marie Fortune and Cindy Enger, *Violence against Women and the Role of Religion* (Harrisburg, PA: National Recourse Center of Domestic Violence, 2005).

26. Num. 5:17–31.

27. Steven R. Tracy, "Patriarchy and Domestic Violence: Challenging

Common Conceptions," *Journal of the Evangelical Theological Society* 50 (2007): 573–94.

28. Annie L. Horton, Melany M. Wilkins, and Wendy Wright, "Women Who Ended Abuse: What Religious Leaders and Religion Did for These Victims," in *Abuse and Religion: When Praying Isn't Enough*, ed. Annie L. Horton and Judith A. Williamson (Lexington, MA: Lexington Books, 1988), 235–46.

29. Shondrah T. Nash and Latonya Hesterberg, "Biblical Framings of and Responses to Spousal Violence in the Narratives of Abused Christian Women," *Violence Against Women* 15 (2009): 340–61.

30. Ibid.

31. Gen. 39: 7–20.

32. Genesis 19:31–36 provides an absurd example. Lot's daughters apparently gave him enough wine to render him totally unaware of having had sex with his daughters, while remaining capable of having sex, on two consecutive nights. The idea of completely innocent men being duped by cunning and manipulative women abounds in the Bible. Samson must have been the stupidest man alive to share the secret of his strength with the scheming Delilah in the wake of three rather obvious attempts to set him up in conjunction with the Philistines (Judges 16:1–5, 15–21). But, apparently, he could not stand her nagging. See also 1 Kings 11:3–9.

33. Jane P. Sheldon and Sandra L. Parent, "Clergy's Attitudes of Blame toward Female Rape Victims," *Violence Against Women* 8 (2002): 233–56.

34. Jerome R. Koch and Inacio L. Ramirez, *Religiosity, Fundamentalism, and Intimate Partner Violence among U.S. College Students* (Lubbock, TX: Texas Tech University, 2009).

35. Nancy T. Ammerman, *Bible Believers: Fundamentalists in the Modern World* (New Brunswick, NJ: Rutgers University Press, 1987).

36. Deut. 22:23–24.

37. See also Alden Roberts, Jerome Koch, and D. Paul Johnson, "Reference Groups and Religion: An Empirical Test," *Sociological Spectrum* 21 (2001): 81–98.

38. Gustav Niebuhr, "Southern Baptists Declare Wife Should 'Submit' to her Husband," *New York Times*, June 10, 1998, http://www.nytimes.com/1998/06/10/us/southern-baptists-declare-wife-should-submit-to-her-husband.html (accessed December 15, 2013).

39. See also Sirach 25:18, 19, 33.

40. Pat Robertson, *700 Club*, December 24, 1973, quoted in *The Sins of the*

Scripture: Exposing the Bible's Texts of Hate to Reveal the God of Love, John S. Spong (New York: HarperCollins, 2005).

41. Michael Gryboski, "Latest NIV Bible Translation Clearer on Homosexual Sins, Says Theologian," *Christian Post*, January 4, 2012, http://www.christianpost.com/news/latest-niv-bible-translation-clearer-on-homosexual-sins-says-theologian-66393/ (accessed July 13, 2013).

42. See, for example, Matt. 5:32, Mark 10:11–12, Luke 16:18, 1 Cor. 7:10–11, 1 Cor. 7:27, and Rom. 7:3.

43. Associated Press, "Haggard Admits 'Sexual Immorality,' Apologizes," *NBC News*, http://www.nbcnews.com/id/15536263/ns/us_news-life/t/haggard-admits-sexual-immorality-apologizes/#.VcyNNj8pqIE (accessed August 13, 2015).

44. Michelle Goldberg, *Kingdom Coming: The Rise of Christian Nationalism* (New York: Norton, 2007).

45. Federal Bureau of Investigation, *Hate Crime Statistics, 2012* (Washington, DC: United States Department of Justice, 2013), http://www.fbi.gov/about-us/cjis/ucr/hate-crime/2012 (accessed June 15, 2014). Attacks against individuals due to their real or perceived sexual orientation make up 19.2 percent of all hate crimes. Hate crime perpetrators do not tend to be the brightest bulbs in the box, so they often mistake their victims for LGBT when they are not.

46. David McConnell, *American Honor Killings: Desire and Rage Among Men* (New York: Akashic Books, 2013).

47. Xiaohe Xu, Yuk-Ying Tung, and R. Gregory Dunaway, "Cultural, Human, and Social Capital as Determinants of Corporal Punishment: Toward an Integrated Theoretical Model," *Journal of Interpersonal Violence* 15 (2000): 603–30.

48. Elizabeth T. Gershoff, Pamela C. Miller, and George W. Holden, "Parenting Influences from the Pulpit: Religious Affiliation as a Determinant of Parental Corporal Punishment," *Journal of Family Psychology* 13 (1999): 307–20.

49. Ibid.

50. Ibid.

51. Christopher G. Ellison, John P. Bartkowski, and Michelle L. Segal, "Conservative Protestantism and the Parental Use of Corporal Punishment," *Social Forces* 74 (1996): 1003–28.

52. Harold G. Grasmick, Robert J. Bursik, Jr., and M'lou Kimpel, "Protestant Fundamentalism and Attitudes toward Corporal Punishment of Children," *Violence and Victims* 6 (1991): 283–98.

53. Vernon R. Wiehe, "Religious Influence on Parental Attitudes toward the Use of Corporal Punishment," *Journal of Family Violence* 5 (1990): 173–86.

54. For information related to child sexual abuse and medical neglect related to religion, see Seth M. Asser and Rita Swan, "Child Fatalities from Religion-Motivated Medical Neglect," *Pediatrics 101* (1998): 625–29; Rebecca M. Bolen, "Predicting Risk to be Sexually Abused: A Comparison of Logistic Regression to Event History Analysis," *Child Maltreatment* 3 (1998): 157–70; Bette L. Bottoms et al., "In the Name of God: A Profile of Religion-Based Child Abuse," *Journal of Social Issues* 51 (1995): 85–111; Lainie F. Ross and Timothy J. Aspinwall, "Religious Exemptions to the Immunization Statutes: Balancing Public Health and Religious Freedom," *Journal of Law, Medicine and Ethics* 25 (1997): 202–209; and Alice Miller, *For Your Own Good: Hidden Cruelty in Child-Rearing and the Roots of Violence* (New York: Farrar, Straus & Giroux, 1983).

55. Though this view is rarely explicit in a generalized form.

56. The Westminster Confession (1647 CE). Also, Clement of Rome (circa 30–96 CE) offered, "The holy Scriptures which are given through the Holy Spirit . . . nothing iniquitous or falsified is written." St. Augustine (354–430 CE) said, "None of these [biblical] authors has erred in any respect of writing." He also wrote, "Therefore, since they wrote the things which He [God] showed and uttered to them, it cannot be pretended that He is not the writer; for his members executed what their head dictated." St. Gregory the Great (circa 540–604 CE; Pope from 590–604 CE) stated, ". . . we loyally believe the Holy Spirit to be the author of the book. He wrote it who dictated it for writing; He wrote it who inspired its execution." See also The Belgic Confessional (1561 CE), Council of Florence (1438–1445), Council of Trent (1545–1563), Council of the Vatican (1869–1870), and Leo XIII in his Encyclical Letter "Providentissimus Deus" (1893), http://www.religioustolerance.org/inerran4.htm (accessed September 27, 2013). What is more alarming, though, given the content, are the number of right-wing politicians who still make such statements.

57. Jeffrey M. Jones, "In U.S., 3 in 10 Say they Take the Bible Literally," *Gallup*, July 8, 2011, http://www.gallup.com/poll/148427/say-bible-literally.aspx (accessed June 16, 2013).

CHAPTER SIX: THE LION OR THE LAMB—THE FUTURE OF CRIME AND JUSTICE IN AMERICA

1. For a notable exception, see Volkan Topalli, Timothy Brezina, and Mindy Bernhardt, "With God on My Side: The Paradoxical Relationship between

Religious Belief and Criminality among Hardcore Street Offenders," *Theoretical Criminology* 17 (2013): 49–69. For examples of this work, see also Ronald L. Akers, "Religion and Crime," *Criminologist* 35 (2010): 2–6; Stephen R. Burkett and Mervin White, "Hellfire and Delinquency: Another Look," *Journal for the Scientific Study of Religion* 13 (1974): 455–62; Stephen R. Burkett and Mervin White, "Perceived Parents' Religiosity, Friends' Drinking and Hellfire: A Panel Study of Adolescent Drinking," *Review of Religious Research* 35 (1993): 134–54; John K. Cochran and Ronald L. Akers, "Beyond Hellfire: An Exploration of the Variable Effects of Religiosity on Adolescent Marijuana and Alcohol Use," *Journal of Research on Crime and Delinquency* 26 (1989): 198–225; Paul C. Higgins and Gary L. Albrecht, "Hellfire and Delinquency Revisited," *Social Forces* 55 (1977): 952–58; Travis Hirschi, *Causes of Delinquency* (Berkeley, CA: University of California Press, 1969); Travis Hirschi and Michael R. Gottfredson, "Control Theory and the Life-Course Perspective," *Studies on Crime & Crime Prevention* 4 (1995): 131–42; Travis Hirschi and Rodney Stark, "Hellfire and Delinquency," *Social Problems* 17 (1969): 202–13; and Rodney Stark, "Religion as Context: Hellfire and Delinquency One More Time," *Sociology of Religion* 57 (1996): 163–73.

2. Michael E. McCullough and Brian L. B. Willoughby, "Religion, Self-Regulation, and Self-Control," *Psychological Bulletin* 135 (2009): 69–93.

3. Hirschi, *Causes of Delinquency*; see also Marvin D. Krohn and James L. Massey, "Social Control and Delinquent Behavior: An Examination of the Elements of the Social Bond," *Sociological Quarterly* 21 (1980): 529–43. For an application to religion at the neighborhood level, see Mark D. Regnerus, "Moral Communities and Adolescent Delinquency: Religious Contexts and Community Social Control," *Sociological Quarterly* 44 (2003): 523–54.

4. Marcus Felson, *Crime and Nature* (Thousand Oaks, CA: Sage, 2006).

5. Jeffrey M. Jones, "Atheists, Muslims see Most Bias as Presidential Candidates," *Gallup*, June 21, 2012, http://www.gallup.com/poll/155285/atheists-muslims-bias-presidential-candidates.aspx (accessed June 23, 2012).

6. Azim F. Shariff and Ara Norenzayan, "God Is Watching You: Priming God Concepts Increases Prosocial Behavior in an Anonymous Economic Game," *Psychological Science* 18 (2007): 803–809; and Ara Norenzayan and Azim F. Shariff, "The Origin and Evolution of Religious Prosociality," *Science* 322 (2008): 58–62.

7. For noncriminologists: Social theorist Jeremy Bentham designed prisons based on his panopticon design in the late eighteenth century. It is based on the

idea of a central guard tower where prisoners would not know if they were being watched at any given time, thus forcing them to always assume—and behave as if—they were being watched. (Jeremy Bentham, *The Panopticon Writings*, ed. Miran Božovič [London: VersoBooks, 1995].)

8. Jamie Arndt et al., "Subliminal Exposure to Death-Related Stimuli Increases Defense of the Cultural Worldview," *Psychological Science* 8 (1997): 379–85; Jamie Arndt et al., "Suppression, Accessibility of Death-Related Thoughts, and Cultural Worldview Defense: Exploring the Psychodynamics of Terror Management," *Journal of Personality and Social Psychology* 73 (1997): 5–18; Jeff Greenberg et al., "Clarifying the Function of Mortality-Salience Induced Worldview Defense: Renewed Suppression or Reduced Accessibility of Death-Related Thoughts?" *Journal of Experimental Social Psychology* 37 (2001): 70–76; Jeff Greenberg, Tom Pyszczynski, and Sheldon Solomon, "The Causes and Consequences of a Need for Self-Esteem: A Terror Management Theory," in *Public Self and Private Self*, ed. Roy F. Baumeister (New York: Springer-Verlag, 1986), 189–212; Jeff Greenberg et al., "Evidence of a Terror Management Function of Cultural Icons: The Effects of Mortality Salience on the Inappropriate Use of Cherished Cultural Symbols," *Personality and Social Psychology Bulletin* 21 (1995): 1221–28; and Jeff Greenberg et al., "Terror Management and Tolerance: Does Mortality Salience Always Intensify Negative Reactions to Others Who Threaten One's Worldview?" *Journal of Personality and Social Psychology* 63 (1992): 212–20.

9. Phil Zuckerman, *Society without God: What the Least Religious Nations Can Tell Us About Contentment* (New York: New York University Press, 2010).

10. As well as lower rates of teen pregnancy and abortion. Gregory S. Paul, "Cross-National Correlations of Quantifiable Societal Health with Popular Religiosity and Secularism in the Prosperous Democracies," *Journal of Religion & Society* 7 (2005): 1–17.

11. Charles D. Ayers et al., "Assessing Correlates of Onset, Escalation and Desistance of Delinquent Behavior," *Journal of Quantitative Criminology* 15 (1999): 277–307; Denise C. Gottfredson, Amanda Cross, and David A. Soulé, "Distinguishing Characteristics of Effective and Ineffective After-School Programs to Prevent Delinquency and Victimization," *Criminology & Public Policy* 6 (2007): 289–318; Denise C. Gottfredson et al., "Do After School Programs Reduce Delinquency?" *Prevention Science* 5 (2004): 253–66; J. David Hawkins, Richard F. Catalano, and Janet Y. Miller, "Risk and Protective Factors for Alcohol and Other Drug Problems in Adolescence and Early Adulthood:

Implications for Substance Abuse in Adolescents," in *Childhood Aggression and Violence: Sources of Influence Prevention and Control*, ed. David H Crowell, Ian M. Evans, and Clifford R. O'Donnell (New York: Plenum, 1992), 263–82; Flavia J. Rivera and Timothy A. McCorry, "An Evaluation of an After-School Program's Effectiveness in Preventing Juvenile Delinquency and Substance Use: A Test of the Social Development Model," *New York Sociologist* 2 (2007): 65–84 (here, the impact was not present in elementary school children but was present in middle school); Task Force on Youth Development and Community Programs, *A Matter of Time: Risk and Opportunity in the Non-School Hours* (New York: Carnegie Corporation, 1992).

12. Regnerus, "Moral Communities and Adolescent Delinquency"; Topalli, Brezina, and Bernhardt, "With God on My Side."

13. For a discussion of the importance of understanding individual traits in the social environments in which they occur, see Robert J. Bursik, Jr. and Harold G. Grasmick, "The Use of Contextual Analysis in Models of Criminal Behavior," in *Delinquency and Crime: Current Theories*, ed. J. David Hawkins (Cambridge, UK: Cambridge University Press, 1996), 236–67.

14. Audrey Barrick, "Study: Christian Divorce Rate Identical to National Average," *Christian Post*, April 4, 2008, http://www.christianpost.com/news/ study-christian-divorce-rate-identical-to-national-average-31815/ (accessed July 24, 2014). New marriage and divorce rates released. Barna Group, https://www. barna.org/family-kids-articles/42-new-marriage-and-divorce-statistics-released (accessed July 20, 2014). While Barna is a group of evangelical pollsters, the Christian right has criticized their methodology over this finding. Specifically, they have taken umbrage with Barna researchers' definitions of born-again and evangelicals, and countered that church attendance is the key to finding a reduction in divorce rates. You will find the details at the following source, but it is worth noting that Barna has been using this definition for quite some time and only drew criticism from the Christian right with the release of this finding. Adelle M. Banks, "Christians Question Divorce Statistics," *StarTribune*, March 16, 2010, http://www.startribune.com/lifestyle/118101934.html (accessed April 2, 2012).

15. The Bible is pretty clear on the issue of divorce. See Mark 10:11–12: "Anyone who divorces his wife and marries another woman commits adultery against her. And if she divorces her husband and marries another man, she commits adultery" (Jesus; NIV). See also Matt. 5:32: "But I tell you that anyone who divorces his wife, except for sexual immorality, makes her the victim of adultery, and anyone who marries a divorced woman commits adultery" (NIV)

Similar commandments are found in Luke 16:18, 1 Cor. 7:10–11, and Rom. 7:3. My personal favorite is 1 Cor. 7:27: "Are you bound to a wife? Do not seek to be free. Are you free from a wife? Do not seek a wife" (ESV). That Paul . . .

16. Topalli, Brezina, and Bernhardt, "With God on My Side."

17. Pew Forum on Religion and Public Life, *U.S. Religious Knowledge Survey*, September 28, 2010, http://www.pewforum.org/files/2010/09/religious-knowledge-full-report.pdf (accessed January 9, 2014). See also Katherine T. Phan, "Survey: More Americans Familiar with Big Mac Ingredients than Ten Commandments," *Christian Post*, October 3, 2007, http://www.christianpost .com/news/survey-more-americans-familiar-with-big-mac-ingredients-than-10 -commandments-29557/ (accessed September 22, 2013). We will talk more about the issue of religious ignorance among the religious a bit later.

18. Topalli, Brezina, and Berhardt, "With God on My Side," 58. See also Robert Agnew, "The Techniques of Neutralization and Violence," *Criminology* 32 (1994): 401–26.

19. Christopher G. Ellison, Jeffrey A. Burr, and Patricia L. McCall, "The Enduring Puzzle of Southern Homicide: Is Regional Religious Culture the Missing Piece?" *Homicide Studies* 7 (2003): 326–52. See also Matthew R. Lee, "Reconsidering Culture and Homicide," *Homicide Studies* 15 (2011): 319–40.

20. See: Theodor W. Adorno, Else Frenkel-Brunswik, Daniel J. Levinson, and Nevitt Sanford, *The Authoritarian Personality* (New York: Harper and Bros, 1950); Bob Altemeyer. "The Other 'Authoritarian Personality,'" *Advances in Experimental Social Psychology* 30 (1998): 47–92; Michael Argyle and Benjamin Beit-Hallahmi, *The Psychology of Religious Behaviour, Belief and Experience* (London: Routledge, 1997); Dan Ariely, *Predictably Irrational: The Hidden Forces that Shape Our Decisions* (New York: HarperCollins, 2008); Pascal Boyer, *Religion Explained: The Evolutionary Origins of Religious Thought* (New York: Basic Books, 2001); John Brockman, ed., *What Have You Changed Your Mind About?* (New York: HarperCollins, 2009); Edmund D. Cohen, *The Mind of the Bible Believer* (Amherst, NY: Prometheus Books, 1988); Christopher G. Ellison and Darren E. Sherkat, "Obedience and Autonomy: Religion and Parental Values Reconsidered," *Journal for the Scientific Study of Religion* 32 (1993): 313–29; Daniel Gardner, *The Science of Fear: How the Culture of Fear Manipulates Your Brain* (New York: Plume, 2008); Joshua Green, "From Neural 'Is' to Moral 'Ought': What are the Moral Implications of Neuroscientific Moral Psychology?" *Nature Reviews Neuroscience* 4 (2003): 847–50; Anthony G. Greenwald, Jacqueline E. Pickrell, and Shelly D. Farnham, "Implicit Partisanship: Taking Sides for No.

Reason," *Journal of Personality and Social Psychology* 83 (2002): 367–79; Ralph W. Hood Jr., Peter C. Hill, and Bernard Spilka, *The Psychology of Religion: An Empirical Approach* (New York: Guilford Press, 2003); Judy J. Johnson, *What's So Wrong With Being Absolutely Right: The Dangerous Nature of Dogmatic Beliefs* (Amherst, NY: Prometheus Books, 2009); Daniel Kahneman and Amos Tversky, "The Psychology of Preferences," *Scientific American* 246 (1982): 160–73; Ryota Kanai, Tom Feilden, Colin Firth, and Geraint Rees. "Political Orientations Are Correlated with Brain Structure in Young Adults," *Current Biology* 21 (2011): 677–80; CarolAnne M. Kardash and Roberta J. Scholes, "Effects of Pre-Existing Beliefs, Epistemological Beliefs, and Need for Cognition on Interpretation of Controversial Issues," *Journal of Educational Psychology* 88 (1996): 260–71; George Lakoff, *Moral Politics: How Liberals and Conservatives Think* (Chicago: University of Chicago Press, 2002); Chris Mooney, "Scientists Are Beginning to Figure Out Why Conservatives Are . . . Conservative," *Mother Jones*, July 15, 2014 (accessed July 15, 2014), http://www.motherjones.com/politics/2014/07/biology-ideology-john-hibbing-negativity-bias; Andrew Newberg, Eugene D'Aquili, and Vince Rause, *Why God Won't Go Away: Brain Science and the Biology of Belief* (New York: Ballentine, 2001); Douglas R. Oxley, Kevin B. Smith, John R. Alford, Matthew V. Hibbing, Jennifer L. Miller, and Mario J. Scalora. "Political Attitudes Vary with Psychological Traits," *Science* 321 (2008): 1667–70; P. Wesley Schultz and Alan Searleman, "Rigidity of Thought and Behavior: 100 Years of Research," *Genetic, Social, and General Psychology Monographs* 128 (2002): 165–209; Hulda Thórisdóttir and John T. Jost, "Motivated Closed-Mindedness Mediates the Effect of Threat on Political Conservatism," *Political Psychology* 32 (2011): 785–811.

21. In 2007, the UN General Assembly adopted resolution 62/149, calling for a worldwide moratorium on capital punishment—104 countries voted in favor of the resolution, with 54 against, and 29 abstentions. In 2008, the UNGA passed a second resolution to this effect, with 106 votes in favor, 46 against, and 34 abstentions. While the resolution is not legally binding, of course, it does carry considerable moral and political weight.

22. And the only other democracies still using the death penalty besides the United States are Japan—very infrequently—and South Korea.

23. James A. Aho, *The Politics of Righteousness: Idaho Christian Patriotism* (Seattle: University of Washington Press, 1990).

24. Except Bill Mahar, Jon Stewart, and Stephen Colbert. Apparently, being a comedian allows one to speak more freely about Christian nationalism.

25. Stephen Prothero, *Religious Literacy: What Every American Needs to Know—And Doesn't* (New York: HarperOne, 2008).

26. Exod. 20:2–17 (NKJV).

27. The list is nearly identical in Deut. 5:6–21.

28. Cathy L. Grossman, "Americans Get an 'F' in Religion," *USA Today*, March 14, 2007, http://usatoday30.usatoday.com/news/religion/2007–03–07-teaching-religion-cover_N.htm (accessed July 30, 2013). An amusing side note: a survey of a thousand high school seniors revealed that 50 percent thought Sodom and Gomorrah were married.

29. Phan, "Survey: More Americans familiar with Big Mac ingredients than Ten Commandments." Only 34 percent were aware of the prohibition against working on the Sabbath, and 29 percent knew the commandment against false idols. On a brighter note, 80 percent of respondents knew that "two all-beef patties" are ingredients in McDonald's Big Mac.

30. Matt Labash, "God and Man in Alabama," *Weekly Standard*, March 2, 1988, 1.

31. Michelle Goldberg, "Kingdom Coming: The Rise of Christian Nationalism," *Salon*, May 12, 2006, http://www.salon.com/2006/05/12/goldberg_14/ (accessed November 20, 2013).

32. Ibid.

33. In fact, the Ten Commandment statue controversy is raging again, this time in New Mexico. Associated Press, "Judge Rules Ten Commandment Monument Must Go," *Huffington Post Politics*, August 8, 2014, http://www.huffingtonpost.com/2014/08/08/judge-ten-commandments_n_5662743.html (accessed August 26, 2014).

34. Dan Wakefield, *The Hijacking of Jesus: How the Religious Right Distorts Christianity and Promotes Prejudice and Hate* (New York: Nation Books, 2006).

35. George Grant, *The Changing of the Guard: The Vital Role Christians Must Play in America's Unfolding Political and Cultural Drama* (Nashville: Broadman and Holman, 1995).

36. Shadee Ashtari, "KKK Leader Disputes Hate Group Label: 'We're a Christian Organization,'" *Huffington Post*, March 21, 2014, http://www.huffington post.com/2014/03/21/virginia-kkk-fliers_n_5008647.html (accessed March 23, 2014).

37. Gregg W. Etter, "Perceived Effects of Religion on White Supremacist Culture," *Journal of Gang Research* 9 (2002): 15–24.

38. Jonathan R. White, "Political Eschatology: A Theology of Anti-governmental Extremism," *American Behavioral Scientist* 44 (2001): 937–56.

39. Ibid.

40. Marian J. Borg, "The Southern Subculture of Punitiveness? Regional Variation in Support for Capital Punishment," *Journal of Research on Crime and Delinquency* 34 (1997): 25–45.

41. Laurence R. Iannacone, "Why Strict Churches are Strong," *American Journal of Sociology* 99 (1994): 1180–211.

42. Ibid., 1181.

43. Gary Potter, "Fundamental Violence: Protestant Fundamentalism and Violent Crime," *Uprooting Criminology: A Reasoned Plot*, November 11, 2013, http://uprootingcriminology.org/essays/fundamental-violence-protestant -fundamentalism-violent-crime-gary-w-potter/ (accessed February 26, 2014).

44. If Jesus indeed existed, and if Jesus were the Son of Man.

45. See, for example, Byron R. Johnson, *More God, Less Crime: Why Faith Matters and How It Could Matter More* (West Conshohocken, PA: Templeton Press, 2011).

46. Kathleen H. Corriveau, Eva E. Chen, and Paul L. Harris, "Judgments about Fact and Fiction by Children from Religious and Nonreligious Backgrounds," *Cognitive Science* (2014): 1–30.

47. Ola Mohamed, "Religion and Violence," *Washington Post*, April 17, 2009, http://onfaith.washingtonpost.com/onfaith/eboo_patel/2009/04/religion _violence.html (accessed October, 19, 2013).

BIBLIOGRAPHY

Abraham, Ken. *Who Are the Promise Keepers? Understanding the Christian Men's Movement*. New York: Doubleday, 1997.

Abramowitz, Alan I., and Kyle L. Saunders. "Is Polarization a Myth?" *Journal of Politics* 70 (2008): 542–55.

Adams, John. "A Defence of the Constitutions of Government of the United States of America (1787–1788)." In *The American Enlightenment: The Shaping of the American Experiment and a Free Society*, edited by Adrienne Koch, 258. New York: George Braziller Press, 1965.

———. *The Portable John Adams*. New York: Penguin Classics, 2004.

———. *Thoughts on Government: Applicable to the Present State of the American Colonies: In a Letter from a Gentleman to his Friend*. Independence, KY: Gale, Sabin Americana, 2012.

Adorno, Theodor W., Else Frenkel-Brunswik, Daniel J. Levinson, and Nevitt Sanford. *The Authoritarian Personality*. New York: Harper and Bros, 1950.

Aebi, Marcelo F., Martin Killias, and Cynthia Tavares. "Comparing Crime Rates through Police or Survey Data? The International Crime (Victim) Survey, the European Sourcebook of Crime and Criminal Justice and Interpol Statistics Compared." *International Journal of Comparative Criminology* 2 (2002): 22–37.

Agnew, Robert. "The Techniques of Neutralization and Violence." *Criminology* 32 (1994): 401–26.

Aho, James A. *The Politics of Righteousness: Idaho Christian Patriotism*. Seattle: University of Washington Press, 1990.

Akers, Ronald L. "Religion and Crime." *Criminologist* 35 (2010): 2–6.

Akers, Ronald L., Jodi Lane, and Lonn Lanza-Kaduce. "Faith-Based Mentoring and Restorative Justice: Overlapping Theoretical, Empirical, and Philosophical Background." In *Restorative Justice: From Theory to Practice*, edited by Holly V. Miller, 139–65. Bingley, UK: Emerald Group Publishing, 2008.

Albrecht, Stan L., and Tim B. Heaton. "Secularization, Higher Education, and Religiosity." *Review of Religious Research* 26 (1984): 43–58.

Alexander, Jeffrey C. "Citizen and Enemy as Symbolic Classification: On the Polarizing Discourse of Civil Society." In *Cultivating Differences: Symbolic Boundaries and the Making of Inequality*, edited by Michèle Lamont and Marcel Fournier, 289–308. Chicago, IL: University of Chicago Press, 1992.

Alford, John R., Carolyn L. Funk, and John R. Hibbing. "Beyond Liberals and Conservatives to Political Genotypes and Phenotypes." *Perspectives on Politics* 6 (2005): 321–28.

Allman, Mark J. *Who Would Jesus Kill?: War, Peace, and the Christian Tradition.* Winona, MN: Anselm Academic, 2008.

Almás, Ingvild, Alexander W. Cappelen, Erik Ø. Sorensen, and Bertil Tungodden. "Fairness and the Development of Inequality Acceptance." *Science* 328 (2010): 1176–78.

Almond, Gabriel A., R. Scott Appleby, and Emmanuel Sivan. *Strong Religion: The Rise of Fundamentalisms around the World.* Chicago: University of Chicago Press, 2003.

Alpert, Geoffrey P., John M. MacDonald, and Roger G. Dunham. "Police Suspicion and Discretionary Decision Making During Citizen Stops." *Criminology* 43 (2005): 407–34.

Altemeyer, Bob. *Enemies of Freedom: Understanding Right-Wing Authoritarianism.* San Francisco: Jossey-Bass, 1988.

———. *The Authoritarian Specter.* Cambridge, MA: Harvard University Press, 1996.

———. "The Other 'Authoritarian Personality.'" *Advances in Experimental Social Psychology* 30 (1998): 47–92.

Altemeyer, Bob, and Bruce Hunsberger. "A Revised Religious Fundamentalism Scale: The Short and Sweet of It." *International Journal for the Psychology of Religion* 14 (2004): 47–54.

Alwin, Duane F. "Religion and Parental Child-Rearing Orientations: Evidence of a Catholic-Protestant Convergence." *American Journal of Sociology* 92 (1986): 412–40.

Ammerman, Nancy T. *Bible Believers: Fundamentalists in the Modern World.* New Brunswick, NJ: Rutgers University Press, 1987.

Amoeteng, Acheampong Y., and Stephen J. Bahr. "Religion, Family, and Adolescent Drug Use." *Sociological Perspectives* 29 (1986): 53–76.

Anderson, Benedict. *Imagined Communities: Reflections on the Origin and Spread of Nationalism.* New York: Versa, 1991.

Anderson, Jocelyn E. *Woman Submit! Christians and Domestic Violence.* Auburndale, FL: One Way Press, 2007.

Anti-Defamation League. *The Religious Right: The Assault on Tolerance and Pluralism in America.* New York: Anti-Defamation League, 1994.

Appiah, Kwame A. *Experiments in Ethics.* Cambridge, MA: Harvard University Press, 2008.

Appleby, R. Scott. *The Ambivalence of the Sacred: Religion, Violence, and Reconciliation.* New York: Rowman & Littlefield, 1999.

Applegate, Brandon K., Francis T. Cullen, and Bonnie S. Fischer. "Public Support for Correctional Treatment: The Continuing Appeal of the Rehabilitative Model." *Prison Journal* 77 (1997): 237–58.

Applegate, Brandon K., Francis T. Cullen, Bonnie S. Fischer, and Thomas Van der Ven, "Forgiveness and Fundamentalism: Reconsidering the Relationship between Correctional Attitudes and Religion." *Criminology* 38 (2000): 719–54.

Applegate, Brandon K., Francis T. Cullen, Bruce G. Link, Pamela J. Richards, and Lonn Lanza-Kaduce. "Determinants of Public Punitiveness toward Drunken Driving: A Factorial Survey Approach." *Justice Quarterly* 13 (1996): 57–79.

Applegate, Brandon K., Francis T. Cullen, Michael G. Turner, and Jody L. Sundt. "Assessing Public Support for Three-Strikes-and-You're-Out Laws: Global versus Specific Attitudes." *Crime & Delinquency* 42 (1996): 517–34.

Arendt, Hannah. *The Origins of Totalitarianism.* 1951. New York: Harcourt, 1994.

Argyle, Michael, and Benjamin Beit-Hallahmi. *The Psychology of Religious Behaviour, Belief and Experience.* London: Routledge, 1997.

Ariely, Dan. *Predictably Irrational: The Hidden Forces that Shape Our Decisions.* New York: HarperCollins, 2008.

Armstrong, Karen. *The Battle for God: A History of Fundamentalism.* New York: Ballantine Books, 2001.

Arndt, Jamie, John J. B. Allen, and Jeff Greenberg. "Traces of Terror: Subliminal Death Primes and Facial Electromyographic Indices of Affect." *Motivation and Emotion* 25 (2001): 253–77.

Arndt, Jamie, Jeff Greenberg, Tom Pyszczynski, and Sheldon Solomon. "Subliminal Exposure to Death-Related Stimuli Increases Defense of the Cultural Worldview." *Psychological Science* 8 (1997): 379–85.

Arndt, Jamie, Jeff Greenberg, Sheldon Solomon, Tom Pyszczynski, and Linda Simon. "Suppression, Accessibility of Death-Related Thoughts, and Cultural Worldview Defense: Exploring the Psychodynamics of Terror Management." *Journal of Personality and Social Psychology* 73 (1997): 5–18.

Arndt, Jamie, Jeff Schimel, and Jamie L. Goldenberg. "Death Can be Good for your Health: Fitness Intentions as Proximal and Distal Defense against Mortality Salience." *Journal of Applied Social Psychology* 38 (2003): 1726–46.

Aronson, Elliot, Timothy D. Wilson, and Robin M. Akert. *Social Psychology: The Heart and the Mind*. New York: HarperCollins, 1994.

Ashtari, Shadee. "KKK Leader Disputes Hate Group Label: 'We're a Christian Organization.'" *Huffington Post*, March 21, 2014. Accessed March 23, 2014. http://www.huffingtonpost.com/2014/03/21/virginia-kkk-fliers_n_5008647.html.

Asser, Seth M., and Rita Swan. "Child Fatalities from Religion-Motivated Medical Neglect." *Pediatrics 101* (1998): 625–29.

Associated Press. "Judge Rules Ten Commandment Monument Must Go." *Huffington Post Politics*, August 8, 2014. Accessed August 26, 2014. http://www.huffingtonpost.com/2014/08/08/judge-ten-commandments_n_5662743.html.

Atran, Scott. *Talking to the Enemy: Faith, Brotherhood, and the (Un) Making of Terrorists*. New York: HarperCollins, 2010.

Atran, Scott, and Joseph Henrich. "The Evolution of Religion: How Cognitive By-Products, Adaptive Learning Heuristics, Ritual Displays, and Group Competition Generate Deep Commitment to Prosocial Religions." *Biological Theory* 5 (2010): 18–30.

Ault, Jr., James M. *Spirit and Flesh: Life in a Fundamentalist Baptist Church*. New York: Knopf, 2005.

Avalos, Hector. *Fighting Words: The Origins of Religious Violence.* Amherst, NY: Prometheus Books, 2005.

Ayers, Charles D., James H. Williams, J. David Hawkins, Peggy L. Peterson, Richard F. Catalano, and Robert D. Abbot. "Assessing Correlates of Onset, Escalation and Desistance of Delinquent Behavior." *Journal of Quantitative Criminology* 15 (1999): 277–307.

Bader, Christopher D., Scott A. Desmond, F. Carson Mencken, and Byron R. Johnson. "Divine Justice: The Relationship between Images of God and Attitudes toward Criminal Punishment." *Criminal Justice Review* 35 (2010): 90–106.

Bader, Christopher D., F. Carson Mencken, and Paul Froese. "American Piety 2005: Content and Methods of the Baylor Religion Survey." *Journal for the Scientific Study of Religion* 46 (2007): 447–63.

Bageant, Joe. *Deer Hunting With Jesus: Dispatches from America's Class War.* New York: Crown, 2007.

Bahr, Stephen J., and John P. Hoffman. "Religiosity, Peers, and Adolescent Drug Use." *Journal of Drug Issues* 38 (2008): 743–70.

Baier, Colin J., and Bradley R. E. Wright. "'If You Love Me, Keep My Commandments': A Meta-Analysis of the Effect of Religion on Crime." *Journal of Research in Crime and Delinquency* 38 (2001): 3–21.

Bainbridge, William S. "The Religious Ecology of Deviance." *American Sociological Review* 54 (1989): 288–95.

Baird, Robert M., and Stuart E. Rosenbaum, eds. *Bigotry, Prejudice and Hatred: Definitions, Causes & Solutions.* Amherst, NY: Prometheus Books, 1992.

Baker, Joseph O. "An Investigation of the Sociological Patterns of Prayer Frequency and Content." *Sociology of Religion* 69 (2008): 169–85.

Balmer, Randall. *God in the White House: How Faith Shaped the Presidency from John F. Kennedy to George W. Bush.* New York: HarperOne, 2008.

———. *Mine Eyes Have Seen the Glory: A Journey into the Evangelical Subculture in America.* New York: Oxford University Press, 1989.

Bandura, Albert, Claudio Baranelli, Gian V. Capara, and Concetta

Pastorelli. "Mechanisms of Moral Disengagement." In *Origins of Terrorism: Psychologies, Ideologies, Theologies, States of Mind*, edited by Walter Reich, 161–91. Washington, DC: Woodrow Wilson Center Press, 1998.

Bandura, Albert, Dorothea Ross, and Sheila A. Ross. "Transmission of Aggression through Imitation of Aggressive Models." *Journal of Abnormal and Social Psychology* 63 (1961): 575–82.

Bandura, Albert, Bill Underwood, and Michael E. Fromson. "Disinhibition of Aggression through Diffusion of Responsibility and Dehumanization of Victims." *Journal of Research in Personality* 9 (1975): 253–69.

Banks, Adelle M. "Christians Question Divorce Statistics." *StarTribune*, March 16, 2010. Accessed April 2, 2012. http://www.startribune.com/ lifestyle/ 118101934.html.

Banner, Stuart. *The Death Penalty: An American History*. Cambridge, MA: Harvard University Press, 2003.

Barber, Benjamin R. *Fear's Empire: War, Terrorism, and Democracy*. New York: Norton, 2003.

Barber, Brian K. "Parental Psychological Control: Revisiting a Neglected Construct." *Child Development* 67 (1996): 3296–319.

Barbour, Ian G. *When Science Meets Religion: Enemies, Strangers, or Partners?* New York: HarperOne, 2000.

Barlet, Chip, and Matthew N. Lyons. "Militia Nation." *PublicEye*, 1995. Accessed February 12, 2014. http://www.publiceye.org/rightist/ milnatbl.html.

Barna Group of Ventura, California. "How Americans View 'Evangelical Voters.'" www.barna.org. September 9, 2008. Accessed June 4, 2013. https://www.barna.org/barna-update/media-watch/24-how -americans-view-evangelical-voters.

Barnes, Ed. "Just or Not, Cost of Death Penalty Is a Killer for State Budgets." Fox News. March 27, 2010. Accessed October 15, 2013. http://www.foxnews.com/us/2010/03/27/just-cost-death-penalty -killer-state-budgets/.

Baron, Jonathan B. *Judgment Misguided: Intuition and the Error in Public Decision Making*. New York: Oxford University Press, 1998.

————. *Thinking and Deciding*. Cambridge: Cambridge University Press, 2000.

Barreto, Manuela, and Naomi Ellemers. "The Perils of Political Correctness: Men's and Women's Responses to Old-Fashioned and Modern Sexist Views." *Social Psychology Quarterly* 68 (2005): 75–88.

Barrett, Justin L. "Exploring the Natural Foundations of Religion." *Trends in Cognitive Sciences* 4 (2000): 29–34.

Barrick, Audrey. "Study: Christian Divorce Rate Identical to National Average." *Christian Post*, April 4, 2008. Accessed July 24, 2014. http://www.christianpost.com/news/study-christian-divorce-rate-identical-to-national-average-31815/.

Bartels, Daniel M. "Principled Moral Sentiment and the Flexibility of Moral Judgment and Decision-Making." *Cognition* 108 (2008): 381–417.

Bartkowski, John P., and Christopher G. Ellison. "Divergent Perspectives on Childrearing in Popular Manuals: Conservative Protestants vs. the Mainstream Experts." *Sociology of Religion* 56 (1995): 21–34.

Bartlett, Tom. "Controversial Gay-Parenting Study is Severely Flawed, Journal's Audit Finds." *Chronicle of Higher Education*, July 26, 2012. Accessed July 27, 2012. http://chronicle.com/blogs/percolator/controversial-gay-parenting-study-is-severely-flawed-journals-audit-finds/30255.

Barton, David. *The Jefferson Lies: Exposing the Myths You've Always Believed About Thomas Jefferson*. New York: Thomas Nelson, 2012.

————. *The Myth of Separation: What is the Correct Relationship between Church and State?* Aledo, TX: WallBuilders Press, 1992.

Basset, Laura. "Rand Paul Fetal Personhood Amendment Stalls Flood Insurance Bill (Update)." *Huffington Post*, June 26, 2012. Accessed January 3, 2015. http://www.huffingtonpost.com/2012/06/26/rand-paul-fetal-personhood-flood-insurance_n_1628128.html.

Batson, C. Daniel. "Altruism and Prosocial Behavior." In *The Handbook of Social Psychology*, 4th ed., vol. 2, edited by Susan T. Fiske, Daniel T. Gilbert, and Gardner Lindzey, 262–316. Boston: McGraw-Hill, 1998.

————. *The Altruism Question: Toward a Social-Psychological Answer.* Hillsdale, NJ: Lawrence Erlbaum, 1991.

Batson, C. Daniel, Elizabeth R. Thompson, Greg Seuferling, Heather Whitney, and Jon A. Strongman. "Moral Hypocrisy: Appearing Moral to Oneself Without Being So." *Journal of Personality and Social Psychology* 77 (1999): 525–37.

Bauckham, Richard. *The Theology of the Book of Revelation*. Cambridge, MA: Cambridge University Press, 1993.

Baumeister, Roy F. *Identity: Cultural Change and the Struggle for Self.* New York: Oxford University Press, 1986.

Baumgartner, Frederic J. *Longing for the End: A History of Millennialism in Western Civilization*. New York: St. Martin's Press, 1999.

Becker, Ernest. *The Birth and Death of Meaning*. New York: Free Press, 1971.

———. *The Denial of Death*. New York: Free Press, 1973.

———. *Escape from Evil*. New York: Free Press, 1975.

Becker, Howard S. *Outsiders: Studies in the Sociology of Deviance*. New York: Free Press, 1963.

Beckett, Katherine, and Theodore Sasson. *The Politics of Injustice: Crime and Punishment in America*. Thousand Oaks, CA: Sage, 2003.

Bekkenkamp, Jonneke, and Yvonne Sherwood. *Sanctified Aggression: Legacies of Biblical and Post-Biblical Vocabularies of Violence*. New York: T & T Clark, 2004.

Bell, Paul. "Would You Believe It?" *Mensa Magazine*, UK edition, February 11, 2002, 12–13.

Bellant, Russ. *The Coors Connection: How Coors Family Philanthropy Undermines Democratic Pluralism*. Boston, MA: South End Press, 1991.

———. *Old Nazis, the New Right, and the Republican Party: Domestic Fascist Networks and Their Effect on the U.S. Cold War Politics*. Boston, MA: South End Press, 1991.

Benda, Brent B. "The Effect of Religion on Adolescent Delinquency Revisited." *Journal of Research in Crime and Delinquency* 32 (1995): 446–65.

———. "An Examination of a Reciprocal Relationship between Religiosity and Different Forms of Delinquency within a Theoretical Model." *Journal of Research in Crime and Delinquency* 34 (1997): 163–87.

————. "Testing Competing Theoretical Concepts: Adolescent Alcohol Consumption." *Deviant Behavior: An Interdisciplinary Journal* 15 (1994): 375–96.

Benda, Brent B., and Robert F. Corwyn. "Are the Effects of Religion on Crime Mediated, Moderated, and Misrepresented by Inappropriate Measures?" *Journal of Social Service Research* 27 (2001): 57–86.

————. "Religion and Delinquency: The Relationship after Considering Family and Peer Influences." *Journal for the Scientific Study of Religion* 36 (1997): 81–92.

Benda, Brent B., Sandra K. Pope, and Kelly J. Kelleher. "Church Attendance and Religiosity: Their Relationship to Adolescents' Use of Alcohol, Other Drugs, and Delinquency." *Alcoholism Treatment Quarterly* 24 (2006): 75–87.

Benda, Brent B., and Nancy J. Toombs. "Religiosity and Violence. Are they Related after Considering the Strongest Predictors?" *Journal of Criminal Justice*, 28 (2002): 483–96.

Bentham, Jeremy. *The Panopticon Writings*. Edited by Miran Božovič. London: VersoBooks, 1995.

Berlet, Chip, and Matthew N. Lyons. *Right-Wing Populism in America*. New York: Guilford Press, 2000.

Berlinerblau, Jacques. *The Secular Bible: Why Nonbelievers Must Take Religion Seriously*. Cambridge: Cambridge University Press, 2005.

Berman, Harold J. *The Interaction of Law and Religion*. Nashville, TN: Abingdon Press, 1974.

Berman, Paul. *Terror and Liberalism*. New York: Norton, 2003.

Bersoff, David M. "Why Good People Sometimes Do Bad Things: Motivated Reasoning and Unethical Behavior." *Personality and Social Psychology Bulletin* 25 (1999): 28–39.

Best, Joel. *Threatened Children: Rhetoric and Concern About Child Victims*. Chicago: University of Chicago Press, 1990.

Bishop, Bill. *The Big Sort: Why the Clustering of Like-Minded Americans is Tearing Us Apart*. Boston: Houghton Mifflin Harcourt, 2008.

Bivins, Jason C. *Religion of Fear: The Politics of Horror in Conservative Evangelicalism*. New York: Oxford University Press, 2010.

Black, Donald. "Crime as Social Control." *American Sociological Review* 48 (1983): 34–45.

Black, Helen K. "Poverty and Prayer: Spiritual Narratives of Elderly African-American Women." *Review of Religious Research* 40 (1999): 359–74.

Blake, John. "Why a President's Faith May Not Matter." *CNN*, June 30, 2012. Accessed August 10, 2014. http://religion.blogs.cnn.com/2012/06/30/why-a-presidents-faith-may-not-matter/.

Blaker, Kimberly, ed. *The Fundamentals of Extremism: The Christian Right in America*. Plymouth, MI: New Boston, 2003.

Bloom, Mia. *Dying to Kill: The Global Phenomenon of Suicide Terror*. New York: Columbia University Press, 2004.

Bloom, Paul. "Religion, Morality, Evolution." *Annual Review of Psychology* 63 (2012): 179–99.

———. "Religious Belief as an Evolutionary Accident." In *The Believing Primate: Scientific, Philosophical, and Theological Reflections on the Origin of Religion*, edited by Jeffrey Schloss and Michael J. Murray, 118–27. Oxford: Oxford University Press, 2009.

Blume, John H., Theodore Eisenberg, and Martin T. Wells. "Explaining Death Row's Population and Racial Composition." *Journal of Empirical Legal Studies* 1 (2004): 165–207.

Blumstein, Alfred., and Jacqueline Cohen. "Sentencing of Convicted Offenders: An Analysis of the Public's Views." *Law & Society Review* 14 (1980): 223–62.

———. "A Theory of the Stability of Punishment." *Journal of Criminal Law and Criminology* 64 (1973): 198–206.

Blumstein, Alfred, and Joel Wallman, eds. *The Crime Drop in America*. New York: Cambridge University Press, 2000.

Bliss, Stephen K., and Cynthia L. Crown. "Concern for Appropriateness, Religiosity, and Gender as Predictors of Alcohol and Marijuana Use." *Social Behavior and Personality* 22 (1994): 227–38.

Boehm, Christopher. "A Biocultural Evolutionary Explanation of Supernatural Sanctioning." In *Evolution of Religion: Studies, Theories, and Critiques*, edited by Joseph Bulbulia, Richard Sosis, Erika Harris,

Russell Genet, Cheryl Genet, and Karen Wyman, 143–52. Santa Margarita, CA: Collins Family Foundation, 2008.

———. *Moral Origins: The Evolution of Virtue, Altruism, and Shame.* New York: Basic Books, 2012.

———. "Retaliatory Violence in Human Prehistory." *British Journal of Criminology* 51 (2011): 518–34.

Bolen, Rebecca M. "Predicting Risk to Be Sexually Abused: A Comparison of Logistic Regression to Event History Analysis." *Child Maltreatment* 3 (1998): 157–70.

Bonomi, Patricia U. "John Jay, Religion, and the State." *New York History* 81 (2000): 8–18.

Borg, Marian J. "The Southern Subculture of Punitiveness? Regional Variation in Support for Capital Punishment." *Journal of Research on Crime and Delinquency* 34 (1997): 25–45.

Boroumand, Ladan, and Roya Boroumand. "Terror, Islam, and Democracy." *Journal of Democracy* 13 (2002): 7–8.

Bottoms, Bette L., Phillip R. Shaver, Gail S. Goodman, and Jianjian Qin. "In the Name of God: A Profile of Religion-Based Child Abuse." *Journal of Social Issues* 51 (1995): 85–111.

Bourgois, Philippe, and Jeffrey Schonberg. *Righteous Dopefiend.* Berkeley, CA: University of California Press, 2009.

Boyd, Gregory A. *The Myth of a Christian Nation: How the Quest for Political Power Is Destroying the Church.* Grand Rapids: Zondervan, 2006.

Boyer, Pascal. *Religion Explained: The Evolutionary Origins of Religious Thought.* New York: Basic Books, 2001.

Braman, Donald. *Doing Time on the Outside: Incarceration and Family Life in Urban America.* Ann Arbor, MI: University of Michigan Press, 2007.

Brant, Irving. *James Madison the Nationalist, 1780–1787.* Morgantown, PA: Sullivan Press, 2008.

Brauer, Markus, Wolfgang Wasel, and Paula Niedenthal. "Implicit and Explicit Components of Prejudice." *Review of General Psychology* 4 (2000): 79–101.

Brenner, Athalya. *The Israelite Woman: Social Role and Literary Type in Biblical Narrative*. Sheffield, England: JSOT Press, 1985.

Brewer, Marilynn B. "The Psychology of Prejudice: Ingroup Love or Outgroup Hate?" *Journal of Social Issues* 55 (1999): 429–44.

———. "Social Identity, Distinctiveness, and In-Group Homogeneity." *Social Cognition* 11 (1993): 150–64.

Brewer, Marilynn B., and Joseph G. Weber. "Self-Evaluation Effects of Interpersonal versus Intergroup Social Comparison." *Journal of Personality and Social Psychology* 66 (1994): 268–75.

Brezina, Timothy, Erdal Tekin, and Volkan Topalli. "'Might Not Be a Tomorrow': A Multi-Methods Approach to Anticipated Early Death and Youth Crime." *Criminology* 47 (2009): 1091–1129.

Brickner, Bryan W. *The Promise Keepers: Politics and Promises*. Lanham, MD: Lexington Books, 1999.

Bridgers, Lynn. *The American Religious Experience: A Concise History*. Lanham, MD: Rowman & Littlefield Publishers, 2006.

Brockman, John, ed. *What Have You Changed Your Mind About?* New York: HarperCollins, 2009.

Brooks, Arthur C. *Who Really Cares: The Surprising Truth About Compassionate Conservatism*. New York: Basic Books, 2006.

Brouwer, Steve, Paul Gifford, and Susan D. Rose. *Exporting the American Gospel: Global Christian Fundamentalism*. New York: Routledge, 1996.

Brown, Karen M. "Fundamentalism and the Control of Women." In *Fundamentalism and Gender*, edited by John S. Hawley, 175–201. New York: Oxford University Press, 1994.

Brown, L. B. "Aggression and Denominational Membership." *British Journal of Social and Clinical Psychology* 4 (2011): 175–78.

Brown, Michael P., and Preston Elrod. "Electronic House Arrest: An Examination of Citizen Attitudes." *Crime & Delinquency* 41 (1995): 332–46.

Brown, Rupert. *Prejudice: Its Social Psychology*. Oxford: Blackwell, 1995.

Bruce, Steve. "Identifying Conservative Protestantism." *Sociological Analysis* 44 (1983): 55–70.

Brückner, Hannah, and Peter Bearman. "After the Promise: The STD Consequences of Adolescent Virginity Pledges." *Journal of Adolescent Health* 36 (2005): 271–78.

Buckman, Rob. *Can We Be Good Without God?* Toronto: Viking Press, 2000.

Bunge, Mario. "Absolute Skepticism Equals Dogmatism." *Skeptical Inquirer* (2000): 34–36.

Bureau of Justice Statistics. *Drug and Crime Facts: Drug Law Violations.* Washington, DC: US Department of Justice, 2012. Accessed April 22, 2013. http://bjs.ojp.usdoj.gov/content/dcf/enforce.cfm.

Bureau of Labor Statistics. "Time Spent in Leisure and Sports Activities for the Civilian Population by Selected Characteristics, 2007 Annual Averages." US Department of Labor. June 18, 2014. Accessed August 17, 2014. http://www.bls.gov/news.release/atus.t11.htm.

Bureau of Prisons. "A Storied Past." Accessed May 14, 2012. http://www.bop.gov/about/history/.

Burkett, Steven R., and Mervin White. "Hellfire and Delinquency: Another Look." *Journal for the Scientific Study of Religion* 13 (1974): 455–62.

———. "Perceived Parents' Religiosity, Friends' Drinking and Hellfire: A Panel Study of Adolescent Drinking." *Review of Religious Research* 35 (1993): 134–54.

Bursik, Jr., Robert J., and Harold G. Grasmick. "The Use of Contextual Analysis in Models of Criminal Behavior." In *Delinquency and Crime: Current Theories*, edited by J. David Hawkins, 236–67. Cambridge, UK: Cambridge University Press, 1996.

———. *Neighborhoods and Crime: The Dimensions of Effective Community Control.* New York: Lexington, 1993.

Bush, George W. "Adjustments of Certain Pay Rates." Executive Order, December 22, 2005. US Office of Personnel Management. Accessed November 15, 2014. http://archive.opm.gov/oca/compmemo/2006/executiveorder2006pay.asp.

———. State of the Union Address. Washington, DC: Official White House version, February 2, 2005. Accessed February 7, 2013. http://www.american rhetoric.com/speeches/stateoftheunion2005.htm.

Butts, Jeffrey A., and Daniel P. Mears. "Reviving Juvenile Justice in a Get-Tough Era." *Youth and Society* 33 (2001): 169–98.

Campbell, Jacquelyn C., et al. "Assessing Risk Factors for Intimate Partner Homicide." *National Institute of Justice Journal* 250 (2003): 14–19.

Caputo, Richard K. "Parent Religiosity, Family Processes, and Adolescent Outcomes." *Journal of Contemporary Social Services* 85 (2004): 495–510.

———. "Religiousness and Adolescent Behaviors: A Comparison of Boys and Girls." *Journal of Religion & Spirituality* 24 (2005): 39–67.

Carlsmith, Kevin M., Timothy D. Wilson, and Daniel T. Gilbert. "The Paradoxical Consequences of Revenge." *Journal of Personality and Social Psychology* 95 (2008): 1316–24.

Carlucci, Kathleen, Jay Genova, Fran Rubackin, Randi Rubackin, and Wesley A. Kayson. "Effects of Sex, Religion, and Amount of Alcohol Consumption on Self-Reported Drinking-Related Problem Behaviors." *Psychosocial Reports* 72 (1993): 983–87.

Carney, Dana R., John T. Jost, Samuel D. Gosling, and Jeff Potter. "The Secret Lives of Liberals and Conservatives: Personality Profiles, Interaction Styles, and the Things They Leave Behind." *Political Psychology* 29 (2008): 807–40.

Caro, Robert A. *The Passage of Power: The Years of Lyndon Johnson.* New York: Knopf, 2012.

Carpenter, Joel A. *Revive Us Again: The Reawakening of American Fundamentalism.* Oxford: Oxford University Press, 1999.

Carter, Jimmy. *A Call to Action: Women, Religion, Violence and Power.* New York: Simon & Schuster, 2014.

———. *Living Faith.* New York: Broadway Books, 1998.

Carter, Stephen L. *The Culture of Disbelief: How American Law and Politics Trivialize Religious Devotion.* New York: Knopf Doubleday, 1994.

Cecero, John J., and Adam L. Fried. "Parental Rejection and Religiosity: Differential Predictors of Mood and Substance Use." *Research on the Social Scientific Study of Religion* 16 (2005): 185–206.

Chadwick, Bruce A., and Brent L. Top. "Religiosity and Delinquency among LDS Adolescents." *Journal for the Scientific Study of Religion* 32 (1993): 51–67.

Chalmers, David M. *Hooded Americanism: The History of the Ku Klux Klan*. Durham, NC: Duke University Press, 1987.

Chapp, Christopher B. *Religious Rhetoric and American Politics: The Endurance of Civil Religion in Electoral Campaigns*. Ithaca, NY: Cornell University Press, 2012.

Chawla, Neharika, Clayton Neighbors, Melissa A. Lewis, Christine M. Lee, and Mary E. Larimer. "Attitudes and Perceived Approval of Drinking as Mediators of the Relationship between the Importance of Religion and Alcohol Use." *Journal of Studies on Alcohol and Drugs* 68 (2007): 410–18.

Chernow, Ron. *Alexander Hamilton*. New York: Penguin Press, 2004.

Chesney-Lind, Meda. *The Female Offender: Girls, Women and Crime*, 2nd ed. Thousand Oaks, CA: Sage, 2004.

Chrnalogar, Mary A. *Twisted Scriptures: Breaking Free From Churches That Abuse*. Grand Rapids, MI: Zondervan, 2000.

Chu, Doris C. "Religiosity and Desistance from Drug Use." *Criminal Justice and Behavior* 34 (2007): 661–79.

Churchill, Ward. *On the Justice of Roosting Chickens: Reflections on the Consequences of the U.S. Imperial Arrogance and Criminality*. Oakland, CA: AK Press, 2003.

Cimino, Richard, and Don Lattin. "Choosing my Religion." *American Demographics* (April 1999): 62.

Citrin, Jack, Beth Reingold, and Donald P. Green. "American Identity and the Politics of Ethnic Change." *Journal of Politics* 52 (1990): 1124–54.

Citrin, Jack, Cara Wong, and Brian Duff. "The Meaning of American National Identity: Patterns of Ethnic Conflict and Consensus." In *Social Identity, Inter-Group Conflict and Conflict Resolution*, edited by Richard D. Ashmore, Lee Jussim, and David Wilder, 71–100. New York: Oxford University Press, 2000.

Clark, Lee. *Worst Cases: Terror and Catastrophe in the Popular Imagination*. Chicago: University of Chicago Press, 2006.

Clarkson, Frederick. *Eternal Hostility: The Struggle between Theocracy and Democracy*. Monroe, ME: Common Courage Press, 1997.

Clear, Todd, and Melvina T. Sumter. "Prisoners, Prison, and Religion: Religion and Adjustment to Prison." *Journal of Offender Rehabilitation* 35 (2002): 127–59.

Clermont, Betty. *The Neo-Catholics: Implementing Christian Nationalism in America*. Atlanta: Clarity Press, 2009.

Clifton, Allen. "Right-wing Christians, Radical Islamic Fundamentalists— They're Pretty Much the Same." *Forward Progressives*, April 20, 2014. Accessed April 22, 2014. http://www.forwardprogressives.com/right-wing-christians-radical-islamic-fundamentalists-theyre-pretty-much-exactly/.

Coates, James. *Armed and Dangerous: The Rise of the Survivalist Right*. New York: Hill & Wang, 1987.

Cochran, John K. "The Effect of Religiosity on Secular and Ascetic Deviance." *Sociological Focus* 4 (1989): 293–306.

———. "The Variable Effects of Religiosity and Denomination on Adolescent Self-Reported Alcohol Use by Beverage Type." *Journal of Drug Issues* 33 (1993): 479–91.

Cochran, John K., and Ronald L. Akers. "Beyond Hellfire: An Exploration of the Variable Effects of Religiosity on Adolescent Marijuana and Alcohol Use." *Journal of Research on Crime and Delinquency* 26 (1989): 198–225.

Cochran, John K., Peter B. Wood, and Bruce J. Arneklev. "Is the Religiosity-Delinquency Relationship Spurious? A Test of Arousal and Social Control Theories." *Journal of Research in Crime and Delinquency* 31 (1994): 92–123.

Cochran, Joshua C., and Patricia Y. Warren. "Racial, Ethnic and Gender Differences in Perceptions of the Police: The Salience of Officer Race within the Context of Racial Profiling." *Journal of Contemporary Criminal Justice* 28 (2012): 206–27.

Coffin, William S. *The Heart Is a Little to the Left: Essays on Public Morality*. Hanover, NH: University Press of New England, 1999.

Cohen, Anthony P. "Belonging: The Experience of Culture." In *Symbolising Boundaries: Identity and Diversity in British Cultures*, edited by Anthony P. Cohen, 1–17. Manchester: Manchester University Press, 1986.

Cohen, Edmund D. *The Mind of the Bible Believer*. Amherst, NY: Prometheus Books, 1988.

Cohn, Edward. "Paul Cassell and the Goblet of Fire." *American Prospect*. December 19, 2001. Accessed on April 16, 2014. http://prospect.org/article/paul-cassell-and-goblet-fire.

Cole, Deborah D., and Maureen G. Dunn. *Sex and Character*. Richardson, TX: Haughton Publishing Company, 1998.

Coleman, Clive. *Understanding Crime Data: Haunted by the Dark Figure*. New York: Free Press, 1996.

Collins, John J. *Does the Bible Justify Violence?* Minneapolis, MN: Augsburg Fortress, 2004.

Conklin, John E. *Why Crime Rates Fell*. Boston: Allyn & Bacon, 2003.

Conover, Pamela J. "The Influence of Group Identification on Political Perception and Evaluation." *Journal of Politics* 46 (1984): 760–85.

———. "The Role of Social Groups in Political Thinking." *British Journal of Political Science* 18 (1988): 51–76.

Cook, Christopher C.H., Deborah Goddard, and Rachel Westall. "Knowledge and Experience of Drug Use amongst Church Affiliated Young People." *Drug and Alcohol Dependence* 46 (1997): 9–17.

Cooper-White, Pamela. *The Cry of Tamar: Violence against Women and the Church's Response*. Minneapolis, MN: Augsburg Fortress, 1995.

Corning, Peter. *Holistic Darwinism: Synergy, Cybernetics, and the Bioeconomics of Evolution*. Chicago: University of Chicago Press, 2005.

Corriveau, Kathleen H., Eva E. Chen, and Paul L. Harris. "Judgments about Fact and Fiction by Children from Religious and Nonreligious Backgrounds." *Cognitive Science* (2014): 1–30.

Cosmides, Leda, and John Tooby. "From Evolution to Behavior: Evolutionary Psychology as the Missing Link." In *The Latest on the Best: Essays on Evolution and Optimality*, edited by John Dupre, 277–306. Cambridge, MA: MIT Press, 1987.

Crenshaw, Martha. "An Organizational Approach to the Analysis of Political Terrorism." *Orbis* 29 (1985): 465–89.

———. "The Psychology of Political Terrorism." In *Political Psychology*, edited by Margaret Hermann, 379–413. San Francisco, CA: Jossey-Bass, 1986.

Cretacci, Michael A. "Religion and Social Control: An Application of a Modified Social Bond on Violence." *College Health and Human Sciences* 28 (2003): 254–77.

Crisafulli, Chuck, and Kyra Thompson. *Go to Hell: A Heated History of the Underworld.* New York: Simon Spotlight, 2005.

Crocker, Jennifer, Leigh L. Thompson, Kathleen M. McGraw, and Cindy Ingerman. "Downward Comparison, Prejudice, and Evaluation of Others: Effects of Self-Esteem and Threat." *Journal of Personality and Social Psychology* 52 (1987): 907–16.

Cronin, Christopher. "Religiosity, Religious Affiliation, and Alcohol and Drug Use among American College Students Living in Germany." *Interdisciplinary Journal of the Addictions* 30 (1995): 231–38.

Crowley, Sharon. *Toward a Civil Discourse: Rhetoric and Fundamentalism.* Pittsburgh: University of Pittsburgh Press, 2006.

Crowne, Douglas P., and David Marlowe. *The Approval Motive.* New York: Wiley, 1964.

Crowson, H. Michael. "Are All Conservatives Alike? A Study of the Psychological Correlates of Cultural and Economic Conservatism." *Journal of Psychology: Interdisciplinary and Applied* 143 (2009): 449–63.

Cullen, Francis T., Bonnie S. Fisher, and Brandon K. Applegate. "Public Opinion about Punishment and Corrections." In *Of Crime and Justice: A Review of Research*, edited by Michael Tonry, 1–79. Chicago: University of Chicago Press, 2000.

Cullen, Francis T., John P. Wright, and Mitchell B. Chamlin. "Social Support and Social reform: A Progressive Crime Control Agenda." *Crime & Delinquency* 45 (1999): 188–207.

Cunningham, William A., Kristopher J. Preacher, and Mahzarin R. Banaji. "Implicit Attitude Measures: Consistency, Stability, and Convergent Validity." *Psychological Science* 12 (2001): 163–70.

Curry, Theodore R. "Conservative Protestantism and the Perceived Wrongfulness of Crimes." *Criminology* 34 (1996): 453–64.

Curtis, Lynn A. "Victim Precipitation and Violent Crime." *Social Problems* 21 (1974): 594–612.

Damasio, Antonio. *Descartes' Error: Emotion, Reason, and the Human Brain*. New York: Putnam, 1994.

Darwin, Charles R. *On the Origin of the Species By Means of Natural Selection, or the Preservation of Favoured Races in the Struggle for Life*. London: John Murray, 1859.

Dasgupta, Nilanjana, David DeSteno, and Matthew Hunsinger. "Fanning the Flames of Prejudice: The Influence of Specific Incidental Emotions on Implicit Prejudice." *American Psychological Association* 9 (2009): 585–91.

David, Henry P. "Born Unwanted: Long-Term Developmental Effects of Denied Abortion." *Journal of Social Issues* 48 (1992): 163–81.

Davidson, James D. "Socioeconomic Status and Ten Dimensions of Religious Commitment." *Sociology and Social Research* 61 (1977): 462–85.

Davidson, James D., and Dean D. Knudsen. "A New Approach to Religious Commitment." *Sociological Focus* 10 (1977): 151–73.

Davies, Martin F. "Dogmatism and Belief Formation: Output Inference in the Processing of Supporting and Contradictory Cognitions." *Journal of Personality and Social Psychology* 75 (1998): 456–66.

Davis, Percival, and Dean H. Kenyon. *Of Pandas and People: The Central Question of Biological Origins*. Richardson, TX: Haughton Publishing, 1989.

Dawkins, Richard. *The God Delusion*. New York: Houghton Mifflin, 2006.
———. "Viruses of the Mind." *Free Inquiry* 13 (1993): 34–38.

Dawson, Myrna, and Rosemary Gartner. "Differences in the Characteristics of Intimate Femicides: The Role of Relationship State and Relationship Status." *Homicide Studies* 2 (1998): 378–99.

Deaux, Kay, Anne Reid, Kim Mizrahi, and Kathleen A. Ethier. "Parameters of Social Identity." *Journal of Personality and Social Psychology* 68 (1995): 280–91.

DeBerg, Betty A. *Ungodly Women: Gender and the First Wave of American Fundamentalism*. Macon, GA: Mercer University Press, 2000.

Dechesne, Mark, Jacques Janssen, and Ad van Knippenberg. "Derogation and Distancing as Terror Management Strategies: The Moderating Role of Need for Structure and Permeability of Group Boundaries." *Journal of Personality and Social Psychology* 79 (2000): 923–32.

Dechesne, Mark, Tom Pyszczynski, Jamie Arndt, Sean Ransom, Kennon M. Sheldon, Ad van Knippenberg, and Jacques Janssen. "Literal and Symbolic Immortality: The Effect of Evidence of Literal Immortality on Self-Esteem Striving in Response to Mortality Salience." *Journal of Personality and Social Psychology* 84 (2003): 722–37.

DeIulio, John J. "Let 'Em Rot." *Wall Street Journal*, January 26, 1994: A14.

Demar, Gary. *Ruler of the Nations: Biblical Principles for Government*. Middlesex, UK: Dominion Press, 1987.

Demerath, N.J., III. *Social Class in American Protestantism*. Chicago: Rand McNally, 1965.

Demos, John. *The Enemy Within: 2000 Years of Witch-Hunting in the Western World*. New York: Viking, 2008.

Dennett, Daniel C. *Breaking the Spell: Religion as a Natural Phenomenon*. New York: Penguin Books, 2006.

Dennis, Kyle M. "The Impact of Religiosity on Deviance and Criminal Activity in Youth and Young Adults." *Research in Race and Ethnic Relations* 12 (2005): 93–130.

Desmond, Scott A., Sarah E. Soper, David J. Purpura, and Elizabeth Smith. "Religiosity, Moral Beliefs, and Delinquency: Does the Effect of Religiosity on Delinquency Depend on Moral Beliefs?" *Sociological Spectrum* 29 (2009): 51–71.

Diamond, Sarah. *Not By Politics Alone: The Enduring Influence of the Christian Right*. New York: Guilford Press, 2000.

———. *Roads to Dominion: Right-Wing Movements and Political Power in the United States*. New York: Guilford Press, 1995.

———. *Spiritual Warfare: The Politics of the Christian Right*. Boston: South End Press, 1989.

Diaz, Joseph D. "Religion and Gambling in Sin-City: A Statistical Analysis of the Relationship between Religion and Gambling Patterns in Las Vegas Residents." *Social Science Journal* 37 (2000): 453–58.

DiMaggio, Paul, John Evans, and Bethany Bryson. "Have Americans' Social Attitudes Become More Polarized?" *American Journal of Sociology* 102 (1996): 90–155.

Dinnerstein, Leonard. *Anti-Semitism and the American Jewish Experience.* New York: Columbia University Press, 1994.

Dion, Kenneth L. "Intergroup Conflict and Intragroup Cohesiveness." In *The Social Psychology of Intergroup Relations*, edited by William G. Austin and Stephen Worchel, 211–24. Monterey, CA: Brooks/Cole, 1979.

Dobson, James. *Bringing Up Boys.* Wheaton, IL: Tyndale House, 2001.

———. *Dare to Discipline.* New York: Bantam Books, 1970.

———. *Marriage Under Fire: Why We Must Win This Battle.* Sisters, OR: Multnomah, 2004.

Dodson, Kimberly D., Leann N. Cabage, and Paul M. Klenowoski. "An Evidence Based Assessment of Faith-Based Programs: Do Faith-Based Programs 'Work' to Reduce Recidivism?" *Journal of Offender Rehabilitation* 50 (2011): 367–83.

Dolan, Raymond J. "On the Neurology of Morals." *Nature Neuroscience* 2 (1999): 927–29.

Donner, Frank J. *The Un-Americans.* New York, NY: Ballantine, 1961.

Douglas, Roger. "Is Chivalry Dead? Gender and Sentence in the Victorian Magistrates' Courts." *Journal of Sociology* 23 (1987): 343–57.

Dovidio, John F., Kerry Kawakami, Craig Johnson, Brenda Johnson, and Adaiah Howard. "On the Nature of Prejudice: Automatic and Controlled Processes." *Journal of Experimental Social Psychology* 33 (1997): 510–40.

Dubose, Lou, and Jan Reid. *The Hammer: Tom DeLay, God, Money, and the Rise of the Republican Congress.* New York: Public Affairs, 2004.

Dunn, Michael S. "The Relationship between Religiosity, Employment, and Political Beliefs on Substance Use among High School Seniors." *Journal of Drug and Alcohol Education* 49 (2005): 43–88.

Durkheim, Emile. *The Elementary Forms of Religious Life.* Translated by Karen E. Fields. New York: Free Press, 1995.

Eck, Diana L. *A New Religious America: How a "Christian Country" Has*

Now Become the World's Most Religiously Diverse Nation. New York: Harper, 2001.

Eckholm, Erik. "History Buff Sets a Course for the Right." *New York Times*, May 5, 2011.

Ecklund, Elaine H., and Jerry Z. Park. "Conflict between Religion and Science among Academic Scientists?" *Journal for the Scientific Study of Religion* 48 (2009): 276–92.

Ecklund, Elaine H., and Christopher P. Scheitle. "Religion among Academic Scientists: Distinctions, Disciplines, and Demographics." *Social Forces* 54 (2007): 289–307.

Economist. "Saving Lives and Money: States Plagued by Fiscal Woes Rethink their Stance on the Death Penalty." *Economist*, March 12, 2009. Accessed March 30, 2013. http://www.economist.com/node/13279051.

Edelson, Jeffrey L. "The Overlap between Child Maltreatment and Woman Battering." *Violence Against Women* 5 (1990): 134–154.

Edgell, Penny, Joseph Gerteis, and Douglas Hartmann. "Atheists as 'Other': Moral Boundaries and Cultural Membership in American Society." *American Sociological Review* 71 (2006): 211–34.

Edsall, Thomas B. *Building Red America: The New Conservative Coalition and the Drive for Permanent Power.* New York: Basic Books, 2006.

Ehrenreich, Barbara. *Nickel and Dimed: On (Not) Getting By in America.* New York: Holt, 2002.

Ehrman, Bart D. *Misquoting Jesus: The Story Behind Who Changed the Bible and Why.* San Francisco: Harper, 2005.

———. *Revealing the Hidden Contradictions in the Bible (and Why We Don't Know About Them).* New York: Harper One, 2009.

———. *Whose Word Is It?* New York: Continuum, 2006.

Eisenberg, Carol. "America Gets Religion (But Do Americans Get Religion?): God Talk is Everywhere." *Newsday*, April 12, 2004: B02.

Elifson, Kirk W., David M. Peterson, and C. Kirk Hadaway. "Religiosity and Delinquency: A Contextual Analysis." *Criminology* 21 (1983): 505–27.

Ellens, J. Harold. *The Destructive Power of Religion: Violence in Judaism, Christianity, and Islam.* New York: Praeger, 2007.

Eller, Jack D. *Cruel Creeds, Virtuous Violence: Religious Violence across Culture and History*. Amherst, NY: Prometheus Books, 2010.

Ellerbe, Helen. *The Dark Side of Christian History*. Orlando, FL: Morningstar & Lark, 1995.

Ellis, Albert. "Is Religiosity Pathological?" *Free Inquiry* 8 (1988): 27–32.

Ellis, Lee. "Denominational Differences in Self-Reported Delinquency." *Journal of Offender Rehabilitation* 35 (2002): 185–98.

Ellison, Christopher G. "Religious Involvement and Subjective Well-Being." *Journal of Health and Social Behavior* 32 (1991): 80–99.

Ellison, Christopher G., John P. Bartkowski, and Kristin L. Anderson. "Are There Religious Variations in Domestic Violence?" *Journal of Family Issues* 20 (1999): 87–113.

Ellison, Christopher G., John P. Bartkowski, and Michelle L. Segal. "Conservative Protestantism and the Parental Use of Corporal Punishment." *Social Forces* 74 (1996): 1003–28.

Ellison, Christopher G., Jason D. Boardman, David R. Williams, and James S. Jackson. "Religious Involvement, Stress, and Mental Health: Findings from the 1995 Detroit Area Study." *Social Forces* 80 (2001): 215–49.

Ellison, Christopher G., Jeffrey A. Burr, and Patricia L. McCall. "The Enduring Puzzle of Southern Homicide: Is Regional Religious Culture the Missing Piece?" *Homicide Studies* 7 (2003): 326–52.

Ellison, Christopher G., and Linda K. George. "Religious Involvement, Social Ties, and Social Support in a Southeastern Community." *Journal for the Scientific Study of Religion* 33 (1994): 46–61.

Ellison, Christopher G., and Darren E. Sherkat. "Obedience and Autonomy: Religion and Parental Values Reconsidered." *Journal for the Scientific Study of Religion* 32 (1993): 313–29.

Ellison, Christopher G., Jenny A. Trinitapoli, Kristin L. Anderson, and Byron R. Johnson. "Religion and Domestic Violence: An Examination of Variations by Race and Ethnicity." *Violence against Women* 13 (2007): 1094–112.

Engs, Ruth C., and Kenneth Mullen. "The Effect of Religion and Religiosity on Drug Use among a Selected Sample of Post Secondary Students in Scotland." *Addiction Research* 7 (1999): 149–70.

Erb, Kelly Phillips. "Death and Taxes: The Real Cost of the Death Penalty." *Forbes*, September 22, 2011. Accessed June 9, 2013. http://www.forbes.com/sites/kellyphillipserb/2011/09/22/death-and -taxes-the-real-cost-of-the-death-penalty/.

Ethier, Kathleen A., and Kay Deaux. "Negotiating Social Identity When Contexts Change: Maintaining Identification and Responding to Threat." *Journal of Personality and Social Psychology* 67 (1994): 243–51.

Etter, Gregg W. "Perceived Effects of Religion on White Supremacist Culture." *Journal of Gang Research* 9 (2002): 15–24.

Evans, Richard J. *The Coming of the Third Reich*. New York: Penguin Books, 2005.

Evans, T. David, Francis T. Cullen, R. Gregory Dunaway, and Velmer S. Burton, Jr. "Religion and Crime Reexamined: The Impact of Religion, Secular Controls, and Social Ecology on Adult Criminality." *Criminology* 33 (1995): 195–224.

Eyssel, Freiderike, and Gerd Bohner. "The Rating of Sexist Humor under Time Pressure as an Indicator of Spontaneous Sexist Attitudes." *Sex Roles* 57 (2007): 651–60.

Fagan, Jeffrey, and Garth Davies. "Policing Guns: Order Maintenance and Crime Control in New York." In *Guns, Crime, and Punishment in America*, edited by Bernard E. Harcourt, 857–953. New York: University Press, 2003.

———. "Street Stops and Broken Windows: Terry, Race, and Disorder in New York City." *Fordham Urban Law Journal* 28 (2000): 457–504.

Fagan, Jeffrey, Franklin E. Zimring, and June Kim. "Declining Homicide in New York: A Tale of Two Trends." *Journal of Criminal Law and Criminology* 88 (1998): 1277–324.

Falwell, Jerry. "The Case of the Offensive Candy Canes." WorldNetDaily, January 11, 2001. Accessed May 24, 2013. http://www.wnd. com/2003/01/16684/.

Farkas, Steve, Jean Johnson, and Tony Foleno. *For Goodness' Sake: Why So Many Want Religion to Play a Greater Role in American Society*. New York: Public Agenda, 2001.

Farley, John E. *Majority-Minority Relations*. Upper Saddle River, NJ: Prentice Hall, 2010.

Farrington, David P., Patrick A. Langan, and Michael Tonry. *National Crime Rates Compared*. Washington, D.C.: Bureau of Justice Statistics, 2004.

Farris, Michael. *The Joshua Generation: Restoring the Heritage of Christian Leadership*. Nashville, TN: Broadman & Holman, 2005.

Fass, Simon M., and Chung-Ron Pi. "Getting Tough on Juvenile Crime: An Analysis of Costs and Benefits." *Crime & Delinquency* 39 (2002): 321–44.

Federal Bureau of Investigation. *Crime in the United States, 2010*. Washington, DC: Department of Justice, 2011. Accessed June 10, 2014. http://www.fbi.gov/about-us/cjis/ucr/crime-in-the-u.s/2010/crime -in-the-u.s.-2010.

———. *Hate Crime Statistics, 2012*. Washington, DC: United States Department of Justice, 2013. Accessed June 15, 2014. http://www.fbi .gov/about-us/cjis/ucr/hate-crime/2012.

———. *Uniform Crime Reports: Crime in the United States, 2012*. Washington, DC: United States Department of Justice, 2013. Accessed June 10, 2014. http://www.fbi.gov/about-us/cjis/ucr/ucr.

Fehr, Ernst. "Human Behavior: Don't Lose Your Reputation." *Nature* 432 (2004): 449–50.

Fehr, Ernst., and Simon Gächter. "Altruistic Punishment in Humans." *Nature* 415 (2002): 137–40.

Feldman, Noah. *Divided by God: America's Church-State Problem—And What We Should Do About It*. New York: Farrar, Straus, and Giroux, 2005.

Felson, Marcus. *Crime and Nature*. Thousand Oaks, CA: Sage, 2006.

———. "Predatory and Dispute-Related Violence: A Social Interactionist Approach." In *Advances in Criminological Theory*, Vol. 5, edited by Ronald V. Clark and Marcus Felson, 103–25. New Brunswick, NJ: Transaction, 1993.

Felson, Marcus, and Rachel Boba. *Crime & Everyday Life*. Thousand Oaks, CA: Sage, 2009.

Fenn, Richard K. *Dreams of Glory: Sources of Apocalyptic Terror*. Burlington, VT: Ashgate, 2006.

Ferling, John. *Adams vs. Jefferson: The Tumultuous Election of 1800*. New York: Oxford University Press, 2004.

Ferngren, Gary B. *Science and Religion: A Historical Introduction*. Baltimore, MD: John Hopkins University Press, 2002.

Fernquist, Robert M. "A Research Note on the Association between Religion and Delinquency." *Deviant Behavior: An Interdisciplinary Journal* 16 (1995): 169–75.

Finckenauer, James O. "Public Support for the Death Penalty: Retribution as Just Deserts or Retribution as Revenge." *Justice Quarterly* 5 (1988): 81–100.

Fiorina, Morris P., Samuel J. Abrams, and Jeremy C. Pope. *Culture War? The Myth of a Polarized America*. New York: Pearson Longman, 2005.

Fischer, Hannah. "Iraq Casualties: U.S. Military Forces and Iraqi Civilians, Police, and Security Forces." Congressional Research Service. Report for Members and Committees of Congress, 2010.

Flippen, Annette R., Harvey A. Hornstein, William E. Siegal, and Eben A. Weitzman. "A Comparison of Similarity and Interdependence as Triggers for In-Group Formation." *Personality and Social Psychology Bulletin* 22 (1996): 882–93.

Florian, Victor, and Mario Mikulincer. "Fear of Death and the Judgment of Social Transgressions: A Multidimensional Test of Terror Management Theory." *Journal of Personality and Social Psychology* 73 (1997): 369–80.

Fontaine, Natalie M. G., Frühling V. Rijsdijk, Eamon J. P. McCrory, and Essi Viding. "Etiology of Different Developmental Trajectories of Callous-Unemotional Traits." *Journal of the American Academy of Child and Adolescent Psychiatry* 49 (2010): 656–64.

Forthun, Larry F., Nancy J. Bell, Charles W. Peek, and Sheh-Wei Sun. "Religiosity, Sensation Seeking, and Alcohol/Drug Use in Denominational and Gender Contexts." *Journal of Drug Issues* 29 (1999): 75–90.

Fortune, Marie, and Cindy Enger. *Violence against Women and the Role of Religion*. Harrisburg, PA: National Recourse Center of Domestic Violence, 2005.

Fox, James A., and Marianne W. Zawitz. *Homicide Trends in the United States, 2003*. Washington, DC: US Department of Justice, Bureau of Justice Statistics, July 1, 2004. Accessed August 16, 2014. http://www.bjs.gov/index.cfm?ty=pbdetail&iid=966.

Frank, Thomas. *What's the Matter with Kansas?* New York: Metropolitan Books, 2004.

Franken, Al. *Lies and the Lying Liars Who Tell Them*. New York: Dutton, 2003.

Frankfurt, Harry G. *On Bullshit*. Princeton: Princeton University Press, 2005.

Frankl, Viktor E. *Man's Search for Meaning*. New York: Simon and Schuster, 1963.

Frazer, Gregg L. *The Religious Beliefs of America's Founding Fathers: Reason, Revelation, Revolution*. Lawrence, KS: University Press of Kansas, 2012.

Frazier, Michael L. *The Enlightenment of Sympathy: Justice and the Moral Sentiments in the Eighteenth Century and Today*. New York: Oxford University Press, 2010.

Free, Jr., Marvin D. "Religiosity, Religious Conservatism, Bonds to School, and Juvenile Delinquency among Three Categories of Drug Users." *Deviant Behavior* 15 (1994): 151–70.

———. "Religious Affiliation, Religiosity, and Impulsive and Intentional Deviance." *Sociological Forum* 25 (1992): 77–91.

Freeman, Richard B. "Who Escapes? The Relation of Churchgoing and Other Background Factors to the Socioeconomic Performance of Black Male Youth from Inner-City Tracts." In *The Black Youth Employment Crisis*, edited by Richard B. Freeman and Harry J. Holzer, 353–76. Chicago: University of Chicago Press, 1986.

Friedman, Richard E. *Who Wrote the Bible?* New York: HarperCollins, 1989.

Froese, Paul, and Christopher D. Bader. "God in America: Why Theology is Not Simply the Concern of Philosophers." *Journal for the Scientific Study of Religion* 46 (2007): 465–81.

Fukuyama, Yoshio. "The Major Dimensions of Church Membership." *Review of Religious Research* 2 (1961): 154–61.

Fulsom, Don. *Nixon's Darkest Secrets: The Inside Story of America's Most Troubled President*. New York: Thomas Dunne Books, 2012.

Fulton, Aubyn S. "Identity Status, Religious Orientation, and Prejudice." *Journal of Youth and Adolescence* 26 (1997): 1–11.

Gaede, Stan. "A Causal Model of Belief-Orthodoxy: Proposal and Empirical Test." *Sociological Analysis* 37 (1976): 205–17.

———. "Religious Participation, Socioeconomic Status, and Belief Orthodoxy." *Journal for the Scientific Study of Religion* 16 (1977): 245–53.

Galanter, Marc. "Psychological Induction into the Large Group: Findings from a Modern Religious Sect." *American Journal of Psychiatry* 136 (1980): 1574–79.

Galbraith, John K. *The Good Society: The Humane Agenda*. New York: Houghton Mifflin, 1996.

Galen, Luke W., and William M. Rogers. "Religiosity, Alcohol Expectancies, Drinking Motives and Their Interaction in the Prediction of Drinking among College Students." *Journal of Studies on Alcohol* 65 (2004): 469–76.

Gallup, Jr., George, and Jim Castelli. *The People's Religion: American Faith in the 90's*. New York: Macmillan, 1989.

Gardner, Daniel. *The Science of Fear: How the Culture of Fear Manipulates Your Brain*. New York: Plume, 2008.

Garland, David. *Peculiar Institution: America's Death Penalty in an Age of Abolition*. New York: Oxford University Press, 2010.

Gershoff, Elizabeth T., Pamela C. Miller, and George W. Holden. "Parenting Influences from the Pulpit: Religious Affiliation as a Determinant of Parental Corporal Punishment." *Journal of Family Psychology* 13 (1999): 307–20.

Gibson, John. *The War on Christmas: How the Liberal Plot to Ban the Sacred Christian Holiday is Worse Than You Thought*. New York: Sentinel Press, 2005.

Gilovich, Thomas. *How We Know What Isn't So: The Fallibility of Human Reason in Everyday Life*. New York: Free Press, 1991.

Gilovich, Thomas, Dale Griffin, and Daniel Kahneman, eds. *Heuristics and Biases: The Psychology of Intuitive Judgment.* New York, Cambridge University Press, 2002.

Girard, René. *Violence and the Sacred.* Baltimore, MD: John Hopkins University Press, 1977.

Gitlin, Todd. "Varieties of Patriotic Experience." In *The Fight Is for Democracy,* edited by George Packer, 105–38. New York: HarperCollins, 2003.

Glassner, Barry. *The Culture of Fear.* New York: Basic Books, 1999.

Glaze, Lauren F., and Laura M. Maruschak. *Parents in Prison and Their Minor Children.* Bureau of Justice Special Report, 2010. Accessed August 1, 2013. http://www.bjs.gov/content/pub/pdf/pptmc.pdf.

Glover, Jonathan. *Humanity: A Moral History of the Twentieth Century.* New Haven, CT: Yale University Press, 2002.

Goffman, Erving. *The Presentation of Self in Everyday Life.* New York: Anchor, 1959.

Goldberg, Jeffrey. "Why Is U.S. Violent Crime Declining? Part 2: Goldberg." *Bloomberg View,* February 15, 2012. Accessed January 10, 2013. http://www.bloomberg.com/news/2012–02–15/why-is-u-s-violent-crime-down-part-2-commentary-by-jeffrey-goldberg.html.

Goldberg, Michelle. *Kingdom Coming: The Rise of Christian Nationalism.* New York: Norton, 2007.

———. "Kingdom Coming: The Rise of Christian Nationalism." *Salon,* May 12, 2006. Accessed November 20, 2013. http://www.salon.com/2006/05/12/goldberg_14/.

Goldenberg, Jamie L., Tom Pyszczynski, Jeff Greenberg, and Sheldon Solomon. "Fleeing the Body: A Terror Management Perspective on the Problem of Human Corporeality." *Personality & Social Psychology Review* 4 (2000): 200–18.

Goldenberg, Jamie L., Tom Pyszczynski, Jeff Greenberg, Sheldon Solomon, Benjamin Kluck, and Robin Cornwell. "I Am Not an Animal: Mortality Salience, Disgust, and the Denial of Human Creatureliness." *Journal of Experimental Psychology* 130 (2001): 427–35.

Goldenberg, Jamie L., Tom Pyszczynski, Shannon K. McCoy, Jeff

Greenberg, and Sheldon Solomon. "Death, Sex, Love, and Neuroticism: Why is Sex Such a Problem?" *Journal of Personality and Social Psychology* 77 (1999): 1173–87.

Golebiowska, Ewa A. "The Gender Gap in Political Tolerance." *Political Behavior* 21 (1999): 43–66.

Gore, Al. *The Assault on Reason*. New York: Penguin Books, 2007.

Gottfredson, Denise C., Amanda Cross, and David A. Soulé. "Distinguishing Characteristics of Effective and Ineffective After-School Programs to Prevent Delinquency and Victimization." *Criminology & Public Policy* 6 (2007): 289–318.

Gottfredson, Denise C., Stephanie A. Gerstenblith, David A. Soulé, Shannon C. Womer, and Shaoli Lu. "Do After School Programs Reduce Delinquency?" *Prevention* Science 5 (2004): 253–66.

Gould, Jon B., and Stephen D. Mastrofski. "Suspect Searches: Assessing Police Behavior under the U.S. Constitution." *Criminology and Public Policy* 3 (2004): 315–61.

Graber, Doris. *Crime News and the Public*. New York: Praeger, 1980.

Graham, Jesse, and Jonathan Haidt. "Beyond Beliefs: Religions Bind Individuals into Moral Communities." *Personality and Social Psychology Review* 14 (2010): 140–50.

Graham, Jesse, Jonathan Haidt, and Brian A. Nosek. "Liberals and Conservatives Rely on Different Sets of Moral Foundations." *Personality and Social Psychology* 96 (2009): 1029–46.

Grann, David. "Where W. Got Compassion." *New York Times*, September, 12 1999. Accessed August 1, 2013. http://www.nytimes.com/1999/09/12/magazine/where-w-got-compassion.html.

Grant, George. *The Changing of the Guard: The Vital Role Christians Must Play in America's Unfolding Political and Cultural Drama*. Nashville: Broadman and Holman, 1995.

———. *The Importance of the Electoral College*. San Antonio, TX: Vision Forum Ministries, 2004.

———. *Killer Angel: A Short Biography of Planned Parenthood's Founder, Margaret Sanger*. Tennessee: Highland Books, 2001.

———. *The Patriot's Handbook: A Citizenship Primer for a New*

Generation of Americans, 2nd ed. Nashville: Cumberland House Publishing, 2004.

Grant, George., and Mark A. Horne. *Legislating Immorality: The Homosexual Movement Comes Out of the Closet*. Chicago: Moody Publishers, 1993.

Grasmick, Harold G., Robert J. Bursik, Jr., and John K. Cochran. "Render unto Caesar What Is Caesar's: Religiosity and Taxpayer's Inclination to Cheat." *Sociological Quarterly* 32 (1991): 251–66.

Grasmick, Harold G., Robert J. Bursik, Jr., and M'lou Kimpel. "Protestant Fundamentalism and Attitudes toward Corporal Punishment of Children." *Violence and Victims* 6 (1991): 283–98.

Grasmick, Harold G., John K. Cochran, Robert J. Bursik, and M'lou Kimpel. "Religion, Punitive Justice, and Support for the Death Penalty." *Justice Quarterly* 10 (1993): 289–314.

Grasmick, Harold G., Elizabeth Davenport, Mitchell B. Chamlin, and Robert J. Bursik, Jr. "Protestant Fundamentalism and the Retributivist Doctrine of Punishment." *Criminology* 30 (1992): 21–45.

Grasmick, Harold G., Karyl Kinsey, and John K. Cochran. "Denomination, Religiosity and Compliance with the Law: A Study of Adults." *Journal for the Scientific Study of Religion* 30 (1991): 99–107.

Grasmick, Harold G., Carolyn S. Morgan, and Mary Baldwin. "Support for Corporal Punishment in the Schools: A Comparison of the Effects of Socioeconomic Status and Religion." *Social Science Quarterly* 73 (1992): 177–87.

Graves, Kersey. *The World's Sixteen Crucified Saviors*. New York: Cosimo Classics, 1875.

Graves, William D. "The Case for Curbing the Federal Courts." *Journal of Christian Reconstructionism Fall* (1996): 168–69.

Grayling, A. C. *What is Good? The Search for the Best Way to Live.* London: Weidenfeld and Nicolson, 2003.

Green, John C., Mark J. Rozell, and Clyde Wilcox, eds. *The Christian Right in American Politics: Marching to the Millennium*. Washington, DC: Georgetown University Press, 2003.

Green, Joshua "From Neural 'Is' to Moral 'Ought': What are the Moral

Implications of Neuroscientific Moral Psychology?" *Nature Reviews Neuroscience* 4 (2003): 847–50.

Greenberg, Jeff, Jamie Arndt, Jeff Schimel, Tom Pyszczynski, and Sheldon Solomon. "Clarifying the Function of Mortality-Salience Induced Worldview Defense: Renewed Suppression or Reduced Accessibility of Death-Related Thoughts?" *Journal of Experimental Social Psychology* 37 (2001): 70–76.

Greenberg, Jeff, and Eva Jonas. "Psychological Motives and Political Orientation—The Left, the Right, and the Rigid: Comment on Jost, et al." *Psychological Bulletin* 129 (2003): 376–82.

Greenberg, Jeff, Andy Martens, and Eva Jonas. "Psychological Defense in Anticipation of Anxiety: Eliminating the Potential for Anxiety Eliminates the Effect of Mortality Salience on Worldview Defense." *Psychological Science* 14 (2003): 516–19.

Greenberg, Jeff, Jonathan Porteus, Linda Simon, Tom Pyszczynski, and Sheldon Solomon. "Evidence of a Terror Management Function of Cultural Icons: The Effects of Mortality Salience on the Inappropriate Use of Cherished Cultural Symbols." *Personality and Social Psychology Bulletin* 21 (1995): 1221–28.

Greenberg, Jeff, Tom Pyszczynski, and Sheldon Solomon. "The Causes and Consequences of a Need for Self-Esteem: A Terror Management Theory." In *Public Self and Private Self*, edited by Roy F. Baumeister, 189–212. New York: Springer-Verlag, 1986.

Greenberg, Jeff, Tom Pyszczynski, Sheldon Solomon, Linda Simon, and Michael Breus. "The Role of Consciousness and Accessibility of Death-Related Thoughts in Mortality Salience Effects." *Journal of Personality and Social Psychology* 67 (1994): 627–37.

Greenberg, Jeff, Linda Simon, Tom Pyszczynski, Sheldon Solomon, and Dan Chatel. "Terror Management and Tolerance: Does Mortality Salience Always Intensify Negative Reactions to Others Who Threaten One's Worldview?" *Journal of Personality and Social Psychology* 63 (1992): 212–20.

Greenberg, Jeff, Sheldon Solomon, and Tom Pyszczynski. "Terror Management Theory of Self-Esteem and Cultural Worldviews:

Empirical Assessments and Conceptual Refinements." In *Advances in Experimental Social Psychology*, edited by Mark Zanna, 61–139. San Diego, CA: Academic Press, 1997.

Greenberg, Jeff, Sheldon Solomon, Tom Pyszczynski, Abram Rosenblatt, John Burling, and Debra Lyon. "Assessing the Terror Management Analysis of Self-Esteem: Converging Evidence of an Anxiety-Buffering Function." *Journal of Personality and Social Psychology* 63 (1992): 913–22.

Greenwald, Anthony G., Jacqueline E. Pickrell, and Shelly D. Farnham, "Implicit Partisanship: Taking Sides for No Reason." *Journal of Personality and Social Psychology* 83 (2002): 367–79.

Grenke, Arthur. *God, Greed, and Genocide: The Holocaust through the Centuries*. Washington, DC: New Academia Publishing, 2005.

Greven, Philip J. *The Protestant Temperament: Patterns of Child-Rearing, Religious Experience, and the Self in Early America*. Chicago: University of Chicago Press, 1988.

———. *Spare the Child: The Religious Roots of Punishment and the Psychological Impact of Physical Abuse*. New York: Vintage Books, 1992.

Griffin, Roger. *The Nature of Fascism*. New York: Routledge, 2003.

Griffin, Roger, ed. *Fascism*. New York: Oxford University Press, 1995.

Grinder, Darrin, and Steve Shaw. *Presidents and Their Faith: From George Washington to Barack Obama*. Boise, ID: Russell Media, 2012.

Gross, Samuel R., and Debra Livingston. "Racial Profiling Under Attack." *Columbia Law Review* 102 (2002): 1413–38.

Grossman, Cathy L. "Americans Get an 'F' in Religion." *USA Today*, March 14, 2007. Accessed July 30, 2013. http://usatoday30.usatoday.com/news/religion/2007-03-07-teaching-religion-cover_N.htm.

Gryboski, Michael. "Latest NIV Bible Translation Clearer on Homosexual Sins, Says Theologian." *Christian Post*, January 4, 2012. Accessed July 13, 2013. http://www.christianpost.com/news/latest-niv-bible-translation-clearer-on-homosexual-sins-says-theologian-66393/.

Gusfield, Joseph R. *Symbolic Crusade: Status Politics and the American Temperance Movement*. Urbana, IL: University of Illinois Press, 1986.

Haidt, Jonathan. *The Righteous Mind: Why Good People Are Divided by Politics and Religion*. New York: Pantheon, 2012.

————. "What the Tea Partiers Really Want." *Wall Street Journal*, October 16, 2010. Accessed May 6, 2014. http://www.wsj.com/articles/SB100 01424052748703673604575550243700895762.

Haidt, Jonathan, and Jesse Graham. "When Morality Opposes Justice: Conservatives Have Moral Intuitions that Liberals May Not Recognize." *Social Justice Research* 20 (2007): 98–116.

Haidt, Jonathan, Silvia H. Koller, and Maria G. Dias. "Affect, Culture, and Morality, or Is it Wrong to Eat Your Dog?" *Journal of Personality and Social Psychology* 65 (1993): 613–28.

Haidt, Jonathan, Evan Rosenberg, and Holly Hom. "Differentiating Diversities: Moral Diversity Is Not Like Other Kinds." *Journal of Applied Social Psychology* 33 (2003): 1–36.

Haidt, Jonathan, J. Patrick Seder, and Selin Kesebir. "Hive Psychology, Happiness, and Public Policy." *Journal of Legal Studies* 37 (2008): S133–S216.

Hamilton, James T. *Channeling Violence: The Economic Market for Violent Television Programming*. Princeton, NJ: Princeton University Press, 1998.

Hamilton, Marci A. *God vs. the Gavel: Religion and the Rule of Law*. New York: Cambridge University Press, 2005.

Hammermeister, Jon, Matt Flint, Julia Havens, and Margaret Peterson. "Psychosocial and Health Related Characteristics of Religious Well-Being." *Psychosocial Reports* 89 (2001): 589–94.

Hanson, David J., and Ruth C Engs. "Religion and Collegiate Drinking Problems over Time." *Psychology* 24 (1987): 10–12.

Harcourt, Bernard E. *Illusion of Order: The False Promise of Broken Windows Policing*. Cambridge: Harvard University Press, 2001.

Harden, Russell. *One for All: The Logic of Group Conflict*. Princeton, NJ: Princeton University Press, 1995.

Harding, Susan F. *The Book of Jerry Falwell: Fundamentalist Language and Politics*. Princeton, NJ: Princeton University Press, 2000.

Hardisty, Jean. "Crime and Political Ideology." *Public Eye*, 2012. Accessed

May 10, 2014. http://www.publiceye.org/magazine/v18n3/hardisty _crime.html.

———. *Mobilizing Resentment*. Boston: Beacon Press, 1999.

Harpur, Tom. *The Pagan Christ: Is Blind Faith Killing Christianity?* New York: Walker & Company, 2004.

Harris, Sam. *The End of Faith: Religion, Terror, and the Future of Reason*. New York: Norton, 2005.

———. *Freewill*. New York: Free Press, 2012.

———. *Letter to a Christian Nation*. New York: Knopf, 2006.

———. *The Moral Landscape: How Science Can Determine Human Values*. New York: Free Press, 2010.

Hart, Joshua, Phillip R. Shaver, and Jamie L. Goldenberg. "Attachment, Self-Esteem, Worldviews, and Terror Management: Evidence for a Tripartite Security System." *Journal of Personality and Social Psychology* 88 (2005): 999–1013.

Hart, Stephen. "Religion and Changes in Family Patterns." *Review of Religious Research* 28 (1986): 51–70.

Hartmann, Douglas, Xuefeng Zhang, and William Windschadt. "One (Multicultural) Nation Under God? The Changing Meanings and Uses of the Term 'Judeo-Christian' in the American Media." *Journal of Media and Religion* 4 (2005): 207–34.

Hatemi, Peter K., Nathan A. Gillespie, Lindon J. Eaves, Brion S. Maher, Bradley T. Webb, Andrew C. Health, Sarah E. Medland, et al. "A Genome-Wide Analysis of Liberal and Conservative Political Attitudes." *Journal of Politics* 73 (2011): 271–85.

Hauser, Marc. *Moral Minds: How Nature Designed Our Universal Sense of Right and Wrong*. New York: HarperCollins, 2006.

Hawkins, J. David, Richard F. Catalano, and Janet Y. Miller. "Risk and Protective Factors for Alcohol and Other Drug Problems in Adolescence and Early Adulthood: Implications for Substance Abuse in Adolescents." In *Childhood Aggression and Violence: Sources of Influence Prevention and Control*, edited by David H Crowell, Ian M. Evans, and Clifford R. O'Donnell, 263–82. New York: Plenum, 1992.

Hedges, Chris. *American Fascism: The Christian Right and the War on America*. New York: Free Press, 2007.

Helzer, Eric G., and David A. Pizarro. "Dirty Liberals! Reminders of Physical Cleanliness Influence Moral and Political Attitudes." *Psychological Science* 22 (2011): 517–22.

Hemeyer, Julia C. *Religion in America*. Englewood Cliffs, NJ: Prentice-Hall, 1990.

Henry, Carl F.H. *The Uneasy Conscience of Modern Fundamentalism*. Grand Rapids, MI: William B. Eerdmans Publishing, 2003.

Herbst, Susan. *Rude Democracy: Civility and Incivility in American Politics*. Philadelphia: Temple University Press, 2010.

Herrenkohl, Todd I., Emiko A. Tajima, Stephen D. Whitney, and Bu Huang, "Protection against Antisocial Behavior in Children Exposed to Physically Abusive Discipline." *Journal of Adolescent Health* 36 (2005): 457–65.

Heyrman, Christine L. *Southern Cross: The Beginnings of the Bible Belt*. Raleigh: University of North Carolina Press, 1998.

Hibbing, John R., Kevin B. Smith, and John R. Alford. "Differences in Negativity Bias Underlie Variations in Political Ideology." *Behavioral and Brain Sciences* 37 (2014): 297–350.

Higgins, Paul C., and Gary L. Albrecht. "Hellfire and Delinquency Revisited." *Social Forces* 55 (1977): 952–58.

Hill, Steven. *Fixing Elections: The Failure of America's Winner Take All Politics*. New York: Routledge, 2002.

Hinde, Robert A. *Why Gods Persist: A Scientific Approach to Religion*. London: Routledge, 2002.

Hinojosa, Victor J., and Jerry Z. Park. "Religion and the Paradox of Racial Inequality Attitudes." *Journal for the Scientific Study of Religion* 42 (2004): 229–38.

Hirschi, Travis. *Causes of Delinquency*. Berkeley, CA: University of California Press, 1969.

Hirschi, Travis, and Michael R. Gottfredson. "Control Theory and the Life-Course Perspective." *Studies on Crime & Crime Prevention* 4 (1995): 131–42.

Hirschi, Travis, and Rodney Stark. "Hellfire and Delinquency." *Social Problems* 17 (1969): 202–13.

Hitchcock, James. "The Enemies of Religious Liberty." *First Things* 140 (2004): 26–29.

Hitchcock, Mark. *101 Answers to the Most Asked Questions about the End Times*. Sisters, OR: Multnomah, 2001.

Hitchens, Christopher. *God Is Not Great: How Religion Poisons Everything*. New York: Twelve/Warner Books, 2007.

———. *Thomas Jefferson: Author of America*. New York: HarperCollins, 2005.

Hodge, David R., Paul Cardenas, and Harry Montoya. "Substance Use: Spirituality and Religious Participation as Protective Factors among Rural Youths." *Social Work Research* 25 (2001): 153–61.

Hoffman, Bruce. *"Holy Terror": The Implications of Terrorism Motivated by a Religious Imperative*. Santa Monica, CA: Rand, 1993.

Hogg, Michael A., and Sarah C. Hains. "Intergroup Relations and Group Solidarity: Effects of Group Identification and Social Beliefs on Depersonalized Attraction." *Journal of Personality and Social Psychology* 70 (1996): 295–309.

Hogg, Michael A., and John C. Turner. "Interpersonal Attraction, Social Identification, and Psychological Group Formation." *European Journal of Social Psychology* 15 (1985): 51–66.

Holloway, Richard. *Godless Morality: Keeping Religion Out of Ethics*. Edinburgh: Canongate, 1999.

———. *Doubts and Loves: What is Left of Christianity*. Edinburgh: Cannongate, 2001.

Holmes, David L. *The Faiths of the Founding Fathers*. New York: Oxford University Press, 2006.

Hood, Ralph W., Jr., Peter C. Hill, and Bernard Spilka. *The Psychology of Religion: An Empirical Approach*. New York: Guilford Press, 2003.

Hood, Roger, and Carolyn Hoyle. *The Death Penalty: A Worldwide Perspective*. New York: Oxford University Press, 2008.

Hoover, Stewart M., and Lynn S. Clark, eds. *Practicing Religion in the Age of the Media: Explorations in Media, Religion, and Culture*. New York: Columbia University Press, 2002.

Horton, Annie L., Melany M. Wilkins, and Wendy Wright. "Women Who

Ended Abuse: What Religious Leaders and Religion Did for these Victims." In *Abuse and Religion: When Praying Isn't Enough*, edited by Annie L. Horton and Judith A. Williamson, 235–46. Lexington, MA: Lexington Books, 1988.

Horton, Ronald A., ed. *Christian Education: Its Mandate and Mission*. Greenville, SC: Bob Jones University Press, 1992.

Hout, Michael, and Claude S. Fischer. "Americans With 'No Religion': Why Their Numbers are Growing." *American Sociological Review* 67 (2002): 165–90.

Hoyles, J.Arthur. *Punishment in the Bible*. London: Epworth Press, 1986.

Huddy, Leonie. "From Social to Political Identity: A Critical Examination of Social Identity Theory." *Political Psychology* 22 (2001): 127–56.

Huett, Jeff. "2012 Shurden Lectures Explore American History." Baptist Joint Committee for Religious Liberty, May 14, 2012. Accessed May 26, 2013. http://bjconline.org/2012-shurden-lectures-explore-american-history/.

Hughes, Richard T. *Myths America Lives By*. Urbana, IL: University of Illinois Press, 2004.

Hull, Kathleen E. *Same-Sex Marriage: The Cultural Politics of Love and Law*. New York: Cambridge University Press, 2006.

Human Rights First. Violence Based on Religious Bias, 2009. Accessed June 10, 2013. http://www.humanrightsfirst.org/our-work/fighting-discrimination/2008-hate-crime-survey/usa/iii-violence-based-on-religious-bias/.

Humphrey, John A., Paul Leslie, and Jean Brittain. "Religious Participation, Southern University Women, and Abstinence." *Deviant Behavior* 10 (1989): 145–55.

Hunsberger, Bruce E., and Bob Altemeyer. *Atheists: A Groundbreaking Study of America's Nonbelievers*. Amherst, NY: Prometheus Books, 2006.

Hunter, James D. *Culture Wars: The Struggle to Define America*. New York: Basic Books, 1991.

Hutson, James H., ed. *The Founders on Religion*. Princeton, NJ: Princeton University Press, 2007.

Iacoboni, Marco. *Mirroring People: The New Science of How We Connect with Others*. New York: Farrar, Straus, and Giroux, 2008.

Iannacone, Laurence R. "Why Strict Churches Are Strong." *American Journal of Sociology* 99 (1994): 1180–1211.

Ibrahim, Raymond. "Are Judaism and Christianity as Violent as Islam?" *Middle East Quarterly* 16 (2009): 3–12.

Inbar, Yoel, David A. Pizarro, and Paul Bloom. "Conservatives Are More Easily Disgusted than Liberals." *Cognition and Emotion* 23 (2009): 714–25.

Inhof, James. *The Greatest Hoax: How the Global Warming Conspiracy Threatens Your Future*. Cave Junction, OR: WND Books, 2012.

International Centre for Prison Studies. Prison Brief—Highest to Lowest Rates. World Prison Brief. London: King's College London School of Law, 2010. Accessed February 2013. http://www.kcl.ac.uk/depsta/law/research/icps/worldbrief/wpb_stats.php?area=all&category=wb_poprate.

Irons, Peter. *God on Trial: Dispatches from America's Religious Battlefields*. New York: Viking, 2007.

Irvine, Janice M. *Talk about Sex: The Battles over Sex Education in the United States*. Berkeley: University of California Press, 2004.

Irwin, John. *Lifers: Seeking Redemption in Prison*. New York: Taylor & Francis, 2009.

Irwin, John, Vincent Schiraldi, and Jason Ziedenberg. *America's One Million Nonviolent Prisoners*. Washington, DC: Justice Policy Institute, 1999.

Jackson, John G. *Christianity Before Christ*. Parsippany, NJ: American Atheist Press, 2002.

Jackson, Linda A., Linda A. Sullivan, Richard Harnish, and Carole N. Hodge. "Achieving Positive Social Identity: Social Mobility, Social Creativity, and Permeability of Group Boundaries." *Journal of Personality and Social Psychology* 70 (1996): 241–54

Jacobs, Bruce A. "Deterrence and Deterrability." *Criminology*, 48 (2010): 417–41.

Jacobs, James B. "Should Hate be a Crime?" *Public Interest* 113 (1993): 3–14.

Jacobs, James B., and Kimberly Potter. *Hate Crimes: Criminal Law & Identity Politics*. New York: Oxford University Press, 1998.

Jacoby, Susan. *Freethinkers: A History of American Secularism.* New York: Holt, 2004.

James, William. *The Varieties of Religious Experience.* Mineola, NY: Dover, 2002.

Jammer, Max. *Einstein and Religion.* Princeton: Princeton University Press, 2002.

Jang, Sung J., Christopher D. Bader, and Byron R. Johnson. "The Cumulative Advantage of Religiosity in Preventing Drug Abuse." *Journal of Drug Issues* 38 (2010): 771–98.

Jang, Sung J., and Byron R. Johnson. "Gender, Religiosity, and Reactions to Strain among African Americans." *Sociological Quarterly* 46 (2005): 323–57.

———. "Neighborhood Disorder, Individual Religiosity, and Adolescent Use of Illicit Drugs: A Test of Multilevel Hypotheses." *Criminology* 39 (2001): 109–44.

Jay, Nancy. *Throughout Your Generations Forever: Sacrifice, Religion, and Paternity.* Chicago: University of Chicago Press, 1992.

Jelen, Ted G. "Biblical Literalism and Inerrancy: Does the Difference Make a Difference?" *Sociological Analysis* 49 (1989): 421–29.

Jenkins, Peter. "Dark Passages." *Boston Globe*, March 8, 2009.

———. *Jesus Wars: How Four Patriarchs, Three Queens, and Two Emperors Decided What Christians Would Believe for the Next 1,500 Years.* New York: HarperOne, 2011.

———. *Laying Down the Sword: Why We Can't Ignore the Bible's Violent Verses.* New York: HarperOne, 2011.

Jensen, Lene A. "Culture Wars: American Moral Divisions across the Adult Lifespan." *Journal of Adult Development* 4 (1997): 107–21.

———. "Moral Divisions Within Countries between Orthodoxy and Progressivism: India and the United States." *Journal for the Scientific Study of Religion* 37 (1998): 90–107.

Jeynes, William H. "Adolescent Religious Commitment and Their Consumption of Marijuana, Cocaine, and Alcohol." *Journal of Health and Social Policy* 21 (2006): 1–20.

Johnson, Byron R. *More God, Less Crime: Why Faith Matters and How It Could Matter More.* West Conshohocken, PA: Templeton Press, 2011.

————. "Religious Programs and Recidivism among Former Inmates in Prison Fellowship Programs: A Long-Term Follow-Up Study." *Justice Quarterly* 21 (2004): 329–54.

Johnson, Byron R., Sung J. Jang, David B. Larson, and Spencer D. Li. "Does Adolescent Religious Commitment Matter? A Re-Examination of the Effects of Religiosity on Delinquency." *Journal of Research in Crime and Delinquency* 38 (2001): 22–44.

Johnson, Byron R., Sung J. Jang, Spencer D. Li, and David B. Larson. "The 'Invisible Institution' and Black Youth Crime: The Church as an Agency of Local Social Control." *Journal of Youth and Adolescence* 29 (2000): 479–98.

Johnson, Byron R., David B. Larson, Spencer D. Li, and Sung J. Jang. "Escaping from the Crime of Inner Cities: Church Attendance and Religious Salience among Disadvantaged Youth." *Justice Quarterly* 17 (2000): 377–91.

Johnson, Byron R., David B. Larson, and Timothy C. Pitts. "Religious Programming, Institutional Adjustment and Recidivism among Former Inmates in Prison Fellowship Programs." *Justice Quarterly* 14 (1997): 145–66.

Johnson, Judy J. *What's So Wrong With Being Absolutely Right: The Dangerous Nature of Dogmatic Beliefs*. Amherst, NY: Prometheus Books, 2009.

Johnson, Michael P. "Patriarchal Terrorism and Common Couple Violence: Two Forms of Violence against Women." *Journal of Marriage and the Family* 57 (1995): 283–94.

Johnson, Phillip. *The Wedge of Truth: Splitting the Foundations of Naturalism*. Downers Grove, IL: InterVarsity Press, 2000.

Johnson, Timothy R., and Andrew D. Martin. "The Public's Conditional Response to Supreme Court Decisions." *American Political Science Review* 92 (1998): 300–309.

Johnston, Robert K. "American Evangelicalism: An Extended Family." In *The Variety of American Evangelicalism*, edited by Donald W. Dayton and Robert K. Johnston, 252–72. Downers Grove, IL: Inter-Varsity Press, 1991.

Jonas, Eva, and Peter Fischer. "Terror Management and Religion: Evidence that Intrinsic Religiousness Mitigates Worldview Defense Following Mortality Salience." *Journal of Personality and Social Psychology* 91 (2006): 553–67.

Jonas, Eva, Jeff Greenberg, and Dieter Frey. "Connecting Terror Management and Dissonance Theories: Evidence that Mortality Salience Increases the Preference for Supportive Information after Decisions." *Personality and Social Psychology Bulletin* 29 (2003): 1181–89.

Jones, Jeffrey M. "Atheists, Muslims see Most Bias as Presidential Candidates." *Gallup*, June 21, 2012. Accessed June 23, 2012. http://www.gallup.com/poll/155285/atheists-muslims-bias-presidential-candidates.aspx.

———. "In U.S., 3 in 10 Say they Take the Bible Literally." *Gallup*, July 8, 2011. Accessed June 16, 2013. http://www.gallup.com/poll/148427/say-bible-literally.aspx.

———. "Some Americans Reluctant to Vote for Mormon, 72-Year-Old Presidential Candidates." *Gallup*, February 20, 2007. Accessed June 23, 2012. http://www.gallup.com/poll/26611/Some-Americans-Reluctant-Vote-Mormon-72YearOld-Presidential-Candidates.aspx.

Jost, John T. "The End of the End of Ideology." *American Psychologist* 61 (2006): 651–70.

Jost, John T., Christopher M. Federico, and Jamie L. "Political Ideology: Its Structure, Functions, and Elective Affinities." *Annual Review of Psychology* 60 (2009): 307–37.

Jost, John T., Jack Glaser, Arie W. Kruglanski, and Frank J. Sulloway. "Political Conservatism as Motivated Social Cognition." *Psychological Bulletin* 129 (2003): 339–75.

Joyce, Kathryn. "Biblical Battered Wife Syndrome: Christian Women and Domestic Violence." *Religion Dispatches*, January 22, 2009. Accessed March 12, 2013. http://religiondispatches.org/biblical-battered-wife-syndrome-christian-women-and-domestic-violence/.

Jowett, Garth S., and Victoria J. O'Donnell. *Propaganda and Persuasion*, 4th ed. Thousand Oaks, CA: Sage, 2006.

Judd, Charles M., and Bernadette Park. "Out-Group Homogeneity: Judgments of Variability at the Individual and Group Levels." *Journal of Personality and Social Psychology* 54 (1988): 778–88.

Juergensmeyer, Mark. *Terror in the Mind of God: The Global Rise of Religious Violence*. Berkeley, CA: University of California Press, 2000.

———. "The Worldwide Rise of Religious Nationalism." *Journal of International Affairs* 50 (1996): 1–20.

Kahneman, Daniel. *Thinking Fast and Slow*. New York: Farrar, Straus and Giroux, 2011.

Kahneman, Daniel, Paul Slovic, and Amos Tversky, eds. *Judgment under Uncertainty: Heuristics and Biases*. New York: Cambridge University Press, 1982.

Kahneman, Daniel, and Amos Tversky. "The Psychology of Preferences." *Scientific American* 246 (1982): 160–73.

Kaminer, Wendy. *The Last Taboo: Why America Needs Atheism*. New York: New Republic, 1996.

Kanai, Ryota, Tom Feilden, Colin Firth, and Geraint Rees. "Political Orientations Are Correlated with Brain Structure in Young Adults." *Current Biology* 21 (2011): 677–80.

Kane, John. *The Politics of Moral Capital*. New York: Cambridge University Press, 2001.

Kaplan, Esther. *With God on Their Side: How Christian Fundamentalists Trampled Science, Policy, and Democracy in George W. Bush's White House*. New York: New Press, 2004.

Karakurt, Gunnur, and Tamra Cumbie. "The Relationship between Egalitarianism, Dominance, and Violence in Intimate Relationships." *Journal of Family Violence* 27 (2012): 115–22.

Karasawa, Minoru. "Toward an Assessment of Social Identity: The Structure of Group Identification and its Effects on In-Group Evaluations." *British Journal of Social Psychology* 30 (1991): 293–307.

Kardash, CarolAnne M., and Roberta J. Scholes. "Effects of Pre-Existing Beliefs, Epistemological Beliefs, and Need for Cognition on Interpretation of Controversial Issues." *Journal of Educational Psychology* 88 (1996): 260–71.

Kellstedt, Lyman, and Corwin Smidt. "Measuring Fundamentalism: An Analysis of Different Operational Strategies." *Journal for the Scientific Study of Religion* 30 (1991): 259–78.

Kelly, Caroline. "Political Identity and Perceived Intragroup Homogeneity." *British Journal of Social Psychology* 28 (1989): 239–50.

Keltner, Dacher, and Jonathan Haidt. "Approaching Awe, a Moral, Spiritual, and Aesthetic Emotion." *Cognition and Emotion* 17 (2003): 297–314.

Kennedy, D. James. *Character and Destiny: A Nation in Search of Its Soul.* Grand Rapids: Zondervan, 1995.

———. *Evangelism Explosion*, 4th ed. Wheaton, IL: Tyndale House, 1996.

Kennedy, D. James, with Jerry Newcombe, *The Gates of Hell Shall Not Prevail: The Attack on Christianity and What You Need to Know to Combat It.* Nashville, TN: Thomas Nelson, 1996.

———. *What If America Were a Christian Nation Again?* Nashville, TN: Thomas Nelson, 2003.

Kepel, Gilles. *The War for Muslim Minds: Islam and the West.* Cambridge, MA: Belknap Press, 2004.

Kerley, Kent R., Marissa C. Allison, and Rachelle D. Graham. "Investigating the Impact of Religiosity on Emotional and Behavioural Coping in Prison." *Journal of Crime and Justice* 29 (2006): 71–96.

Kerley, Kent R., and Heith Copes. "'Keepin' My Mind Right': Identity Maintenance and Religious Social Support in the Prison Context." *International Journal of Offender Therapy and Comparative Criminology* 53 (2009): 228–44.

Kerley, Kent R., and Heith Copes, Richard Tewksbury, and Dean A. Dabney. "Examining the Relationship between Religiosity and Self-Control as Predictors of Prison Deviance." *International Journal of Offender Therapy and Comparative Criminology* 55 (2011): 1251–71.

Kida, Thomas E. *Don't Believe Everything You Think: The Six Basic Mistakes We Make in Thinking.* Amherst, NY: Prometheus Books, 2006.

Kilgore, Ed. "'Religious Liberty' Revisited in Hobby Lobby's Wake." *Talking Points Memo*, July 2, 2014. Accessed July 3, 2014.

http://talkingpointsmemo.com/cafe/religious-liberty-revisited-in -hobby-lobby-s-wake.

Kinder, Donald R., and Howard Schuman. "Racial Attitudes: Developments and Divisions in Survey Research." In *A Telescope on Society: Survey Research and Social Science at the University of Michigan and Beyond*, edited by James S. House, F. Thomas Juster, Robert Kahn, Howard Schuman, and Eleanor Singer, 365–92. Ann Arbor, MI: University of Michigan Press, 2004.

Kintz, Linda, and Julia Lesage, eds. *Media, Culture, and the Religious Right*. Minneapolis: University of Minneapolis Press, 1998.

Kleck, Gary. *Point Blank: Guns and Violence in America*. Piscataway, NJ: Aldine Transaction, 2005.

Klein, Joe. "Why the 'War President' is Under Fire." *Time*, February 15, 2004. Accessed April 23, 2014. http://content.time.com/time/nation/ article/ 0,8599,591270,00.html

Koch, Jerome R., and Inacio L. Ramirez. *Religiosity, Fundamentalism, and Intimate Partner Violence among U.S. College Students*. Lubbock, TX: Texas Tech University, 2009.

Koenigsberg, Richard A. *Nations Have the Right to Kill: Hitler, the Holocaust and War*. New York: Library of Social Science, 2009.

Kohler, Pamela K., Lisa E. Manhart, and William E. Lafferty. "Abstinence-Only and Comprehensive Sex Education and the Initiation of Sexual Activity and Teen Pregnancy." *Journal of Adolescent Health* 42 (2008): 344–51.

Kosmin, Barry A., and Ariela Keysar, with Ryan Cragun, and Juhem Navarro-Rivera. *American Nones: The Profile of the No Religion Population*. Hartford, CT: Trinity College, 2009.

Kosmin, Barry A., and Seymour P. Lachman. *One Nation under God: Religion in Contemporary American Society*. New York: Random House, 1993.

Krakauer, Jon. *Under the Banner of Heaven: A Story of Violent Faith*. New York: Anchor Books, 2003.

Kramnick, Isaac, and R. Laurence Moore. *The Godless Constitution: The Case against Religious Correctness*. New York: Norton, 1997.

Krause, Neal. "Church-Based Social Support and Health in Old Age: Exploring Variations by Race." *Journal of Gerontology* 57 (2002): S332–347.

———. "God-Mediated Control and Psychological Well-Being in Late Life." *Research on Aging* 27 (2005): 136–64.

———. "Religiosity and Self-Esteem among Older Adults." *Journal of Gerontology* 50 (1995): 236–46.

———. "Religious Meaning and Subjective Well-Being in Late Life." *Journal of Gerontology* 58 (2003): S160–170.

———. "Social Involvement in Religious Institutions and God-Mediated Control Beliefs: A Longitudinal Investigation." *Journal for the Scientific Study of Religion* 46 (2007): 519–37.

Kregeloh, Hubert. *There Goes Christmas?!* Belmont, MA: American Opinion, 1959.

Krohn, Marvin D., and James L. Massey. "Social Control and Delinquent Behavior: An Examination of the Elements of the Social Bond." *Sociological Quarterly* 21 (1980): 529–43.

Kuo, David. *Tempting Faith: An Inside Story of Political Seduction.* New York: Free Press, 2006.

Kurtz, Paul, ed. *Science and Religion: Are They Compatible?* Amherst, NY: Prometheus Books, 2003.

Kurtz, Paul, and Timothy J. Madigan, eds. *Challenges to the Enlightenment: In Defense of Reason and Science.* Amherst, NY: Prometheus Books, 1994.

Kurzban, Robert. *Why Everyone (Else) Is a Hypocrite: Evolution and the Modular Mind.* Princeton, NJ: Princeton University Press, 2010.

Labash, Matt. "God and Man in Alabama." *Weekly Standard*, March 2, 1988.

LaHaye, Tim. *Battle for the Mind.* Old Tappan, NJ: Fleming H. Revell Press, 1980.

———. *The Merciful God of Prophecy: His Loving Plan for You in the End Times.* New York: Warner Faith, 2002.

LaHaye, Tim, and Thomas Ice. *Charting the End Times.* Eugene, OR: Harvest House, 2001.

LaHaye, Tim, and Jerry B. Jenkins. *Desecration: Antichrist Takes the Throne*. Wheaton, IL: Tyndale House, 2001.

——. *Glorious Appearing: The End of Days*. Wheaton, IL: Tyndale House, 2004.

——. *The Remnant*. Wheaton, IL: Tyndale House, 2002.

Lakoff, George. *Moral Politics: How Liberals and Conservatives Think*. Chicago: University of Chicago Press, 2002.

——. *Moral Politics: What Conservatives Know That Liberals Don't*. Chicago: University of Chicago Press, 1996.

Lamont, Michael, and Marcel Fournier. *Cultivating Differences: Symbolic Boundaries and the Making of Inequality*. Chicago, IL: University of Chicago Press, 1992.

Landau, Mark J., Michael Johns, Jeff Greenberg, Tom Pyszczynski, Andy Martens, Jamie L. Golderberg, and Sheldon Solomon. "A Function of Form: Terror Management and Structuring the Social World." *Journal of Personality & Social Psychology* 87 (2004): 190–210.

Landau, Mark J., Sheldon Solomon, Jaime Arndt, Jeff Greenberg, Tom Pyszczynski, Claude H. Miller, Florette Cohen, and Daniel M. Ogilvie. "Deliver Us from Evil: The Effects of Mortality Salience and Reminders of 9/11 on Support for President George W. Bush." *Personality and Social Psychology Bulletin* 30 (2004): 1136–50.

Langton, Lynn, Michael Planty, and Jennifer Truman. Criminal Victimization, 2012. Washington, DC: Bureau of Justice Statistics, 2013. Accessed March 12, 2014. http://www.bjs.gov/index.cfm?ty =pbdetail&iid=4781

Larson, Edward J. *Summer for the Gods: The Scope Trial and America's Continuing Debate over Science and Religion*. New York: Basic Books, 1997.

Lattman, Peter. "Judge Paul Cassell Resigns, Bemoaning Low Judicial Pay." *Wall Street Journal* (Law Blog), September 21, 2007. Accessed October 3, 2013. http://blogs.wsj.com/law/2007/09/21/judge-paul -cassell-resigning/.

Lawler, Peter A. "Manliness, Religion, and Our Manly Scientists." *Social Science and Modern Society* 45 (2008): 155–58.

Lawrence, Charles R., III "The Id, the Ego, and Equal Protection: Reckoning with Unconscious Racism." *Stanford Law Review* 39 (1987): 317–88.

Laythe, Brian, Deborah G. Finkel, Robert G. Bringle, and Lee A. Kirkpatrick. "Religious Fundamentalism as a Predictor of Prejudice: A Two-Component Model." *Journal for the Scientific Study of Religion* 41 (2002): 623–35.

Leary, Mark R. *The Curse of the Self: Self-Awareness, Egotism, and the Quality of Human Life.* Oxford: Oxford University Press, 2004.

Lee, Jerry W., Gail T. Rice, and V. Bailey Gillespie. "Family Worship Patterns and their Correlation with Adolescent Behaviour and Beliefs." *Journal of the Scientific Study of Religion* 36 (1997): 372–81.

Lee, Matthew R. "Reconsidering Culture and Homicide." *Homicide Studies* 15 (2011): 319–40.

Lee, Matthew R., and John P. Bartkowski. "Love Thy Behaviour? Moral Communities, Civic Engagement, and Juvenile Homicide in Rural Areas." *Social Forces* 82 (2004): 1001–35.

Leibow, Elliot. *Tally's Corner: A Study of Negro Streetcorner Men* (2nd ed.). New York: Rowman & Littlefield, 1967.

Lemert, Edwin. *Human Deviance, Social Problems and Social Control.* Englewood Cliffs, NJ: Prentice Hall, 1969.

Leonard, Bill J. *Baptists in America.* New York: Columbia University Press, 2005.

Leonard, Kathleen C., Kaye V. Cook, Chris J. Boyatzis, Cynthia N. Kimball, Kelly S. Flanagan. "Parent-Child Dynamics and Emerging Adult Religiosity: Attachment, Parental Beliefs, and Faith Support." *Psychology of Religion and Spirituality* 5 (2013): 5–14.

Lepore, Jill. *The Whites of Their Eyes: The Tea Party's Revolution and the Battle over American History.* Princeton: Princeton University Press, 2010.

Levin, Jack, and Jack McDevitt. *Hate Crimes: The Rising Tide of Bigotry and Bloodshed.* New York: Plenum Press, 1993.

Levitas, Daniel. *The Terrorist Next Door.* New York: St. Martin's Press, 2002.

Levitt, Heidi M., and Kimberly Ware. "'Anything with Two Heads Is a

Monster': Religious Leaders' Perspective on Marital Equality and Domestic Violence." *Violence against Women* 12 (2006): 1169–90.

Linder, Douglas O. *Putting Evolution on the Defensive: William B. Riley and the Rise of Fundamentalism in America*, 2005. Accessed October 3, 2013. http://law2.umkc.edu/faculty/projects/ftrials/conlaw/Fundamentalism.html.

Linville, Deanna C., and Angela J. Huebner. "The Analysis of Extracurricular Activities and Their Relationship to Youth Violence." *Journal of Youth and Adolescence* 34 (2005): 483–92.

Lively, Scott, and Kevin Abrams. *The Pink Swastika*. Sacramento, CA: Veritas Aeterna Press, 2002.

Loehr, Davidson. *America, Fascism and God: Sermons from a Heretical Preacher*. White River Junction, VT: Chelsea Green Publishing, 2005.

Loftus, Jeni. "America's Liberalization in Attitudes toward Homosexuality, 1973 to 1998." *American Sociological Review* 66 (2001): 762–82.

Longest, Kyle C., and Stephen Vaisey. "Control or Conviction: Religion and Adolescent Initiation of Marijuana Use." *Journal of Drug Issues* 38 (2008): 689–715.

Loughlin, Sean. "Santorum under Fire for Comments on Homosexuality." CNN, April 22, 2003. Accessed July 6, 2014. http://www.cnn.com/2003/ALLPOLITICS/04/22/santorum.gays/.

Loveland, Matthew T. "Religious Switching: Preference Development, Maintenance and Change." *Journal for the Scientific Study of Religion* 41 (2003): 147–57.

Lucas, Stephen E., ed. *The Quotable George Washington: The Wisdom of an American Patriot*. Madison, WI: Madison House, 1999.

Luo, Michael. "Preaching a Gospel of Wealth in a Glittery Market, New York." *New York Times*, January 15, 2006. Accessed July 10, 2014. http://www.nytimes.com/2006/01/15/nyregion/15prosperity.html.

Lupfer, Michael B., Karla F. Brock, and Stephen J. DePaola. "The Use of Secular and Religious Attributions to Explain Everyday Behavior." *Journal for the Scientific Study of Religion* 31 (1992): 486–503.

Lupfer, Michael B., Patricia L. Hopkinson, and Patricia Kelley. "An Exploration of the Attributional Styles of Christian Fundamentalists and Authoritarians." *Journal for the Scientific Study of Religion* 27 (1988): 389–98.

Lupfer, Michael B., and Kenneth Wald. "An Exploration of Adults' Religious Orientations and their Philosophies of Human Nature." *Journal for the Scientific Study of Religion* 24 (1985): 293–304.

Lynch, Aaron. *Thought Contagion: How Belief Spreads Through Society.* New York: Basic Books, 1996.

Lynch, James P. "Problems and Promise of Victimization Surveys for Cross-National Research." *Crime and Justice* 34 (2006): 229–87.

Lynn, Richard, John Harvey, and Helmuth Nyborg. "Average Intelligence Predicts Atheism Rates across 137 Nations." *Intelligence* 37 (2009): 11–15.

MacDonald, John M., Alex R. Piquero, Robert F. Valois, and Keith J. Zulig. "The Relationship between Satisfaction, Risk-Taking Behaviours, and Youth Violence." *Journal of Interpersonal Violence* 20 (2005): 1495–1518.

MacLeod, Colin, and Lynlee Campbell. "Memory Accessibility and Probability of Judgments: An Experimental Evaluation of the Availability Heuristic." *Journal of Personality and Social Psychology* 63 (1992): 890–902.

Madison, James. *James Madison on Religious Liberty.* Robert S. Alley, editor. Amherst, NY: Prometheus Books, 1985.

———. *James Madison: Writings, 1772–1836.* Des Moines, IA: Library of America, 1999.

Manis, Melvin, Jonathan Shelder, John Jonides, and Thomas E. Nelson. "Availability Heuristic in Judgments of Set Size and Frequency of Occurrence." *Journal of Personality and Social Psychology* 65 (1993): 448–57.

Mansfield, Stephen. *The Faith of Barack Obama.* Nashville, TN: Thomas Nelson, 2008.

———. *The Faith of George W. Bush.* New York: Tarcher, 2003.

Margolis, Harold. *Dealing With Risk: Why the Public and the Experts Disagree on Environmental Issues.* Chicago: University of Chicago Press, 1996.

Markoe, Lauren. "My Country 'Tis of Thee: Evangelicals Score Highest on Patriotism." Religion News Service, June 27, 2013. Accessed March 13, 2014. http://www.religionnews.com/2013/06/27/some-religious -groups-wave -the-flag-more-than-others/ Retrieved June 28, 2013.

Markus, Hazel R., and Shinobu Kitayama. "Culture and the Self: Implications for Cognition, Emotion, and Motivation." *Psychological Review* 98 (1991): 224–53.

Marsden, George M. *Fundamentalism and American Culture*. Oxford: Oxford University Press, 2006.

———. "Fundamentalism as an American Phenomenon, A Comparison with English Evangelicalism." *Church History* 46 (1977): 215–32.

———. *Understanding Fundamentalism and Evangelicalism*. Grand Rapids, MI: William B. Eerdmans, 1991.

Martin, Michael. *Atheism, Morality, and Meaning*. Amherst, NY: Prometheus Books, 2002.

Martin, William C. *With God on Our Side: The Rise of the Religious Right in America*. New York: Broadway Books, 1996.

Martinson, Robert. "What Works?—Questions and Answers about Prison Reform." *Public Interest* 35 (1974): 22–54.

Marty, Martin E., and R. Scott Appleby. *The Glory and the Power: The Fundamentalist Challenge to the Modern World*. Boston: Beacon Press, 1992.

Maslow, Abraham H. *Religions, Values, and Peak-Experiences*. Columbus, OH: Ohio State University Press, 1964.

Mason, W. Alex, and Michael Windle. "Family, Religious, School and Peer Influences on Adolescent Alcohol Use and Alcohol-Related Problems." *Journal of Adolescent Research* 17 (2001): 346–63.

Matthews, Shelly, and E. Leigh Gibson. *Violence in the New Testament*. New York: T & T Clark, 2005.

Maurer, Adah. "Religious Values and Child Abuse." In *Institutional Abuse of Children and Youth*, edited by Ranae Hanson, 57–63. New York: Haworth Press, 1982.

McAdams, Dan P. *The Redemptive Self: Stories Americans Live By*. New York: Oxford University Press, 2006.

McAdams, Dan P., Jeffrey Reynolds, Martha Lewis, Allison H. Patten, and Phillip J. Bowman. "When Bad Things Turn Good and Good Things Turn Bad: Sequences of Redemption and Contamination in Life Narrative and their Relation to Psychosocial Adaptation in Midlife Adults and in Students." *Personality and Social Psychology Bulletin* 27 (2001): 474–85.

McCullough, Michael E., and Brian L. B. Willoughby. "Religion, Self-Regulation, and Self-Control." *Psychological Bulletin* 135 (2009): 69–93.

McGirr, Lisa. *Suburban Warriors: The Origins of the New American Right.* Princeton, NJ: Princeton University Press, 2001.

McGrath, Alister. *The Twilight of Atheism: The Rise and Fall of Disbelief in the Modern World.* New York: Doubleday, 2004.

McGreal, Chris. "America's Serious Crime Rate Is Plunging, But Why? Sociologists Have Offered Explanations Including Abortion Laws, a Fall in Crack Use and—Most Contentiously—Longer Sentences." *Guardian*, August 21, 2011. Accessed December 8, 2013. http://www.guardian. co.uk/world/2011/aug/21/america-serious-crime-rate-plunging.

McGregor, Holly A., Joel D. Lieberman, Jeff Greenberg, Sheldon Solomon, Jamie Arndt, Linda Simon, and Tom Pyszczynski. "Terror Management and Aggression: Evidence that Mortality Salience Motivates Aggression against Worldview-Threatening Others." *Journal of Personality and Social Psychology* 74 (1998): 590–605.

McGregor, Ian, Mark P. Zanna, John G. Holmes, and Steven J. Spencer. "Compensatory Conviction in the Face of Personal Uncertainty: Going to Extremes and Being Oneself." *Journal of Personality and Social Psychology* 80 (2001): 472–88.

McLaren, Brian D. *Finding Faith: A Search for What Makes Sense.* Grand Rapids, MI: Zondervan, 1999.

Mears, Daniel P. "Getting Tough with Juvenile Offenders: Explaining Support for Sanctioning Youths as Adults." *Criminal Justice and Behavior* 28 (2001): 206–26.

Meckler, Laura. "U.S. Gave $1 Billion in Faith-Based Funds." Associated Press, January 3, 2005. Accessed November 16, 2014. http://

www.truth-out.org/archive/component/k2/item/51552:ap-us-gave-1b -in-faithbased-funds.

Melling, Phillip H. *Fundamentalism in America: Millennialism, Identity, and Militant Religion*. Edinburgh: Edinburgh University Press, 2001.

Merrill, Ray M., Richard D. Salazar, and Nicole W. Gardner. "Relationship between Family Religiosity and Drug Use Behavior among Youth." *Social Behavior and Personality* 29 (2001): 347–58.

Merrill, Ray M., Jeffrey A. Folsom, and Susan S. Christopherson. "The Influence of Family Religiosity on Adolescent Substance Use According to Religious Preference." *Society for Personality Research* 33 (2005): 821–36.

Messner, Steven F. and Richard Rosenfeld. *Crime and the American Dream*. 4th ed. Belmont, CA: Wadsworth, 2007.

Miles, Jack. *God: A Biography*. New York: Knopf, 1995.

Milgram, Stanley. *Obedience to Authority: An Experimental View*. New York: Harper and Row, 1974.

Miller, Alice. *For Your Own Good: Hidden Cruelty in Child-Rearing and the Roots of Violence*. New York: Farrar, Straus & Giroux, 1983.

Miller, Arthur H., Patricia Gurin, Gerald Gurin, and Oksana Malanchuk. "Group Consciousness and Political Participation." *American Journal of Political Science* 25 (1981): 494–511.

Miller, Charles E., and Patricia D. Anderson. "Group Decision Rules and the Rejection of Deviates." *Social Psychology Quarterly* 42 (1979): 354–63.

Mohamed, Ola. "Religion and Violence." *Washington Post*, April 17, 2009. Accessed October, 19, 2013. http://onfaith.washingtonpost.com/ onfaith/eboo_patel/2009/04/religion_violence.html.

Monroe, Kristen R., James Hankin, and Renee B. Van Vechten. "The Psychological Foundations of Identity Politics: A Review of the Literature." *Annual Review of Political Science* 3 (2000): 419–47.

Montgomery, Alice, and Leslie J. Francis. "Relationship between Personal Prayer and School-Related Attitudes among 11- to 16-year-old Girls." *Psychological Reports* 78 (1996): 787–93.

Mooney, Chris. *The Republican War on Science*. Cambridge, MA: Basic Books, 2005.

———. "Scientists Are Beginning to Figure Out Why Conservatives Are . . . Conservative." *Mother Jones*, July 15, 2014. Accessed July 15, 2014. http://www.motherjones.com/politics/2014/07/biology -ideology-john-hibbing -negativity-bias.

Moore, Solomon. "Prison Spending Outpaces All But Medicaid." *New York Times*, March 2, 2009. Accessed April 10, 2013. http://www .nytimes.com/2009/03/03/us/03prison.html?_r=0.

Morris, Richard B. *Seven Who Shaped Our Destiny: The Founding Fathers as Revolutionaries*. New York: HarperCollins, 1973.

———, ed. *John Jay: The Winning of the Peace; Unpublished Papers, 1780–1784*. New York: Harper & Row Publishers, 1980.

Morrison, Melanie A., Todd G. Morrison, Gregory A. Pope, Bruno D. Zumbo. "An Investigation of Measures of Modern and Old-Fashioned Sexism." *Social Indicators Research* 48 (1999): 39–50.

Moseley, James G. *A Cultural History of Religion in America*. Westport, CT: Greenwood Press, 1981.

Moser, Bob. "The Crusaders: Christian Evangelicals Are Plotting to Remake America in their Own Image." *Rolling Stone*, 2005. Accessed December 15, 2013. http://www.rollingstone.com/politics/ story/7235393/the_crusaders.

Moss, Candida. "The Myth of Christian Persecution." *HuffPost Religion*, August 9, 2014. Accessed August 9, 2014. http://www.huffingtonpost .com/candida-moss/the-myth-of-christian-persecution_b_2901880 .html.

———. *The Myth of Persecution: How Early Christians Invented a Story of Martyrdom*. New York: HarperOne, 2014.

Mosse, George L. *The Nationalization of the Masses: Political Symbolism and Mass Movements in Germany from the Napoleonic Wars through the Third Reich*. Ithaca, NY: Cornell University Press, 1991.

Mueller, John. *Overblown: How Politicians and the Terrorism Industry Inflate National Security Threats and Why We Believe Them*. New York: Free Press, 2006.

Mummendey, Amélie, Thomas Kessler, Andreas Klink, and Rosemary Mielke. "Strategies to Cope with Negative Social Identity: Predictions by Social Identity Theory and Relative Deprivation Theory." *Journal of Personality and Social Psychology* 76 (1999): 229–45.

Mummendey, Amélie, and Hans-Joachim Schreiber. "'Different' Just Means 'Better': Some Obvious and Some Hidden Pathways to In-Group Favouritism." *British Journal of Social Psychology* 23 (1984): 363–68.

Nagin, Daniel S., and John V. Pepper, eds. *Deterrence and the Death Penalty*. Washington, DC: National Academies Press, 2012.

Nash, Shondrah T., and Latonya Hesterberg. "Biblical Framings of and Responses to Spousal Violence in the Narratives of Abused Christian Women." *Violence against Women* 15 (2009): 340–61.

Nelson, Hart M., and James F. Rooney. "Fire and Brimstone, Lager and Pot: Religious Involvement and Substance Use." *Sociological Analysis* 43 (1982): 247–56.

Nelson, Jack. *Terror in the Night: The Klan's Campaign against the Jews*. Jackson, MS: University of Mississippi Press, 1996.

Neuberg, Steven L., and Jason T. Newsom. "Personal Need for Structure: Individual Differences in the Desire for Simple Structure." *Journal of Personality and Social Psychology* 65 (1993): 113–31.

Newberg, Andrew, Eugene, D'Aquili, and Vince Rause. *Why God Won't Go Away: Brain Science and the Biology of Belief*. New York: Ballentine, 2001.

Newberg, Andrew, and Mark R. Waldman. *Born to Believe: God, Science, and the Origin of Ordinary and Extraordinary Beliefs*. New York: Free Press, 2006.

———. *Why We Believe What We Believe*. New York: Free Press, 2007.

Newport, Frank. "In U.S., 42% Believe Creationist View of Human Origins." Princeton, NJ: Gallup Politics, 2014. Accessed June 5, 2014. http://www.gallup.com/poll/170822/believe-creationist-view-human -origins.aspx?ref=image.

———. "In U.S., Support for Death Penalty Falls to 39-Year Low." Princeton, NJ: Gallup Politics, 2011. Accessed June 5, 2014. http:// www.gallup.com/poll/150089/support-death-penalty-falls-year-low .aspx.

Nibbing, John R., Kevin B. Smith, and John R. Alford. "Differences in Negativity Bias Underlie Variations in Political Ideology." *Behavioral and Brain Sciences* 37 (2014): 297–350.

Nichols, Stephen J. *Jesus Made in America: A Cultural History from the Puritans to the Passion of Christ*. Westmont, IL: IVP Academic, 2008.

Nickerson, Raymond S. "Confirmation Bias: A Ubiquitous Phenomenon in Many Guises." *Review of General Psychology* 2 (1998): 175–220.

Niebuhr, Gustav. "Southern Baptists Declare Wife Should "Submit" to her Husband." *New York Times*, June 10, 1998. Accessed December 15, 2013. http://www.nytimes.com/1998/06/10/us/southern-baptists-declare-wife-should-submit-to-her-husband.html.

Nisbitt, Richard E., and Dov Cohen. *Culture of Honor: The Psychology of Violence in the South*. Boulder, CO: Westview, 1996.

Nocera, Joe. "The Last Moderate." *New York Times*, September 6, 2011. Accessed August, 1, 2013. http://www.nytimes.com/2011/09/06/opinion/the-last-moderate.html.

Noel, Jeffrey G., Daniel L. Wann, and Nyla R. Branscombe. "Peripheral Ingroup Membership Status and Public Negativity toward Outgroups." *Journal of Personality and Social Psychology* 68 (1995): 127–137.

Nord, Warren A. *Religion and American Education: Rethinking a National Dilemma*. Chapel Hill: University of North Carolina Press, 1995.

Norenzayan, Ara, and Azim F. Shariff. "The Origin and Evolution of Religious Prosociality." *Science* 322 (2008): 58–62.

Norris, Pippa, and Ronald Inglehart. *Sacred and Secular: Religion and Politics Worldwide*. Cambridge, UK: Cambridge University Press, 2004.

Novosad, Nancy. "God Squad: The Promise Keepers Fight for a Man's World." *Progressive*, 60 (1996): 25–30.

Numbers, Ronald L. *The Creationists: From Scientific Creationism to Intelligent Design*. Berkeley: University of California Press, 1992.

———. "The Dilemma of Evangelical Scientists." In *Evangelicalism in Modern America*, edited by George M. Marsden, 150–60. Grand Rapids, MI: Eerdmans, 1984.

Nussbaum, Martha. "Patriotism and Cosmopolitanism." *Boston Review* 19 (1994): 1–12.

O'Connor, Thomas P., Jeff Duncan, and Frank Quillard. "Criminology and Religion: The Shape of an Authentic Dialogue." *Criminology and Public Policy* 5 (2006): 559–70.

O'Connor, Thomas P., and Michael Perreyclear. "Prison Religion in Action and Its Influence on Offender Rehabilitation." *Journal of Offender Rehabilitation* 35 (2002): 11–33.

Olasky, Marvin. *Renewing American Compassion*. New York: Free Press, 1996.

———. *The Tragedy of American Compassion*. Washington, D.C.: Regnery Gateway, 1992.

O'Leary, Stephen D. *Arguing the Apocalypse: A Theory of Millennial Rhetoric*. New York: Oxford University Press, 1994.

Oleckno, William A. "Relationship of Religiosity to Wellness and Other Health-Related Behaviors and Outcomes." *Psychological Reports* 68 (1991): 819–26.

Olsen, Richard G. *Science and Religion, 1450–1900: From Copernicus to Darwin*. Baltimore, MD: John Hopkins University Press, 2006.

Olson, Michael A., and Robert H. Fazio. "Relations Between Implicit Measures of Prejudice: What Are We Measuring?" *Psychological Science* 14 (2003): 636–639.

Oppel, Jr., Richard A. "Steady Decline in Major Crime Baffles Most Experts." *New York Times*, May 23, 2011. Accessed February 13, 2014. http://www.nytimes.com/2011/05/24/us/24crime.html.

Osarchuk, Michael, and Sherman J. Tatz. "Effect of Induced Fear of Death on Belief in the Afterlife." *Journal of Personality and Social Psychology* 27 (1973): 256–60.

Oxley, Douglas R., Kevin B. Smith, John R. Alford, Matthew V. Hibbing, Jennifer L. Miller, and Mario J. Scalora. "Political Attitudes Vary with Psychological Traits." *Science* 321 (2008): 1667–70.

Pagel, Mark. *Wired for Culture: Origins of the Human Social Mind*. New York: W. W. Norton & Company, 2012.

Palaez, Vicky. "The Prison Industry in the United States: Big Business or a New Form of Slavery?" *Centre for Research on Globalization*, 2008. Accessed June 14, 2014. http://www.globalresearch.ca/the

-prison-industry-in-the-united-states-big-business-or-a-new-form-of
-slavery/8289.

Pape, Robert A. *Dying to Win: The Strategic Logic of Suicide Terrorism.* New York: Random House, 2005.

Parfrey, Adam, ed. *Extreme Islam: Anti-American Propaganda of Muslim Fundamentalism.* Port Townsend, WA: Ferel House, 2002.

Pargament, Kenneth I. *The Psychology of Religion and Coping: Theory, Research, Practice.* New York: Guilford Press, 1997.

Park, Hae-Seong, Lauri Ashton, Tammie Causey, and Sung S. Moon. "The Impact of Religious Proscriptiveness on Alcohol Use Among High School Students." *Journal of Alcohol and Drug Education* 44 (1999): 34–46.

Paul, Gregory S. "Cross-National Correlations of Quantifiable Societal Health with Popular Religiosity and Secularism in the Prosperous Democracies." *Journal of Religion & Society* 7 (2005): 1–17.

Pavlak, Thomas J. "Social Class, Ethnicity, and Racial Prejudice." *Public Opinion Quarterly* 37 (1973): 225–31.

Paxton, Robert O. *The Anatomy of Fascism.* New York: Vintage, 2005.

Pearce, Lisa D., and Dana L. Haynie. "Intergenerational Religious Dynamics and Adolescent Delinquency." *Social Forces* 82 (2004): 1553–72.

Pearce, Michelle J., Stephanie M. Jones, Mary E. Schwab-Stone, and Vladislav Ruchkin. "The Protective Effects of Religiousness and Parent Involvement on the Development of Conduct Problems among Youth Exposed to Violence." *Child Development* 74 (2003): 1682–96.

Pearson, Adam R., John F. Dovidio, and Samuel L. Gaertner. "The Nature of Contemporary Prejudice: Insights from Aversive Racism." *Social and Personality Compass* 3 (2009): 314–38.

Peek, Charles W., Eric W. Curry, and Heather P. Chalfant. "Religiosity and Delinquency over Time: Deviance Deterrence and Deviance Amplification." *Social Science Quarterly* 66 (1985): 120–31.

Peek, Charles W., George D. Lowe, and L. Susan Williams. "Gender and God's World: Another Look at Religious Fundamentalism and Sexism." *Social Forces* 69 (1991): 1205–22.

Peretz, Evgenia. "Going After Gore." *Vanity Fair*, October, 14, 2007.

Accessed March 10, 2013. http://www.vanityfair.com/politics/features/2007/10/gore 200710.

Perkins, H. Wesley. "Parental Religion and Alcohol Use Problems as Intergenerational Predictors of Problem Drinking among College Youth." *Journal for the Scientific Study of Religion* 26 (1987): 340–57.

Perlstein, Rick. *Before the Storm*. New York: Hill & Wang, 2000.

Perreault, Stéphane, and Richard Y. Bourhis. "Ethnocentrism, Social Identification, and Discrimination." *Personality and Social Psychology Bulletin* 25 (1999): 92–103.

Perugini, Marco, and Luigi Leone. "Implicit Self-Concept and Moral Actions." *Journal of Research in Personality* 43 (2009): 747–54.

Peters, Rudolf. *Jihad in Classical and Modern Islam*. Princeton, NJ: Marcus Weiner, 1996.

Peterson, Elicka S. L. "Murder as Self-Help: Women and Intimate Partner Homicide." *Homicide Studies* 3 (1999): 30–46.

Pettersson, Thorleif. "Religion and Criminality: Structural Relationships between Church Involvement and Crime Rates in Contemporary Sweden." *Journal for the Scientific Study of Religion* 30 (1991): 279–91.

Petts, Richard J. "Family and Religious Characteristics' Influence on Delinquency Trajectories from Adolescence to Young Adulthood." *American Sociological Review* 74 (2009): 465–83.

Petts, Richard J., and Chris Knoester. "Parents' Religious Heterogamy and Children's Well-Being." *Journal for the Scientific Study of Religion* 46 (2007): 373–89.

Pew Charitable Trusts. "One in 100: Behind Bars in America." February 8, 2008. Accessed September 3, 2012. http://www.pewtrusts .org/en/research-and-analysis/reports/2008/02/28/one-in-100-behind-bars -in-america-2008.

Pew Forum on Global Attitudes and Trends. "The American-Western European Values Gap: American Exceptionalism Subsides." Pew Research Center. November 17, 2011. Accessed June 6, 2013. http://www.pewglobal.org/2011/11/17/the-american-western -european-values-gap/.

Pew Forum on Religion and Public Life. "Global Christianity—A Report on the Size and Distribution of the World's Christian Population." Pew Research Center. December 19, 2011. Accessed February 2, 2012. http://www.pewforum.org/2011/12/19/global-christianity-exec/.

Pew Forum on Religion & Public Life. "Income Distribution within U.S. Religious Groups," Pew Research Center. January 30, 2009. Accessed April 6, 2014. http://www.pewforum.org/Income-Distribution-Within-US-Religious-Groups.aspx.

Pew Forum on Religion and Public Life. "Not All Nonbelievers Call Themselves Atheists." Pew Research Center. April 2, 2009. Accessed January 9, 2014. http://www.pewforum.org/2009/04/02/not-all -nonbelievers-call-themselves-atheists/.

Pew Forum on Religion and Public Life. "U.S. Religious Knowledge Survey." Pew Research Center. September 28, 2010. Accessed January 9, 2014. http://www.pewforum.org/files/2010/09/religious -knowledge-full-report.pdf.

Pew Forum on Religion and Public Life. "U.S. Religious Landscape Survey, 2012." Pew Research Center, 2013. Accessed April 6, 2014. http://religions.pewforum.org/reports.

Pew Forum on U.S. Politics and Policy. "Continued Majority Support for Death Penalty." Pew Research Center. January 6, 2012. Accessed May 23, 2014. http://www.people-press.org/2012/01/06/continued -majority -support-for-death-penalty/.

Pew Forum on U.S. Politics and Policy. "The Generation Gap and the 2012 Election, Section 4: Views of the Nation." *Pew Research Center*. November 3, 2011. Accessed January 3, 2014. http://www.people -press.org/2011/11/03/section-4-views-of-the-nation/.

Phan, Katherine T. "Survey: More Americans Familiar with Big Mac Ingredients than Ten Commandments." *Christian Post*, October 3, 2007. Accessed September 22, 2013. http://www.christianpost.com/ news/survey-more-americans-familiar-with-big-mac-ingredients -than-10-commandments-29557/.

Phillips, Kevin. *American Theocracy*. New York: Viking Press, 2006.

Piatelli-Palmarini, Massimo. *Inevitable Illusions: How Mistakes of Mind*

Rule Our Minds. New York: Wiley, 1996.

Pidgeon, Nick, Roger E. Kasperson, and Paul Slovic, eds. *The Social Amplification of Risk*. New York: Cambridge University Press, 2003.

Pildes, Richard H. "Why the Center Does Not Hold: The Causes of Hyperpolarized Democracy in America." *California Law Review* 99 (2011): 273–334.

Pinker, Stephen. *The Better Angels of Our Nature: Why Violence Has Declined*. New York: Viking Press, 2011.

———. *The Blank State: The Modern Denial of Human Nature*. New York: Penguin Putnam, 2003.

Pollner, Melvin. "Divine Relations, Social Relations, and Well-Being." *Journal of Health and Social Behavior* 22 (1989): 92–104.

Potter, Gary. "Fundamental Violence: Protestant Fundamentalism and Violent Crime." *Uprooting Criminology: A Reasoned Plot*. November 11, 2013. Accessed February 26, 2014. http://uprootingcriminology .org/essays/fundamental-violence-protestant-fundamentalism-violent -crime-gary-w-potter/.

Powell, Russell, and Steve Clarke. "Religion as an Evolutionary Byproduct: A Critique of the Standard Model." *British Journal for the Philosophy of Science* 63 (2012): 457–86.

Pratt, Travis C. *Addicted to Incarceration: Corrections Policy and the Politics of Misinformation in the United States*. Thousand Oaks, CA: Sage, 2009.

Press, Bill. *How the Republicans Stole Christmas: The Republican Party's Declared Monopoly on Religion and What Democrats Can Do to Take it Back*. New York: Doubleday, 2005.

Preston, James D. "Religiosity and Adolescent Drinking Behavior." *Sociological Quarterly* 10 (2005): 372–83.

Prothero, Stephen. *American Jesus: How the Son of God Became a National Icon*. New York: Farrar, Straus, and Giroux, 2003.

———. *Religious Literacy: What Every American Needs to Know—And Doesn't*. New York: HarperOne, 2008.

Putnam, Robert D., and David E. Campbell. *American Grace: How Religion Divides and Unites Us*. New York: Simon & Schuster, 2010.

Pyle, Ralph E. "Trends in Religious Stratification: Have Religious Groups Socioeconomic Distinctions Declined in Recent Decades?" *Sociology of Religion* 67 (2006): 61–79.

Pyszczynski, Tom, Adolhossein Abdollahi, Sheldon Solomon, Jeff Greenberg, Florette Cohen, and David Weise. "Mortality Salience, Martyrdom, and Military Might: The Great Satan Versus the Axis of Evil." *Personality and Social Psychology Bulletin* 32 (2006): 525–37.

Pyszczynski, Tom, Jeff Greenberg, and Sheldon Solomon. "A Dual-Process Model of Defense against Conscious and Unconscious Death-Related Thoughts: An Extension of Terror Management Theory." *Psychological Review* 106 (2007): 835–45.

———. "Why Do We Need What We Need? A Terror Management Perspective on the Roots of Human Social Motivation." *Psychological Inquiry* 8 (1997): 1–20.

Pyszczynski, Tom, Sheldon Solomon, and Jeff Greenberg. *In the Wake of 9/11: The Psychology of Terror*. Washington DC: American Psychological Association, 2002.

Raine, Adrian, Todd Lencz, Susan Bihrle, Lori Lacasse, and Patrick Colletti. "Reduced Prefrontal Gray Matter Volume and Reduced Autonomic Activity in Antisocial Personality Disorder." *Archives of General Psychiatry* 57 (2000): 119–27.

Ranstorp, Magnus. "Terrorism in the Name of Religion." *Journal of International Affairs* 50 (1996): 41–63.

Rapaport, David C. "Fear and Trembling: Terrorism in Three Religious Traditions." *American Political Science Review* 78 (1984): 658–76.

Reed, Ralph. *Active Faith*. New York: Free Press, 1996.

Reese, William J. "Public Schools and the Great Gates of Hell." *Educational Theory* 32 (1982): 9–17.

———. "Soldiers for Christ in the Army of God: The Christian School Movement in America." *Educational Theory* 32 (1985): 175–94.

Reeves, Richard. *President Nixon: Alone in the White House*. New York: Simon & Schuster, 2002.

Reeves, Thomas C. *The Empty Church: The Suicide of Liberal Christianity*. New York: Simon & Schuster, 1996.

Regnerus, Mark D. "How Different Are the Adult Children of Parents Who have Same-Sex Relationships? Findings from the New Family Structures Study." *Social Science Research* 41 (2012): 752–70.

———. "Moral Communities and Adolescent Delinquency: Religious Contexts and Community Social Control." *Sociological Quarterly* 44 (2003): 523–54.

Reiman, Jeffrey H. *The Rich Get Richer and the Poor Get Prison: Ideology, Class, and Criminal Justice*. 7th ed. Boston: Allyn & Bacon, 2005.

Reynolds, Barbara. "Christian Coalition a Model for UnChristian Conduct." *USA Today*, May 26, 1995: A15.

Richards, Robert J. *Was Hitler a Darwinian? Disputed Questions in the History of Evolutionary Theory*. Chicago, IL: University of Chicago Press, 2013.

Ridley, Matt. *The Origins of Virtue*. New York: Penguin Press, 1997.

Riley, Naomi S. *God on the Quad: How Religious Colleges and the Missionary Generation Are Changing America*. New York: St. Martin's Press, 2005.

Rivera, Flavia J., and Timothy A. McCorry. "An Evaluation of an After-School Program's Effectiveness in Preventing Juvenile Delinquency and Substance Use: A Test of the Social Development Model." *New York Sociologist* 2 (2007): 65–84.

Roberts, Alden, Jerome Koch, and D. Paul Johnson. "Reference Groups and Religion: An Empirical Test." *Sociological Spectrum* 21 (2001): 81–98.

Roberts, Julian V. *Public Opinion, Crime, and Criminal Justice*. Boulder, CO: Westview Press, 2000.

Roberts, Julian V., and Mike Hough. *Understanding Public Attitudes to Criminal Justice*. Maidenhead, UK: Open University Press, 2005.

Roberts, Michael K., and James D. Davidson. "The Nature and Sources of Religious Involvement." *Review of Religious Research* 25 (1984): 334–50.

Robertson, Pat. *The Collected Works of Pat Robertson*. New York: Inspirational Press, 1994.

———. *The New World Order*. Nashville: Word Publishing, 1995.

Robins, Robert S., and Jerrold Post. *Political Paranoia: The Psychopolitics of Hatred.* New Haven, CT: Yale University Press, 1997.

Robinson, Matthew B. *Death Nation: The Experts Explain American Capital Punishment.* Upper Saddle River, NJ: Prentice Hall, 2007.

Robison, James. "The Enemy's Plan." *James Robison, A Weekly Commentary,* July 22, 2011. Accessed May 27, 2012. http://jamesrobison.net/?q=node/90.

Rodda, Chris. *Liars for Jesus: The Religious Right's Alternate Version of American History.* Charleston, SC: CreateSpace Publishing, 2006.

Roes, Frans L., and Michel Raymond. "Belief in Moralizing Gods." *Evolution and Human Behavior* 24 (2003): 126–35.

Rose, Brigid M., and Michael J. O'Sullivan. "Afterlife Beliefs and Death Anxiety: An Exploration of the Relationship between Afterlife Expectations and Fear of Death in an Undergraduate Population." *Journal of Death and Dying* 45 (2002): 229–43.

Rosenbaum, Janet E. "Patient Teenagers? A Comparison of the Sexual Behavior of Virginity Pledgers and Matched Nonpledgers." *Pediatrics* 123 (2009): e110–20.

———. "Reborn a Virgin: Adolescents' Retracting of Virginity Pledges and Sexual Histories." *American Journal of Public Health* 96 (2006): 1098–1103.

Rosenberg, Scott. "Did Gore Invent the Internet?" *Salon.* October 5, 2000. Accessed December 13, 2013. http://www.salon.com/2000/10/05/gore_internet/.

Rosenblatt, Abram, Jeff Greenberg, Sheldon Soloman, Tom Pyszczynski, and Debra Lyon. "Evidence For Terror Management Theory: I. The Effects of Mortality Salience on Reactions to Those Who Violate or Uphold Cultural Values." *Journal of Personality and Social Psychology* 57 (1989): 681–90.

———. "Evidence for Terror Management Theory: II. The Effects of Mortality Salience on Reactions to Those Who Threaten or Bolster the Cultural Worldview." *Journal of Personality and Social Psychology* 58 (1990): 308–18.

Ross, Lainie F., and Timothy J. Aspinwall. "Religious Exemptions to the Immunization Statutes: Balancing Public Health and Religious Freedom." *Journal of Law, Medicine and Ethics* 25 (1997): 202–209.

Ross, Lee E. "Religion and Deviance: Exploring the Impact of Social Control Elements." *Sociological Spectrum* 14 (1994): 65–86.

Rothman, Stanley, Robert S. Lichter, and Neil Nevitte. "Politics and Professional Advancement among College Faculty." *Forum* 3, no. 1, article 2 (2005), http://www.cwu.edu/~manwellerm/academic%20 bias.pdf.

Routledge, Clay, and Jamie Arndt. "Self-Sacrifice as Self-Defense: Mortality Salience Increases Efforts to Affirm a Symbolic Immortal Self at the Expense of the Physical Self." *European Journal of Social Psychology* 38 (2008): 531–41.

Rozell, Mark J., and Clyde Wilcox, eds. *God at the Grassroots*. Lanham, MD: Rowman and Littlefield, 1995.

Rudman, Laurie A., and Richard D. Ashmore. "Discrimination and the Implicit Association Test." *Group Processes & Intergroup Relations* 10 (2007): 359–72.

Rushdie, Salman. "Fighting the Forces of Invisibility." *Washington Post*, October 2, 2001.

Rushdooney, Rousas J. "Christian Reconstructionism as a Movement." *Journal of Christian Reconstructionism*, Fall 1996: 21.

———. *The Institutes of Biblical Law*. Nutley, NJ: The Craig Press, 1973.

Russell, Bertrand. *Religion and Science*. Oxford: Oxford University Press, 1997.

Ruthven, Malise. *The Divine Supermarket: Travels in Search of the Soul of America*. London: Chatto & Windus, 1989.

Saletan, William. *Bearing Right: How Conservatives Won the Abortion War*. Berkeley: University of California Press, 2003.

Saloma, John S., III. *Ominous Politics: The New Conservative Labyrinth*. New York: Hill and Wang, 1984.

Saltzstein, Herbert D., and Tziporah Kasachkoff. "Haidt's Moral Intuitionist Theory: A Psychological and Philosophical Critique." *Review of General Psychology* 8 (2004): 273–82.

Sanford, Charles B. *The Religious Life of Thomas Jefferson*. Charlotte: University of North Carolina Press, 1987.

Santelli, John, Mary A. Ott, Maureen Lyon, Jennifer Rogers, and Daniel Summers. "Abstinence-Only Education Policies and Programs: A Position Paper of the Society for Adolescent Medicine." *Journal of Adolescent Health* 38 (2006): 83–87.

Savitsky, Douglas. "Is Plea Bargaining a Rational Choice? Plea Bargaining as an Engine of Racial Stratification and Overcrowding in the United States Prison System." *Rationality and Society* 24 (2012): 131–67.

Scarborough, Rick. *Enough is Enough: A Practical Guide to Political Action (Plus: Why Christians Must Engage)*. Incline Village, NV: Frontline Books, 2008.

———. *In Defense of Mixing Church and State*. Houston: Vision American, 1999.

———. *Liberalism Kills Kids*. Springfield, MO: 21st Century Press, 2006.

Schacter, Daniel I. *The Seven Sins of Memory: How the Mind Forgets and Remembers*. Boston: Houghton Mifflin, 2001.

Schaeffer, Francis A. *A Christian Manifesto*. Westchester, IL: Crossway Books, 1981.

Schatz, Robert T., Ervin Staub, and Howard Lavine. "On the Varieties of National Attachment: Blind versus Constructive Patriotism." *Political Psychology* 20 (1999): 151–74.

Schieman, Scott, and Alex Bierman. "Religious Activities and Changes in the Sense of Divine Control: Dimensions of Stratification as Contingencies." *Sociology of Religion* 68 (2007): 361–81.

Schieman, Scott, Tetyana Pudrovska, Leonard I. Pearlin, and Christopher G. Ellison. "The Sense of Divine Control and Psychological Distress: Variations by Race and Socioeconomic Status." *Journal for the Scientific Study of Religion* 45 (2006): 529–50.

Schimel, Jeff, Linda Simon, Jeff Greenberg, Tom Pyszczynski, Sheldon Solomon, Jeannette Waxmonsky, and Jamie Arndt. "Stereotypes and Terror Management: Evidence that Mortality Salience Enhances Stereotypic Thinking and Preferences." *Journal of Personality and Social Psychology* 77 (1999): 905–26.

Schnall, Simone, Jonathan Haidt, Gerald L. Clore, and Alexander H. Jordan. "Disgust as Embodied Moral Judgment." *Personality and Social Psychology Bulletin* 34 (2008): 1096–1109.

Schneidau, Herbert N. *Sacred and Discontent: The Bible and Western Tradition*. Berkeley: University of California Press, 1977.

Schreck, Christopher J. "Contemporary Retrospective on Social Control Theories." In *Criminological Theory: Readings and Retrospectives*, edited by Heith Copes and Volkan Topalli, 49–69. New York: McGraw-Hill, 2009.

Schuessler, Jennifer. "And the Worst Book of History is . . ." *New York Times*, July 16, 2012. Accessed July 10, 2013. http://artsbeat.blogs. nytimes.com/2012/07/16/and-the-worst-book-of-history-is/?_r=0.

Schultz, P. Wesley, and Alan Searleman. "Rigidity of Thought and Behavior: 100 Years of Research." *Genetic, Social, and General Psychology Monographs* 128 (2002): 165–209.

Schwartz, Regina. *The Curse of Cain: The Violent Legacy of Monotheism*. Chicago: University of Chicago Press, 1997.

Schwarz, Norbert. "Ease of Retrieval as Information: Another Look at the Availability Heuristic." *Journal of Personality and Social Psychology* 61 (1991): 195–202.

Schwitzgebel, Eric. "Do Ethicists Steal More Books?" *Philosophical Psychology* 22 (2009): 711–25.

Sears, Alan, and Craig Osten. *The Homosexual Agenda: Exposing the Principle Threat to Religious Freedom Today*. Nashville: Broadman & Holman, 2003.

Selengut, Charles. *Sacred Fury: Understanding Religious Violence*. Berkeley, CA: Altamira Press, 2004.

Sells, Michael. *The Bridge Betrayed: Religion and Genocide in Bosnia*. Berkeley: University of California Press, 1996.

Seltzer, Rick, and Joseph P. McCormick. "The Impact of Crime Victimization and Fear of Crime on Attitudes toward Death Penalty Defendants." *Violence & Victims* 2 (1987): 99–114.

Sentencing Project. Women in the Criminal Justice System: Briefing Sheets. Washington, DC, May, 2007. http://www.sentencingproject. org/doc/publications/womenincj_total.pdf.

———. *Incarcerated Parents and their Children: Trends 1991–2007*. Washington, DC: The Sentencing Project, 2009. http://www

.sentencingproject.org/doc/publications/publications/inc_incarcerate
dparents.pdf.

Sexton, Stephen. "Suffer the Children: A Vermont Sect Believes It's Wrong
to Spare the Rod." *Boston Globe*, July 14, 1983.

Shariff, Azim F., and Ara Norenzayan. "God is Watching You: Priming God
Concepts Increases Prosocial Behavior in an Anonymous Economic
Game." *Psychological Science* 18 (2007): 803–809.

Sharlet, Jeff. *The Family: The Secret Fundamentalism at the Heart of
American Power*. New York: Harper, 2008.

———. "Through a Glass Darkly: How the Christian Right is Reimagining
U.S. History." *Harper's Magazine*, December 2006. Accessed October
12, 2014. http://jeffsharlet.com/content/wp-content/uploads/2008/09/
through_a_glass.pdf.

Sheldon, Jane P., and Sandra L. Parent. "Clergy's Attitudes of Blame
toward Female Rape Victims." *Violence Against Women* 8 (2002):
233–56.

Sherkat, Darren E., and Christopher G. Ellison. "Recent Developments and
Current Controversies in the Sociology of Religion." *Annual Review
of Sociology* 25 (1999): 363–94.

Sherman, Lawrence W. "Reducing Gun Violence: What Works, What
Doesn't, What's Promising." *Criminology and Criminal Justice* 1
(2001): 11–25.

Shermer, Michael. *The Science of Good and Evil: Why People Cheat,
Gossip, Care, Share, and Follow the Golden Rule*. New York: Henry
Holt, 2004.

Shibley, Mark. *Resurgent Evangelicalism in the United States: Mapping
Cultural Change Since 1970*. Columbia: University of South Carolina
Press, 1996.

Shieman, Scott. "Socioeconomic Status and Beliefs about God's Influence
in Everyday Life." *Sociology of Religion* 71 (2010): 25–51.

Shiner, Larry. "The Concept of Secularization in Empirical Research."
Journal for the Scientific Study of Religion 6 (1967): 207–20.

Shweder, Richard A., Nancy C. Much, Manamohen Mahapatra, and
Lawrence Park. "The 'Big Three' of Morality (Autonomy, Community,

and Divinity), and the 'Big Three' Explanations of Suffering." In *Morality and Health*, edited by Allan Brandt and Paul Rozin, 119–69. New York: Routledge, 1997.

Sidanius, Jim, Michael Mitchell, Hillary Haley, and Carlos D. Navarrete. "Support for Harsh Criminal Sanctions and Criminal Justice Beliefs: A Social Dominance Perspective." *Social Justice Research* 19 (2006): 433–49.

Sikkink, David, and Mark Regnerus. "For God and the Fatherland: Protestant Symbolic Worlds and the Rise of National Socialism." In *Disruptive Religion: The Force of Faith in Social Movement Activism*, edited by Christian Smith, 166–91. New York: Routledge, 1996.

Silver, Lee M. *Challenging Nature: The Clash of Science and Spirituality at the New Frontier of Life*. New York: HarperCollins, 2006.

Silverman, Dave. "It's No Surprise that Atheists Know More about Religion than Most Americans." Fox News. September 28, 2010. Accessed May 14, 2014. http://www.foxnews.com/opinion/2010/09/28/dave-silverman-pew-survey-atheists-Bible-preacher-god-islam-holy-american/#ixzz1zfrPJd1j.

Simons, Lesley G., Ronald L. Simons, and Rand D. Conger. "Identifying the Mechanisms Whereby Family Religiosity Influences the Probability of Adolescent Antisocial Behavior." *Journal of Comparative Family Studies* 25 (2004): 547–63.

Sinha, Jill W., Ram A. Cnaan, and Richard W. Gelles. "Adolescent Risk Behaviors and Religion: Findings from a National Study." *Journal of Adolescence* 30 (2007): 231–49.

Sjöberg, Lennart, and Elisabeth Engelberg. "Risk Perception and Movies: A Study of Availability as a Factor in Risk Perception." *Risk Analysis* 30 (2010): 95–106.

Slack, Gordy. "Inside the Creation Museum." *Salon*, August 5, 2007. Accessed November 6, 2014. http://www.salon.com/news/feature/2007/05/31/creation_museum/index.html.

Sloan, Douglas M., and Raymond H. Potvin. "Religion and Delinquency: Cutting Through the Maze." *Social Forces* 65 (1986): 87–105.

Slovic, Paul. *The Perception of Risk*. London: Earthscan, 2000.

Slovic, Paul, James Flynn, and Howard Kunreuther, eds. *Risk, Media and Stigma: Understanding Public Challenges to Modern Science and Technology*. London: Earthscan, 2001.

Smidt, Corwin E. "Identifying Evangelical Respondents: An Analysis of Born-Again and Bible Questions Used across Different Surveys." In *Religion and Political Behavior in the United States*, edited by Ted G. Jelen, 23–43. New York: Praeger, 1989.

Smith, Christian. *American Evangelicalism: Embattled and Thriving*. Chicago: University of Chicago, 1998.

———. *Christian America? What Evangelicals Really Want*. Los Angeles: University of California Press, 2000.

———. "Why Christianity Works: An Emotions-Focused Phenomeno-logical Account." *Sociology of Religion* 68 (2007): 165–78.

Smith, Christian, and Robert Faris. "Socioeconomic Inequality in the American Religious System." *Journal for the Scientific Study of Religion* 44 (2005): 95–104.

Smith, M. Dwayne, and Margaret A. Zahn, eds. *Homicide: A Sourcebook for Social Research*. Thousand Oaks, CA: Sage, 1998.

Smith, Tom W. "Religious Diversity in America: The Emergence of Muslims, Buddhists, Hindus, and Others." *Journal for the Scientific Study of Religion*, 41 (2002): 577–85.

Sober, Elliot, and David S. Wilson. *Unto Others: The Evolution and Psychology of Unselfish Behavior*. Cambridge, MA: Cambridge University Press, 1998.

Soering, Jens. *An Expensive Way to Make Bad People Worse: An Essay on Prison Reform from an Insider's Perspective*. Lebanon, PA: Lantern Books, 2004.

Soldiers in the Army of God. DVD. Directed by Marc Levin and Daphne Pinkerson. New York: HBO Home Video, 2000.

Solomon, Sheldon, Jeff Greenberg, and Tom Pyszczynski. "Terror Management Theory of Self-Esteem." In *Handbook of Social and Clinical Psychology: The Health Perspective*, edited by C.R. Snyder and Donelson R. Forsyth, 21–40. New York: Pergamon Press, 1991.

———. "The Terror Management Theory of Social Behavior: Psychological Functions of Self Esteem and Cultural Worldviews." *Advances in Experimental Social Psychology* 24 (1991): 93–116.

Solomon, Sheldon, Jeff Greenberg, Linda Schimel, Jamie Arndt, and Tom Pyszczynski. "Human Awareness of Death and the Evolution of Culture." In *The Psychological Foundations of Culture*, edited by Mark Schaller and Christian S. Crandal, 15–40. Mahwah, NJ: Erlbaum, 2004.

Sosis, Richard. "Religion and Intragroup Cooperation: Preliminary Results of a Comparative Analysis of Utopian Communities." *Cross-Cultural Research* 34 (2000): 70–87.

Sosis, Richard, and Candace S. Alcorta. "Signaling, Solidarity, and the Sacred: The Evolution of Religious Behavior." *Evolutionary Anthropology* 12 (2003): 264–74.

Sowell, Thomas. *A Conflict of Visions: The Ideological Origins of Political Struggles*. New York: Basic Books, 2002.

Spong, John S. "Q & A on the Bible as a Weapon of Control." *Bishop Spong Q&A*, weekly newsletter. October 31, 2007. http://johnshelbyspong .com/ 2007/10/31/the-fifth-fundamental-the-second-coming/.

———. *The Sins of Scripture: Exposing the Bible's Texts of Hate to Reveal the God of Love*. New York: HarperCollins, 2005.

Sprinzak, Ehud. "Rational Fanatics." *Foreign Policy* 120 (2000): 66–74.

Stacey, Judith. *Brave New Families: Stories of Domestic Upheaval in Late-Twentieth-Century America*. Oakland, CA: University of California Press, 1998.

Stahr, Walter. *John Jay: Founding Father*. London: Hambledon Continuum Press, 2005.

Stalans, Loretta J. "Citizens' Crime Stereotypes, Biased Recall, and Punishment Preferences in Abstract Cases." *Law and Human Behavior* 17 (1993): 451–69.

Stanovich, Keith E. *The Robot's Rebellion: Finding Meaning in the Age of Darwin*. Chicago: University of Chicago Press, 2004.

Stark, Rodney. *Discovering God: The Origins of the Great Religions and the Evolution of Belief*. New York: Harper, 2007.

———. "The Economics of Piety: Religious Commitment and Social

Class." In *Issues in Social Inequality*, edited by Gerald W. Thielbar, and Saul D. Feldman, 483–503. Boston: Little, Brown and Company, 1972.

———. *One True God: Historical Consequences of Monotheism.* Princeton: Princeton University Press, 2001.

———. "Religion as Context: Hellfire and Delinquency One More Time." *Sociology of Religion* 57 (1996): 163–73.

———. "The Rise of a New World Faith." *Review of Religious Research* 26 (1984): 18–27.

Stark, Rodney, and Roger Finke. *Acts of Faith: Explaining the Human Side of Religion.* Berkeley: University of California Press, 2000.

Stark, Rodney, and Charles Y. Glock. *American Piety: The Nature of Religious Commitment.* Berkeley: University of California Press, 1968.

Stark, Rodney, Lori Kent, and Daniel P. Doyle. "Religion and Delinquency: The Ecology of a "Lost" Relationship." *Journal of Research in Crime and Delinquency* 19 (1982): 4–24.

Staub, Ervin. *The Roots of Evil: The Origins of Genocide and Other Group Violence.* Cambridge, MA: Cambridge University Press, 1989.

Steensland, Brian, Jerry Z. Park, Mark D. Regnerus, Lynn D. Robinson, W. Bradford Wilcox, and Robert D. Woodberry. "The Measure of American Religion: Toward Improving the State of the Art." *Social Forces* 79 (2000): 291–324.

Stenger, Victor J. *Has Science Found God? The Latest Results in the Search for Purpose in the Universe.* Amherst, NY: Prometheus Books, 2003.

Stenner, Karen. *The Authoritarian Dynamic.* New York: Cambridge University Press, 2005.

Stern, Fritz R. *The Politics of Cultural Despair: A Study in the Rise of Germanic Ideology.* Berkeley: University of California Press, 1989.

Stern, Jessica. *Terror in the Name of God: Why Religious Militants Kill.* New York: HarperCollins, 2003.

———. *The Ultimate Terrorists.* Cambridge, MA: Harvard University Press, 1999.

Stewart, Chris. "The Influence of Spirituality on the Substance Use of College Students." *Journal of Drug Education* 21 (2001): 343–51.

Stewart, Chris, and John M. Bolland. "Parental Style as a Possible Mediator of the Relationship between Religiosity and Substance Use in African-American Adolescents." *Journal of Ethnicity in Substance Abuse* 1 (2002): 63–81.

Stolberg, Sheryl G. "You Want Compromise. Sure You Do." *New York Times*, August 14, 2011. Accessed May 4, 2014. http://www.nytimes.com/2011/08/14/sunday-review/you-want-compromise-sure-you-do.html?_r=0.

Strozier, Charles B. *Apocalypse: On the Psychology of Fundamentalism in America*. Boston: Beacon Press, 1994.

Struch, Naomi, and Shalom H. Schwartz. "Intergroup Aggression: Its Predictors and Distinctness from In-Group Bias." *Journal of Personality and Social Psychology* 56 (1989): 364–73.

Stylianou, Stelios. "The Role of Religiosity in the Opposition to Drug Use." *International Journal of Offender Therapy and Comparative Criminology* 48 (2004): 429–48.

Suarez, Ray. *The Holy Vote: The Politics of Faith in America*. New York: Harper Collins, 2006.

Sumter, Melvina, and Clear, Todd R. "Religion in the Correctional Setting." In *Key Correctional Issues*, edited by Roslyn Muraskin, 86–113. Upper Saddle River, NJ: Pearson, 1996.

Sunstein, Cass R. "Moral Heuristics." *Brain and Behavioral Science* 28 (2005): 531–73.

Surette, Ray. *Media, Crime, and Criminal Justice*. Pacific Grove, CA: Brooks/Cole, 1992.

Swineburne, Richard. *The Existence of God*. Oxford: Oxford University Press, 2004.

Taber, Charles S., and Milton Lodge. "Motivated Skepticism in the Evaluation of Political Beliefs." *American Journal of Political Science* 50 (2006): 755–69.

Task Force on Youth Development and Community Programs. *A Matter of Time: Risk and Opportunity in the Non-School Hours*. New York: Carnegie Corporation, 1992.

Taverne, Dick. *The March of Unreason: Science, Democracy and the New Fundamentalism*. Oxford: Oxford University Press, 2005.

Taylor, Charles. "Democracy, Inclusive and Exclusive." In *Meaning and Modernity: Religion, Polity and the Self*, edited by Richard Madsen, William M. Sullivan, Ann Swidler, and Steven M. Tipton, 181–94. Berkeley, CA: University of California Press, 2002.

Taylor, D. Garth, Kim L. Scheppele, and Arthur L. Stinchcombe. "Salience of Crime and Support for Harsher Criminal Sanctions." *Theory and Evidence in Criminology: Correlations and Contradictions* 26 (1979): 413–24.

Taylor, Donald M. *The Quest for Identity: From Minority Groups to Generation Xers*. Westport, CT: Praeger, 2002.

Taylor, Donald M., Fathali M. Moghaddam, Ian Gamble, and Evelyn Zellerer. "Disadvantaged Group Responses to Perceived Inequality: From Passive Acceptance to Collective Action." *Journal of Social Psychology* 127 (1987): 259–72.

Tedin, Kent L. "Religious Preference and Pro/Anti Activism on the Equal Rights Amendment Issue." *Sociological Review* 21 (1978): 55–66.

Teehan, John. *In the Name of God: The Evolutionary Origins of Religious Ethics and Violence*. .5th ed. New York: Wiley-Blackwell, 2010.

Templin, Daniel P., and Martin M. Martin. "The Relationship between Religious Orientation, Gender, and Drinking Patterns among Catholic College Students." *College Student Journal* 33 (1999): 488–96.

Thompson, J. Anderson, and Claire Aukofer. *Why We Believe in God(s): A Concise Guide to the Science of Faith*. Charlottesville, VA: Pritchstone Publishing, 2011.

Thórisdóttir, Hulda, and John T. Jost. "Motivated Closed-Mindedness Mediates the Effect of Threat on Political Conservatism." *Political Psychology* 32 (2011): 785–811.

Thornhill, Randy, Corey L. Fincher, and Devaraj Aran. "Parasites, Democratization, and the Liberalization of Values across Contemporary Countries." *Biological Reviews of the Cambridge Philosophical Society* 84 (2009): 113–31.

Tiger, Lionel. *Optimism: The Biology of Hope*. New York: Simon & Schuster, 1979.

Timmer, Doug A., and William H. Norman. "The Ideology of Victim Precipitation." *Criminal Justice Review* 9 (1984): 63–68.

Tittle, Charles R., and Michael R. Welch. "Religiosity and Deviance: Toward a Contingency Theory of Constraining Effects." *Social Forces* 61 (1983): 653–82.

Tocqueville, Alexis de. *Democracy in America.* Translated by Henry Reeve. London: Saunders and Otley, 2007.

Tomczak, Larry. *God, the Rod, and Your Child's Bod: The Art of Loving Correction for Christian Parents.* Old Tappan, NJ: Fleming H. Revell Co, 1982.

Topalli, Volkan, Timothy Brezina, and Mindy Bernhardt. "With God on My Side: The Paradoxical Relationship between Religious Belief and Criminality among Hardcore Street Offenders." *Theoretical Criminology* 17 (2013): 49–69.

Tracy, Steven R. "Patriarchy and Domestic Violence: Challenging Common Conceptions." *Journal of the Evangelical Theological Society* 50 (2007): 573–94.

Trawick, Michelle W., and Roy M. Howsen. "Crime and Community Heterogeneity: Race, Ethnicity, and Religion." *Applied Economic Letters* 13 (2006): 341–45.

Tremblay, Pierre, and Paul-Philippe Paré. "Crime and Destiny: Patterns in Serious Offenders' Mortality Rates." *Canadian Journal of Criminology and Criminal Justice* 45 (2003): 299–326.

Trollinger, Jr., William V. *God's Empire: William Bell Riley and Midwestern Fundamentalism.* Madison, WI: University of Wisconsin Press, 1991.

Truman, Jennifer I. "Criminal Victimization, 2010." *National Crime Victimization Survey.* US Department of Justice. September 2011. http://www.bjs.gov/content/pub/pdf/cv10.pdf.

Turner, Carol J., and Robert J. Willis. "The Relationship between Self-Reported Religiosity and Drug Use by College Students." *Journal of Drug Education* 9 (1979): 67–78.

Tversky, Amos, and Daniel Kahneman. "Availability: A Heuristic for Judging Frequency and Probability." *Cognitive Psychology* 5 (1973): 207–33.

Twitchell, James B. *Shopping for God: How Christianity Went from in Your Heart to in Your Face.* New York: Simon and Schuster, 2007.

Vakalahi, Halaevalu F. "Family-Based Predictors of Adolescent Substance Use." *Journal of Child and Adolescent Substance Abuse* 11 (2002): 1–15.

Vanberkum, Jos J.A., Bregje Holleman, Mante Nieuwland, Marte Otten, and Jaap Murre. "Right or Wrong? The Brain's Fast Response to Morally Objectionable Statements." *Psychological Science* 20 (2009): 1092–99.

Van den Bos, Kees, and Joost Miedema. "Toward Understanding Why Fairness Matters: The Influence of Mortality Salience on Reactions to Procedural Fairness." *Journal of Personality and Social Psychology* 79 (2000): 355–66.

Vanderford, Marsha L. "Vilifications and Social Movements: A Case Study of Pro-Life and Pro-Choice Rhetoric." *Quarterly Journal of Speech* 25 (1989): 166–82.

Van Doran, Carl. *Benjamin Franklin.* 1938. New York: Viking Press, 2002.

Van Hiel, Alain, and Ivan Mervielde. "Explaining Conservative Beliefs and Political Preferences: A Comparison of Social Dominance Orientation and Authoritarianism." *Journal of Applied Social Psychology* 32 (2002): 965–76.

Van Vugt, Mark, David De Cremer, and Dirk P. Janssen. "Gender Differences in Cooperation and Competition: The Male-Warrior Hypothesis." *Psychological Science* 18 (2007): 19–23.

Vidmar, Neil, and Dale T. Miller. "Social Psychological Processes Underlying Attitudes toward Legal Punishment." *Law & Society Review* 14 (1980): 565–602.

Voegeli, William. *Never Enough: America's Limitless Welfare State.* New York: Encounter Books, 2010.

Voerding, Philip. *The Trouble with Christianity: A Concise Outline of Christian History: From the Traditional Western Birth of Christ (PBUH) to Contemporary American Evangelical Fundamentalism.* Bloomington, IN: Authorhouse, 2009.

Voll, Daniel. "Neal Horsley and the Future of the Armed Abortion Conflict." *Esquire*, February 1999, 110–19.

Vries, Hent de, and Samuel Weber, eds. *Religion and Media.* Stanford, CA: Stanford University Press, 2001.

Waal, Frans B. M. de. *Good Natured: The Origins of Right and Wrong in Humans and Other Animals.* Cambridge, MA: Harvard University Press, 1996.

Wade, Nicholas. *The Faith Instinct: How Religion Evolved and Why It Endures.* New York: Penguin, 2009.

———. "Is 'Do Unto Others' Written Into Our Genes?" *New York Times*, September 18, 2007. Accessed March 12, 2013. http://www.nytimes.com/2007/09/18/science/18mora.html?_r=0.

Wade, Nicholas, and William Broad. *Betrayers of the Truth: Fraud and Deceit in the Halls of Science.* New York: Simon and Schuster, 1982.

Wakefield, Dan. *The Hijacking of Jesus: How the Religious Right Distorts Christianity and Promotes Prejudice and Hate.* New York: Nation Books, 2006.

Wald, Kenneth D., Dennis E. Owen, and Samuel S. Hill, Jr. "Churches as Political Communities." *American Political Science Review* 82 (1988): 531–47.

Wallace, John M., and Jerald G. Bachman. "Explaining Racial/Ethnic Differences in Adolescent Drug Use: The Impact of Background and Lifestyle." *Social Problems* 38 (1991): 333–55.

Wallace, John M., Tony N. Brown, Jerald G. Bachman, and Thomas A. Laveist. "The Influence of Race and Religion on Abstinence from Alcohol, Cigarettes, and Marijuana among Adolescents." *Journal of Studies on Alcohol* 64 (2003): 843–48.

Wallace, John M., Ryoko Yamaguchi, Jerald G. Bachman, Patrick M. O'Malley, John E. Schulenberg, and Lloyd D. Johnson. "Religiosity and Adolescent Substance Use: The Role of Individual and Contextual Influences." *Social Problems* 54 (2007): 308–27.

Warner, R. Stephen. "Work in Progress toward a New Paradigm for the Sociological Study of Religion in the United States." *American Journal of Sociology* 98 (1993): 1044–93.

Warraq, Ibn. *Why I am Not a Muslim.* Amherst, NY: Prometheus Books, 1995.

Watters, Wendell W. *Deadly Doctrine: Health, Illness, and Christian God-Talk.* Amherst, NY: Prometheus Books, 1992.

Wechsler, Henry, George W. Dowdall, Andrea Davenport, and Sonia Castillo. "Correlates of College Student Binge Drinking." *American Journal of Public Health* 85 (1995): 921–26.

Weeks, Matthew, and Michael B. Lupfer. "Complicating Race: The Relationship between Prejudice, Race, and Social Class Categorizations." *Personality and Social Psychology Bulletin* 30 (2004): 972–84.

Weems, Renita J. *Battered Love: Marriage, Sex, and Violence in the Hebrew Prophets.* Minneapolis: Fortress Press, 1995.

Weitzer, Ronald. "Racialized Policing: Residents' Perceptions in Three Neighborhoods." *Law & Society Review* 34 (2000): 129–55.

Weitzer, Ronald, and Steven A. Tuch. "Perceptions of Racial Profiling: Race, Class and Personal Experience." *Criminology* 50 (2002): 435–56.

Welch, Michael R., Charles R. Tittle, and Harold G. Gramick. "Christian Religiosity, Self-Control, and Social Conformity." *Social Forces* 84 (2006): 1605–23.

Wellman, James K., and Kyoko Tokuno. "Is Religious Violence Inevitable?" *Journal for the Scientific Study of Religion* 43 (2004): 291–96.

Welton, Gary L., A. Gelene Adkins, Sandra L. Ingle, and Wayne A. Dixon. "God Control: the Fourth Dimension." *Journal of Psychology and Theology* 24 (1996): 13–25.

Werleman, C. J. "The Results Are In: America is Dumb and on the Road to Getting Dumber." *Alternet.* June 4, 2014. Accessed June 12, 2014. http://www.alternet.org/education/results -are-america-dumb-and-road-getting-dumber.

Westen, Drew. *The Political Brain: The Role of Emotion in Deciding the Fate of the Nation.* New York: Public Affairs, 2007.

Whatley, Stuart. (2010). "Democratic Values, Islam and the Judeo-Christian Tradition Fallacy." *Huffington Post*, August 10, 2010. Accessed August 11, 2010. http://www.huffingtonpost.com/stuart -whatley/islam-america-democratic_b_675756.html?ir=Technology.

White, Jonathan R. "Political Eschatology: A Theology of Antigovernmental Extremism." *American Behavioral Scientist* 44 (2001): 937–56.

White, Mel. *Stranger at the Gate: To Be Gay and Christian in America.* New York: Plume, 1995.

Whitehead, John W. "Jailing Americans for Profit: The Rise of the Prison Industrial Complex." *Huffington Post*, April 10, 2012. Accessed May 5, 2013. http://www.huffingtonpost.com/john-w-whitehead/prison-privatization_b_1414467.html.

Whithnall, Adam. "Saudi Arabia Declares All Atheists are Terrorists in New Law to Crack Down on Political Dissidents." *Independent*, April 1, 2014. Accessed April 2, 2014. http://www.independent.co.uk/news/world/middle-east/saudi-arabia-declares-all-atheists-are-terrorists-in-new-law-to-crack-down-on-political-dissidents-9228389.html.

Whitley, Bernard E., and Mary E. Kite. *The Psychology of Prejudice and Discrimination.* 2nd ed. South Melbourne, Australia: Cengage Learning, 2010.

Whitman, James Q. *Harsh Justice: Criminal Punishment and the Widening Divide between America and Europe.* Oxford: Oxford University Press, 2005.

Wiehe, Vernon R. "Religious Influence on Parental Attitudes toward the Use of Corporal Punishment." *Journal of Family Violence* 5 (1990): 173–86.

Wilcox, Clyde, and Ted Jelen. "Evangelicals and Political Tolerance." *American Politics Quarterly* 18 (1990): 25–46.

Williams, Rhys H., and Susan M. Alexander. "Religious Rhetoric in American Populism: Civil Religion as Movement Ideology." *Journal for the Scientific Study of Religion* 33 (1994): 1–15.

Willis, Clint, and Nate Hardcastle, eds. *Jesus is Not a Republican: The Religious Right's War on America.* New York: Thunder's Mouth Press, 2005.

Wills, Garry. *Head and Heart: American Christianities.* New York: Penguin, 2007.

———. *Under God: Religion and American Politics.* New York: Simon and Schuster, 1990.

Wills, Thomas A., Alison M. Yaeger, and James M. Sandy. "Buffering Effect of Religiosity for Adolescent Substance Use." *Psychology of Addictive Behaviors* 17 (2003): 24–31.

Wilson, Glenn D. *The Psychology of Conservatism*. New York: Academic Press, 1973.

Wimberley, Dale W. "Religion and Role-Identity: A Structural Symbolic Interactionist Conceptualization of Religiosity." *Sociological Quarterly* 30 (1989): 125–42.

Winn, Denise. *The Manipulated Mind: Brainwashing, Conditioning and Indoctrination*. Cambridge, MA: Malor Books, 2000.

Wolfe, Alan. "The God Gap." *Boston Globe*, September 19, 2004.

———. *One Nation After All: What Middle-Class Americans Really Think About: God, Country, Family, Racism, Welfare, Immigration, Homosexuality, Work, The Right, The Left, and Each Other*. New York: Penguin, 1999.

———. *The Transformation of American Religion: How We Actually Live Our Faith*. New York: Free Press, 2003.

———. "What God Owes Jefferson: A Review of 'God's Politics and Taking Faith Seriously.'" *New Republic*, May 23, 2005: 35–41.

Wolfgang, Marvin E. *Patterns in Criminal Homicide*. Philadelphia: University of Pennsylvania Press, 1958.

Wolpert, Lewis. *Six Impossible Things before Breakfast: The Evolutionary Origins of Belief*. London: Faber & Faber, 2006.

Woodberry, Robert D., and Christian S. Smith. *Fundamentalism et al: Conservative Protestants in America*. Palo Alto, CA: Annual Reviews, 1998.

Worden, Robert E., and Robin L. Shepard. "Demeanor, Crime, and Police Behavior: A Reexamination of the Police Services Study Data." *Criminology* 34 (1996): 83–105.

Wright, Richard T., and Scott H. Decker. *Armed Robbers In Action: Stickups and Street Culture*. Boston, MA: Northeastern, 1997.

———. *Burglars on the Job: Streetlife and Residential Break-Ins*. Boston, MA: Northeastern, 1996.

Wright, Robert. *The Evolution of God*. New York: Little, Brown, 2009.

Wright, Stuart A., ed. *Armageddon in Waco: Critical Perspectives of the Branch Davidian Conflict*. Chicago: University of Chicago Press, 1995.

Wuthnow, Robert. "The World of Fundamentalism." *Christian Century*, April 22, 1992: 426–29.

Xu, Xiaohe, Yuk-Ying Tung, and R. Gregory Dunaway. "Cultural, Human, and Social Capital as Determinants of Corporal Punishment: Toward an Integrated Theoretical Model." *Journal of Interpersonal Violence* 15 (2000): 603–30.

Young, Mark C., John Gartner, Thomas O'Connor, David Larson, and Kevin N. Wright. "Long-Term Recidivism among Federal Inmates Trained as Volunteer Prison Ministers." *Journal of Offender Rehabilitation* 22 (1995): 97–118.

Young, Matt and Taner Edis, eds. *Why Intelligent Design Fails: A Scientific Critique of the New Creationism*. New Brunswick: Rutgers University Press, 2006.

Zak, Paul J. "The Physiology of Moral Sentiments." *Journal of Economic Behavior and Organization* 77 (2011): 53–65.

Zaller, John R. *The Nature and Origins of Mass Opinion*. New York: Cambridge University Press, 1992.

Zhong, Chen-Bo, and Katie Liljenquist. "Washing Away Your Sins: Threatened Morality and Physical Cleansing." *Science* 313 (2006): 1451–52.

Zhong, Chen-Bo, Brendon Strejcek, and Niro Sivanathan. "A Clean Self Can Render Harsh Moral Judgment." *Journal of Experimental Social Psychology* 46 (2010): 859–62.

Zimbardo, Phillip G. *The Lucifer Effect: Understanding How Good People Turn Evil*. New York: Random House, 2007.

Zimmerman, Mark A., and Kenneth I. Maton. "Lifestyle and Substance Use among Male African-American Urban Adolescents: A Cluster Analytic Approach." *American Journal of Community Psychology* 20 (1992): 121–38.

Zimring, Franklin E. *The Contradictions of American Capital Punishment*. Oxford: Oxford University Press, 2003.

———. *The Great American Crime Decline*. New York: Oxford University Press, 2007.

Zimring, Franklin E., and Gordon Hawkins. *Crime is Not the Problem: Lethal Violence in America*. New York: Oxford University Press, 1997.

Zoll, Rachel. "Poll: Religious Devotion High in U.S." *Los Angeles Times*, June 6, 2005.

Zuckerman, Phil. "Atheism: Contemporary Numbers and Patterns." In *The Cambridge Companion to Atheism*, edited by Michael Martin, 248–69. Cambridge: Cambridge University Press, 2007.

————. *Society Without God: What the Least Religious Nations Can Tell Us About Contentment*. New York: New York University Press, 2010.

INDEX